S0-CFR-101

$ 9.95

Persuasion

Reception and Responsibility

Persuasion
Reception and Responsibility

Charles U. Larson

Northern Illinois University

Wadsworth Publishing Company, Inc.
Belmont, California

© 1973 by Wadsworth Publishing Company, Inc., Belmont, California 94002. All rights reserved. No part of this book may be reproduced, stored in a retrieval system or transcribed, in any form or by any means, electronic, mechanical, photocopying, recording or otherwise, without the prior written permission of the publisher.

ISBN 0–534–00336–2

L. C. Cat. Card No. 73–85134

Printed in the United States of America

4 5 6 7 8 9 10—77

Preface

Persuasion: Reception and Responsibility is intended primarily for students of persuasion at the undergraduate level. The perspective of this text is largely from the viewpoint of the receiver of persuasive messages. Most of us are only dimly aware of what is happening in the persuasive process and tend to respond in a knee-jerk fashion—we see or hear advertisements, political presentations, appeals from advertisers or agents for social change and respond according to how we feel at that moment, not with any kind of critical standard.

This text, then, attempts to present a series of analytical tools, which we can use to judge the persuasion aimed at us. These tools are by no means exhaustive, and each student and each teacher is encouraged to go further in his study of persuasion and to discover more tools that can make his responses to persuasive appeals more critical and intelligent. Though we all need to seek out persuasive messages to help us make decisions in a world overloaded with information, we also need to analyze these messages carefully, trying to discover what motives lie beneath them, what implications they might have, and what effects they might have upon us and our interests. The tools are divided into four basic categories: those that deal with style and language use, those that concern the psychological or intrapersonal processes operating within each of us, those that are rule-governed by the nature of interpersonal interaction, and those that relate to our cultural training and preparation. Tied to these considerations are several other issues that are integrally tied to persuasion—the power and nature of television in our society, the importance of sustained efforts in persuasion (campaigns or movements), and a consideration of ethical judgments in persuasion. In each of these, you should be able to see a shift in focus from the traditional concern with the persuader or *source* of persuasion to the persuadee or *receiver* of persuasion—you should see the receiver's need to analyze the style and effect of suasory language, the receiver's need to determine what interpersonal and intrapersonal premises are being appealed to, the receiver's desire to understand appeals to his cultural predispositions, and the receiver's need to understand how campaigns and movements operate, especially in an information age, and finally how it is that the receiver is ultimately responsible for making ethical decisions. (It makes little difference to say that Hitler was unethical, but it is extremely important to observe how and why the German people made their ethical decisions.)

Finally, this book is designed to get students involved in the reception process at a critical level. To help, there are annotated bibliographies at the end of each chapter as well as suggestions for individual and group projects. These, along with the study questions, are designed to spark your imagination about critical and responsible reception of persuasion. Hopefully, you will read some of the suggested readings and will decide to participate in some of the projects or to think about the study questions, thereby broadening your perspective and becoming actively involved in receiving persuasion responsibly.

We live in a frightening and sometimes depressing world, and we need to be wary in our responses to persuasion in this kind of world. We need to keep before us the ideal of critical reception of persuasion—the testing and analysis of persuasive messages for the wisdom of their advice, their motives, their techniques, and above all their implications. All these concerns rest ultimately on two premises that underlie this book:

1. The human making of symbols, and the use of them, is the most ego-involving and motive-revealing activity in which we engage.
2. We tend to see the world as made up of dramatic settings and episodes capable of being organized and understood as playlets, in which each of us acts and engages with others in minidramas, all of which have meaning.

If we are to avoid the world painted by George Orwell in his book *1984*—a world in which human beings are treated as robots to be controlled and watched—we need to engage in the act of persuasion with our primary focus on the act of reception. We need to do it actively, critically, and responsibly.

Anytime one writes a book, whether it is a novel, a book of theory, or a textbook, he finds he must admit to having received help from a multitude of sources. That is certainly the case with *Persuasion: Reception and Responsibility*—many persons helped to make this book possible. I want to extend my thanks to the many people who aided me in getting this manuscript from my typewriter to the printing presses and finally to you. The primal and most essential help was from my colleagues and my students who helped me with the content of this book. Especially I want to thank my two office partners during the writing of this book—Charles O. Tucker and Robert E. Sanders; their insights were of immense value to me and often caused me to rethink parts of the text. Richard L. Johannesen was of great help in editorial stages of writing as well as in earlier parts of the creative process. Halbert E. Gulley was most helpful in offering encouragement when the project seemed to be endless and in giving wise counsel on how to proceed. Probably the most important resource in the writing of this book was the input of ideas from the many students in my persuasion classes and seminars—they are the heart of this book.

During the preparation of the manuscript, several persons were of incalculable help—Maxine Mohrbacher, Rita Johnson, Dianne Spahn, Susi Gersonde, and Barbara Anderson; they all helped in getting the manuscript in presentable form. Often they went out of their way to get work done when it was inconvenient.

Finally, I want to thank those teachers who read this manuscript in its early or final stages, offering wise advice and encouragement: Mary Strom Larson, Bernard J. Brommel, George W. Dell, Don F. Faules, Robert F. Forston, Richard E. Porter, and David H. Smith; and Rebecca Hayden of Wadsworth Publishing Company.

Without all of these persons, there would not be a *Persuasion: Reception and Responsibility*. Thank you all.

Charles U. Larson

Contents

3

Tools for Analysis of Language   42

4

Process Premises for Persuasion   74

5

6

7

1

The Study of Persuasion

How and why does a person discuss a concept as complex and as broad as *persuasion,* and how can one arrive at any conclusions about it? There is little reason against studying persuasion—it is one of the major means of settling controversy in a democratic society, and it aims to change beliefs and actions in many noncontroversial situations. Furthermore, all of us must surely be persuaded, if we are to live in the twentieth century, that the only way some persons gain support for their beliefs is through persuasion. At the same time, responding to persuasion is often the major method of making decisions for each of us—we hear advertisers attempt to persuade us to buy their product; we listen to candidates as they try to persuade us to vote for them; and we listen to the direct salesmen of magazine subscriptions, books, or land opportunities in order to decide whether and when we want to buy or reject these ideas or products.

Perhaps the best way to study persuasion is to observe it at work around us and to extract characteristics about it from its workings. In a sense, that is the purpose of this book: to present descriptions of persuasion and discussions of how it works in our everyday lives. There are several reasons for this description and discussion: first, for the sake of knowledge about persuasion (we ought to study something as widespread and impactful as persuasion); second, to prepare ourselves as *students* of persuasion to become intelligent *consumers* of persuasion; third, to prepare ourselves to present persuasive messages.

To observe persuasion at work, we must do at least four things:

1. We must note the context in which persuasion, as we know it, occurs. As students of persuasion, we must be aware of the social

1

fabric in which it functions. We need to know *how persuasion is used, by whom, for what purposes, how often,* and so forth.

2. We also need to differentiate persuasion from other means of communication—particularly those forms intended to settle or reduce controversy—for persuasion is perhaps the technique most often used for achieving agreement and consensus in controversial situations. (Even in the discussion group or committee, we constantly see persuasion at work, as each discussant vies with other members of his group for the acceptance of certain courses of action or for certain interpretations of evidence.)

3. We need, next, to define what persuasion *is*, including such particulars as how persuasion works, what tools are used, what cause-effect relationships operate, and so forth.

4. Finally, we need to discuss how persuasion relates to each of us as student and as consumer of suasory discourse. Examining this relationship involves developing *methods* or *tools* for analyzing persuasion in order to determine how persuasion is operating in a given situation, how it has worked in the past, and how it might work in some future situation. This task is both descriptive and predictive. In a sense, these four tasks form the skeletal organization of this book and particularly of this chapter.

Some persons argue that persuasion is inherently inhumane and manipulative and hence unethical. They conclude that since persuasion aims at the change of action or attitude, at the imposition of a persuader's view on one or more receivers, it must be a mode of communication that exploits other people. Accordingly, if the student of communication really believes that communication ought to be used to encourage agreement, improve interpersonal relationships, and increase the predictability of life, he must be either a heretic or a hypocrite to study persuasion. Persons maintaining this position consider persuasion as serving only a competitive and dehumanizing milieu.[1] Though all of these criticisms are to some degree true, when one observes the extent to which persuasive messages touch us each day, it seems untenable to argue that we shouldn't study it. That is like saying "Since the mass media are profit motivated, no one should examine them except to see if they had a good or bad year financially speaking." We do investigate the mass media for other reasons—to see if they present pap or art to the public, to see if they engage in deceit or not, and for a hundred other reasons. Furthermore, as David K. Berlo argues, all communication is *affective*—we communicate, even with ourselves, in order to secure change.[2] Even the most selfless kinds of communication contain within them the kernels of persuasion—they are motivated in some way.

---

[1] For an evaluation of and partial reply to this position, see Richard L. Johannesen's "The Emerging Concept of Communication as Dialogue," *Quarterly Journal of Speech, 57* (December 1971), 373–382.

[2] Language, as some rhetorical theorists have noted, is inherently sermonic; it contains some degree of persuasive force. The words we choose inherently select

Having thus set the stage, let us begin by trying to explore the first task in any study of persuasion—investigation of the context in which it occurs and how persuasion operates in that context. The persuasion of Nazi Germany, for example, was different from that of Mao's China, which in turn is different from persuasion in America in the 1970s.

Persuasion in an Age of Information Overload

Since the end of World War II man has become increasingly aware of a terrifying and complex problem that he faces—and it is not pollution or war or racism, though it is related to all of those problems. The problem is simply that he lives in an information age that is highly sophisticated and intricate, and yet he is facing that age with antiquated tools. In short, there appears to be no way of processing the tremendous quantity of information that bombards us every day. Moreover, the problem will increase; in fact, the major product of the last half of the twentieth century is likely to be information—masses of it.[3] Technology has offered the institution with adequate resources some help in the form of computers, microfilms, microfiche, and so forth, but the individual processor of information has been largely neglected and left to handle the problem in the best way he can. Consider a few of the frightening aspects of this information explosion: If we were to hire human hands to sort, tally, and compute the transactions of the checking accounts in the banks of the United States, our employees would consist of over half the population of our country; or if a person desired to become an expert in a fairly narrow field of study, he would have to begin reading at birth and continue to read twenty-four hours a day until death, and even with that effort he would fall farther and farther behind; or consider the fact that even the most powerful and complex computers in operation today have continual traffic jams of information and need to be programmed with informational stop-and-go lights. We are only halfway through the last half of the twentieth century, yet the

and interpret facts and values; thus even the most "objective" of words channels our perceptions. For examples of this perspective, see Richard M. Weaver in *Language Is Sermonic*, ed. Richard L. Johannesen, Rennard Strickland, and Ralph T. Eubanks (Baton Rouge: Louisiana State University Press, 1970), pp. 201–225; Paul N. Campbell, *Rhetoric-Ritual* (Encino, Calif.: Dickenson Publishing Co., 1972), pp. 15–21; David K. Berlo, *The Process of Communication* (New York: Holt, Rinehart and Winston, 1960), pp. 228–234.

[3] For further elaboration on this point, see *Future Shock* by Alvin Toffler (New York: Random House, 1970), especially Chs. 2, 15, 16, 18. See also Ch. 5 of *Persuasion: Theory and Practice* by Kenneth E. Andersen (Boston: Allyn and Bacon, 1971).

information problem appears to be getting more difficult not less difficult. Certainly one of man's major problems now is, and will continue to be, focused on the question of how to deal with total emersion in a sea of information—some of which is irrelevant, some of which is slightly relevant, and some of which is essential to the continuance of life as we now know it.

Against the backdrop of this information age, the findings of a fifty-year-old study are still important. In 1926, a professor named Paul Rankin decided to determine what part of the average human day was spent in the communication process. Rankin asked sixty-five white-collar workers to log their communication day, determining just how much time they spent communicating and just how that time was divided among the four constituents of the communication process (reading, writing, speaking, and listening). He found that between 70 and 80 percent of our waking hours are spent communicating in some form or another and almost three-fourths of that time is spent in speaking or listening, with listening accounting for almost half of the average individual's communication activities. Rankin's results have been verified time and time again since 1926.[4] In an information age such as we live in, the percentages of oral-aural communication have probably increased, and it is highly likely, considering the influence of electronic media, that the reception of messages has increased. In other words, our most often used tools of communication are those involved in receiving information —particularly information designed to advise—or *to persuade.*

Most people would agree that, more often than not, we communicate with one another about information that will help us to make decisions. The decision might be to strike up a friendship with another, to buy a certain product, or to vote for a certain candidate. Yet we often seem to overlook this important interactional aspect of communication, especially of persuasive communication. Considering the influx of messages and the importance of the reception process, we seem to have misplaced our priorities—the mail-order courses sold to businessmen and professionals emphasize *the persuader's* ability to manipulate his subordinates; popular books focus on how a person can become a successful, well-liked, and influential *communicator;* and the emphasis of many of the textbooks used in college persuasion courses seek to train efficient and clever *persuaders.*[5]

In some of the most essential and vital areas of our lives, the eyes of scholars and students have been trained on the *source* of persuasive messages. In politics, for example, the assumption is that if an image

---

[4] Larry A. Samovar, Robert D. Brooks, and Richard E. Porter, "A Survey of Adult Communication Activities," *Journal of Communication, 19* (December 1969), 301–307.

[5] For the most part, texts spend time talking about what one ought to do to devise arguments, analyze audiences, and so forth.

man puts enough makeup on a candidate for political office, that candidate is a sure winner; or if Madison Avenue is clever enough about weaving a story concerning toilet-bowl cleaner, the public will rush pell-mell to the local supermarket and completely clear the shelves of that product.[6] Carried to its extreme, this mentality implies that a cadaver can be elected president of the United States if he gets an ingenious agency and a good makeup man working for him. The position of this book is that such a view of man is just not accurate. Man isn't just a robot that operates in a fickle series of opinion-modifying ways, responding to a stimulus here and another there. At times some people may act that way, but for the most part we assimilate information and react to it in patterned if not totally "logical" ways. Furthermore, our most important activity as human beings in a democratic society is to become critical and knowing consumers of information—particularly of information that seeks to advise us to certain courses of action. With the advent of the "electronic revolution," most of this overwhelming information comes to us orally via television and radio. Thus, as receivers of oral language, we need to become critical and aware—not to immunize ourselves from persuasive effects but to enable us to choose among the persuasive messages surrounding us.

Settling Controversy

Whenever two people or institutions become involved in a controversy over an issue, there are several ways that the controversy can be settled: Mr. A may coerce Mr. B to agree at least tacitly with A's position; Mr. A may submit to Mr. B's position without a battle; Mr. A and Mr. B may agree to sit down and talk it out asking the aid of others perhaps; *or* A and B can try to persuade one another of the wisdom of their positions. Even in the context of cooperative group meetings and discussions, persuasion is certainly operating, and perhaps coercion and submission also occur. The student of persuasion may be interested in several of the various methods of settling controversy; but if persuasion is his focus, he will be most interested in the persuasive aspects of achieving consensus. Taken in the broadest sense, *communication* is the genus and *persuasion* is the species. Compared with other

---

[6] In the late 1950s and early 1960s, this belief was articulated by Vance Packard in his *The Hidden Persuaders* (New York: Pocket Books, 1958). More recently, Joe McGinniss notes that the casting bureaus and videotape editors have had a tremendous effect on presidential campaigns—see his book *The Selling of the President* (New York: Trident Press, 1969).

methods of settling controversy or of determining courses of action, persuasion advises action or change. Discussion searches for courses of action or change. Coercion and submission demand or force action or comply with imperative courses of action. And argumentation attempts to demonstrate the relationship between evidence, information, and courses of action—not for the sake of achieving the action but more for the demonstration of proof itself. Thus, though persuasion may utilize the tools and techniques of argument in obtaining agreement, argumentation does not truly employ persuasion. Especially formal argument, but informal argument as well, aims not at swaying an audience to belief or action but rather at demonstrating skills in proof. The three activities most often experienced by persons who are seeking to make a decision about an activity that concerns them are *coercion, submission,* and *persuasion.*[7]

Coercion and Controversy

Coercion is a difficult activity to maintain. The only way Mr. A can be certain that Mr. B follows directions is by setting up a system of inspection or force to make sure that Mr. B is indeed following directions. One look at increasing crime rates suggests that this method doesn't work very well even with increased police forces and increased police sophistication. The problem is that the process of inspection requires an inspector for every inspectee, and then someone must inspect the inspector at least occasionally. Furthermore, the individual who is coerced is not likely to feel satisfied with his position, and his esprit de corps will be minimal. Eventually this dissatisfaction exhibits itself in serious ways—some violent, like riots or rebellions; some destructive, like industrial sabotage or theft; and some merely lethargic, like the worker who found a way to sleep four hours of his eight-hour shift when forced to work the 4 P.M. until midnight shift. In short, coercion doesn't engender a feeling of responsibility or loyalty on the part of participants. The coercer feels constantly threatened, and the coercee feels continually oppressed.

Submission and Controversy

Submission as a means of settling controversy is not very satisfactory either. All of us have been involved in a disagreement with an extremely dogmatic and persistent person. We may finally weary of

---

[7] Particular thanks for help in clarifying the roles of these various forms of communication goes to my graduate students in the Seminar in Persuasion; they gave me many insights.

getting nowhere and weakly agree that our opponent is right or that it makes little difference to us, but we will rarely act on our agreement. *Submission* by its very nature implies the *subsuming* of important goals. Since they are goals and since they are important, dissatisfaction is also a likely by-product of submission.

Persuasion and Controversy

Persuasion is by far the most preferred method of re-solving controversy, at least in a democracy. The negative by-products of both submission and coercion are avoided in the suasory process. How-ever, this process is an extremely delicate one and implies certain char-acteristics. Suppose, as a persuader, I have as a goal the attainment of political office. If I choose to organize a coup and take the position for my own, I run the risk of producing dissatisfaction and low morale. If I achieve the office uncontested, I am somewhat better off, but marshal-ing spirited support will be difficult—there is no issue over which po-tential supporters can become excited. But if I must face another contestant, the goal, the process of achieving the goal, and the likelihood of a satisfied and energized electorate are all increased.

Persuasion in a Democracy

Before proceeding further, we must stop and observe how this preferred means of settling controversy operates in a democracy and with what checks and deterrents. It seems logical to choose and use persuasion, if possible, whenever we want to settle controversy; how-ever, the problem is not as simple as it seems. Persuasion, to operate effectively and fairly, needs a properly tended environment. It doesn't happen automatically—there are conditions that are essential if per-suasion is to operate. We ought to keep in mind that what follows is a description of what ideally happens. Many times in the hurly-burly of the marketplace, these ideals do not operate as neatly as in a textbook. The perfect environment is rare—there are many occasions when per-suasion operates in spite of handicaps.

Aristotle noted that the dialectical process would eventually result in the emergence of truth, if both sides of the controversy had the ad-vantage of equally competent advocates. This is the *first* delicate condi-tion for persuasion to operate in a democratic society.

But we face an information age, also. As noted earlier, the individual dealing with the problems of an information age must, because of the overwhelming amount of information available, act out of partial ignorance. He does have the option, however, of being choosy about information. He can observe and assimilate information most likely to be useful and accurate. He can also spend most of his time listening to equally qualified advocates, when he is not being one himself. So, the *second* condition for the operation of persuasion in a democratic, information-filled society is aware and critical auditors.

The *third* condition necessary for persuasion to be truly effective as a tool for conflict resolution in a democratic society, can be illustrated in this brief example: In the 1950s, Vance Packard in his classic study, *The Hidden Persuaders*, reported the effects of subliminal advertising. For this study, mini-messages were flashed on a movie screen between the frames of the movie being viewed. The messages urged the viewer to purchase a product at the refreshment stand of the theater; but the individual viewer was never consciously aware of the message—what it said or that it was even there. But the message was recorded on the subconscious mind. The light flashes were recorded through the viewer's retina and then on through his central nervous system. The results of this experiment were frightening—the theater sold out of the advertised product and even had problems with indignant customers who demanded that they be allowed to purchase the product.[8] A requisite for the successful operation of persuasion in an information age ought to be the revelation of motives on the part of the persuaders. They ought to make clear what they are up to and why they are up to it. In other words, no hidden agendas. The word "ought" is purposely used in discussing this requisite because, given fulfillment of the first two requisites and enough time, motivations will emerge and will be exposed to the audience. In the case of the subliminal light flashes, the persuaders were not aware or critical, and there was only *one* message presented by the persuader. Presumably, if a contrary message had been presented, the movie viewers would have been psychologically torn between the alternatives to such a degree that either they would not have acted or else they would have demanded that management tell them what was causing their frustration. If they had been aware of the hidden messages, they would also have been able to resist the subliminal demand.

The process of persuasion in a democratic society ideally demands (1) equivalence among advocates, (2) an aware and critical set of persuadees, and (3) hopefully, an a priori revelation of motives. As one examines the various successful persuasive campaigns that have occurred in the history of public address, at least in democratic societies, a pattern is clear. When these three elements are present, persuasion can occur, and the inherent disadvantages of coercion or submission are

---

[8] Packard, pp. 35–36. See fn. 6.

avoided. Given the preceding argument, the student of persuasion faces a challenge he has not had to face so directly at any other time in history. That challenge is how to train himself to be an aware and critical *processor* of information—particularly of persuasive information—as opposed to training himself to be a clever *user* of persuasive techniques to sway others to one's own point of view. Richard M. Weaver, in his *Ethics of Rhetoric*, puts it this way:

> . . . the student of rhetoric must realize that in the contemporary world he is confronted not only by evil practitioners (of rhetoric), but also, and probably to an unprecedented degree, by men who are conditioned by the evil created by others. The machinery of propagation and inculcation is today so immense that no one avoids entirely the assimilation and use of some terms that have a downward tendency. It is especially easy to pick up a tone without realizing its trend. *Perhaps the best that any of us can do is to hold a dialectic with himself to see what the wider circumferences of his terms of persuasion are. This process will not only improve the consistency of one's thinking but it will also, if the foregoing analysis is sound, prevent his becoming a creature of evil public forces and a victim of his own thoughtless rhetoric.*[9]

It is clear the roles of persuader and persuadee are not mutually exclusive, and becoming an aware and critical persuadee does not preclude becoming a successful persuader—in fact, it ought to encourage it. Understanding what it is that persuades us and why it persuades us ought to enable us to become more effective persuaders. The student of persuasion in an information age ought to observe himself being persuaded and ought to try to discover means of applying this self-analysis to the "real world" and the marketplace of ideas.

Persuasion: A Definition

Thus far, we have set the context for the study of persuasion in the last half of the twentieth century and have examined persuasion as a means of settling controversy. We have also compared persuasion with other forms of communication like argumentation and discussion. To fulfill the role of the student of persuasion outlined earlier, we should start at the beginning—with a definition of what

[9] Richard M. Weaver, *The Ethics of Rhetoric* (Chicago: Henry Regnery Co., 1953), p. 232. Italics added.

persuasion is and what it does. The definition of persuasion offered here, like all definitions, is limited and forces us to limit our study correspondingly. It does not focus on the source, the message, or the receiver but on the interaction of all of these elements. Hopefully, this kind of focus allows for maximum flexibility in our study of persuasive messages and effects. Here is our working definition:

> *Persuasion* is a process whereby decision options are intentionally limited or extended through the interaction of messages, sources, and receivers, and through which attitudes, beliefs, opinions, or behaviors are changed by a cognitive restructuring of one's image of the world or of his frame of reference.

The astute reader will probably be saying to himself, "Why, that includes all communication!" In a sense it does, in that all communication does affect, to some degree, one's image of the world and hence his attitudes or beliefs (see footnote 2). However, notice that our interest here is in situations in which human beings feel the necessity of making a decision. There are numerous occasions in our life when we communicate about topics that do not imply the making of decisions (e.g., ritualistic communication like "How are ya?" or "How do you do?") or that are intended for the transmission of information (e.g., a lecture on The History of Greece). But there is something distinctive about communication in the context of decision making. This distinction is closely related to information and how it is presented to us. Let us examine this distinction further, keeping in mind that we are dealing with intended, not accidental, change in decision options. We should also note that the change need not be dramatic or immediate. It may occur months after the message has interacted with the source and receiver, and it may result in minor change only.

Persuasion, Information, and Decision Making

People are constantly faced with the necessity for making decisions; they are forced to make them every minute of the day, and, for the most part, they make decisions on the basis of information —logical information gleaned from research or received from persuasive sources or emotional-psychological information that is a part of one's own personal background, needs, and goals. When the necessity for a decision presents itself, we tend to sift the logical and emotional information at hand and to determine what our options are in reference to that information. Persuasion occurs when those options are either limited or increased by the input of new information and the interaction of that new information with existing sets of information—logical or psychological. In other words, when we are about to make a decision, we need to be persuaded. The problem is deciding how to allow oneself to be persuaded wisely—how to avoid being flim-flammed.

Let's examine an example of persuasion in action. Suppose that I am interested in purchasing a new car and that I view the Fiat as the most likely auto to purchase on the basis of its economy, styling, and utility. I haven't completely made up my mind and am considering the possibility of other foreign autos. But, at the moment, my image of the automobile world within the frame of reference of utility, economy, and styling favors Fiat over other options. Now suppose there is an input of information. A persuader, in the form of a newspaper advertisement, presents me with information about safety and economy of the new Gremlin. My frame of reference heretofore included economy, styling, and utility—but not safety. I am informed that the death ratio in foreign automobiles is 50 percent higher than in American compacts, while utility remains essentially equivalent and economy favors the foreign-made machines. I am now faced with reviewing the automobile world from a new frame of reference—one that includes safety. My decision options are increased because of this new viewpoint, and I must resift all available information, taking into account the new information and the source of that new information. I may ultimately purchase a Fiat; but, operating under the present definition, *persuasion* has occurred because there has been an altering of decision alternatives through a shift in my view of the world—my frame of reference.

In the preceding case, the information concerned with safety in automobiles worked in concert with my preconceived and held biases about death in an auto accident (a psychological fear) and worked its effect largely through a factual argument—the percentage ratio for auto deaths in foreign-made autos. It would be difficult to assign *a* cause for my decision—there probably were many interacting causes each with varying effect, but we can probably say that new *information* had the effect of increasing my alternatives. Something occurred—under the present definition, it was a process called persuasion. The key elements operating were my frame of reference, the necessity of a single decision in the face of alternatives, my characteristics as a receiver of information, and information itself. Finally, the elements do not cease to have effect once I have decided—though I have purchased my Fiat, I continue to mull over my decision as I receive particles of information.

Clearly, persuasion is important in the making of decisions. People are persuaded to limit or to extend their decision alternatives on the basis of information that is persuasively presented. In the example involving automobile purchases, the information about *safety* was persuasive in extending decision alternatives.

Role of the Persuadee in Decision Making

When we think of persuasion, it is natural for us to look to the source of persuasive messages—the "man of words" who is able to sway audiences through his charisma, his knowledge of issues, and his ability to appeal to emotions through the artful use of language and symbols. History is studded with examples of this kind of persuader: Marc Anthony, Daniel Webster, Abraham Lincoln, Adolf Hitler, Franklin D. Roosevelt, John F. Kennedy, for a few examples. Rarely, though, do we stop to think of the audiences these superstars were appealing to in their persuasion. We don't think of the Roman crowd listening to Marc Anthony's funeral oration or of the mass audiences who listened to Adolf Hitler lead the world to war. Yet this element of the persuasive transaction—the element that really gives the "man of words" his power —is the key element in persuasion.

Considering the three criteria mentioned earlier (equal advocates with equal opportunity to persuade, a revelation of motive or intention, and an aware auditor), it is clear that the persuadee also has responsibilities—in fact, his responsibilities are heavy. Given a critical and aware persuadee, the first two criteria need not be fulfilled. If the persuadee is alert to the persuasive process, to the pressures forcing him toward decision, to the information surrounding him and to his own susceptibility to persuasion, then neither equal advocates with equal opportunity nor motive revelation is essential. An alert persuadee who watches himself being appealed to can counteract all of the disadvantages of unequal advocacy, hidden agendas, or unethical persuaders. Unfortunately, many persuadees are like the proverbial sucker in the shell game—responding to diversion, irrelevant information, and deception. Examples of this carelessness are everywhere and face us continually. A television special entitled "The Selling of the Pentagon" recently demonstrated that many persuadees are and have been uncritical. In that special, various pieces of film were spliced out of sequence, thus distorting the truth. In some cases, answers to certain questions were spliced to appear as answers to different questions.

How can the persuadee protect himself from the shell game—the deception he is faced with? How can he distinguish between essential information and that which is merely interesting? How can he spot his own susceptibility to persuasion? How can he allow himself to be persuaded without letting his susceptibility make him an easy mark for manipulation?

There is no easy answer, of course, but two activities will be essential if he is to meet any of these challenges. First, he must be willing to become a *critical persuadee* (i.e., he must watch himself being persuaded and ask why he chose one alternative as opposed to another);

second, he must become aware of the devices of persuasion that compete for his attention and action. How does one become such a person? Most of us are already at least partially along that path. When we lose our bet at the shell game, we say to ourselves, "Where did I get misled? Let's see if I can figure it out by watching closely." Being deceived once, our immediate and natural response is to look at the case and see where we were first miscued, and we say to ourselves that we will never make that mistake again. Initially, that is what the aware persuadee does—he searches for the cues that led him to action or change, and then he decides whether he wants to be moved in the same way again. If he does, he remains susceptible to the same kinds of appeals; if not, his defenses react negatively to those earlier persuasive appeals. There is a danger here, though. Remember, the persuadee is constantly being bombarded with information, often competing information. If he a priori rejects information that comes clothed in the same garb as that which fooled him the first time, he may well reject necessary and pertinent information just because of its "look." When I find that I have been gypped by a magazine salesman offering five separate magazines for $1.50 a week, I am immediately suspicious of the next magazine salesman making a similar appeal. The second salesman may be making a legitimate and honest offer; but because I ordered magazines from the first salesman, only to discover that the five publications were monthly or semimonthly, I reject the legitimate offer out of hand. As a persuadee, I have made a move in the right direction by being aware and by guarding myself against bogus appeals; but since I lack the tools by which to judge the appeals, to question them, or to investigate them thoroughly, my rejection may be unwise.

The persuadee has two major responsibilities if he is to be a member of the "aware and critical" audience mentioned earlier as the key element in persuasion in a democratic society. First, he must watch himself as he is persuaded or as he is subjected to persuasive appeals; second, he must find some way to systematize his awareness by applying carefully considered criteria to the appeals he processes, judging their relevance, their truth, and their applicability to him. This brings us to the fourth task described at the beginning of this chapter, a task that will be more fully developed later. For the present, though, we ought to sketch out the tools or methods of analysis the persuadee uses in his role of receiving, judging, and ultimately deciding whether or not to act on the advice of the persuader. We need to *learn* to be persuaded, instead of blindly responding to the conflicting and confusing appeals being made to us.

Levels of Judgment

Since the time of Aristotle, persuasion theorists have focused their attention on the mechanisms and techniques the persuader can use to move audiences to action. Unfortunately, little has been said of what the receiver can do to alert himself to the use and purposes of these techniques. Perhaps the best we can do for the persuadee, many have said, is to give him some tests of evidence, so that if he is persuaded, at least he can justify his change to others. Or we can urge him to investigate other alternatives before deciding by researching or by exposing himself to an equal advocate holding an opposite or contrary point of view.

Looking at the problem of preparing the persuadee to receive suasory discourse from a realistic point of view, though, we realize he has other things to do, other decisions to make, before he can view and review his alternatives. He doesn't have a great deal of time in this hectic and complex world to run to the library and check up on the "facts" a persuader has presented him with. He probably won't even have the chance to expose himself to an advocate who represents a position contrary to that of the persuader now advising him to purchase a certain product, to vote for a certain candidate, or to follow a certain course of action. If research concerning people's willingness to expose themselves to information that is not supportive of their own beliefs is correct, the persuadee not only lacks the time to investigate all sides of a question, but he may also lack the will to investigate them—especially if that kind of deep examination of the facts requires real effort.[10]

What the persuadee needs for his own self-defense as a receiver of suasory discourse is a set of tools of analysis that have *adaptability*, so that they can be used with ethical and unethical persuaders, with large audiences and small audiences, in formal and informal situations, in issues of great moment and in more mundane issues, and so forth. In subsequent chapters the persuadee's tools of analysis will be presented in four classes or on four levels that relate to varying aspects of persuasion: (1) language, (2) psychological or intrapersonal, (3) organizational or interpersonal, and (4) cultural or societal.

---

[10] Recent findings related to self-persuasion and selective exposure suggest that the ability and/or desire to expose oneself to information counter to already held attitudes is limited. See, for example, Timothy C. Brock and Joe L. Balloun, "Behavioral Receptivity to Dissonant Information," *Journal of Personality and Social Psychology, 5* (1967), 413–428; or Robert J. Mertz, Gerald R. Miller, and Lee Ballance, "Open- and Closed-Mindedness and Cognitive Conflict," *Journalism Quarterly, 43* (Autumn 1966), 429–434.

Language Level

The first major kind of analytical tool relates to the nature and uses of language. Since the information explosion we are facing thrives on oral or written signs and/or symbols to affect decision making, a critical and rather sophisticated analysis of language is a necessary and potent self-defense mechanism for the persuadee. The appeals and suggestions made by various persuaders (advertisers, politicians, employers, political action groups, etc.) all rely to some degree on language as a basic channel for messages. This language may take various forms ranging from the public speech to the leaflet or one-word placard, but the message is nonetheless based on the symbolic nature of linguistic activity in persuaders and their audiences. If "the style is the man," then the reliance upon language provides an opening glimpse into what persuaders are up to. We not only have to ask what words mean when we hear them, but we must also ask what lies behind the words—why did the persuader choose the words he did and what might his choices reveal about himself and his motives?

If you have been persuaded by this chapter to become, or to try to become, an aware and critical persuadee, you have done so by reacting to the symbols you have read and are now reading. If you decide to buy a Fiat instead of a Gremlin, you are reacting to the linguistic signs and symbols the dealer presents to you. Even if you persuade yourself to start saving 10 percent of your salary this month, you will have been persuaded by communicating with yourself through language, even though it is subvocal or silent language. It is your responsibility, if you are to become the "aware" persuadee we talk about here, to examine carefully the language used to persuade you and the language you use to persuade yourself. Chapters 2 and 3 discuss methods for investigating style in language.

Psychological or Intrapersonal Level

Every human being is different. He reacts to deep-seated feelings, beliefs, attitudes, opinions, and character traits. When he is persuaded, these internal and personal elements play an important part in his ultimate choice or decision. Whenever you, as a persuadee, receive some message from a persuader, you process it through your emotional and intellectual "transformers" or converters of information *outside* your skin to information *inside* your skin. The ways in which you transform the appeals or advice of the persuader are complex and interrelated. They affect the language and content of the information the persuader is sending you. For example, your father may never have been an affectionate person. You may have feared him, and that memory may affect your reaction to information coming from "father-type" persons; you may feel fearful of your own ability to succeed, and that fear may affect your response to challenges; or you may be intolerant of chaotic and confusing situations, and that intolerance may affect your response to organized or unorganized appeals. This "Freudian analysis" of your internal state as a persuadee probably interacts with a variety of other "transformers" of information, such as past schedules of positive and negative reinforcement and reward, your aspirations in reference to the persons with whom you associate, and a host of others. In other words, your internal frame of reference will determine your responses to persuasion to some degree. Chapter 4 discusses several of these transformers or processors of information. That discussion should give you insights into why you respond the way you do and why persuaders focus their appeals to you in the way they do.

Organizational or Interpersonal Level

When we deal with ourselves, as in the internal or intrapersonal level of persuasion, we are fairly free to set our own rules. What may be totally consistent to us may be totally inconsistent to someone else. When we begin to consider persuasion in settings involving other persons, however, this freedom diminishes. When others are involved as we send or receive persuasion and decide to react or not react to it, we must not only make our decisions in reference to the language or symbols used to appeal to us and to the characteristics of our own individual personalities and frames of reference, but we must also respond or appeal within bounds of certain rules of procedure that are acceptable to the others involved. We have discovered that when we deal with others, we need at least a minimal set of regulations or "rules of proceeding" that *most* persons would accept as reasonable and consistent. Thus, the Fiat dealer doesn't ask you to buy a car because it will make him rich. Instead he tells you that you ought to buy the car because you need it and will save money by having it. In this case, one of our rules is that we operate in our own self-interest first; only then do we operate in the self-interest of others. Persuaders know this "rule" and present their appeals in such a way as to cause their persuadees to believe that they are operating or deciding in their own self-interest. There are other such rules for proceeding or for agreeing to agree that operate between persuaders and persuadees. Most of them are not as formal as the types of "logical" reasoning discussed by many theoreticians but are probably closer to the informal notion of consistency (i.e., a persuader is "following" the rules if his evidence seems related to his appeals and if it seems to support them sufficiently).[11] To be sure, these methods interact with the individual's intrapersonal frame of reference, but they are also understood as reasonable or acceptable to most persons and seem consistent with the ways people deal with one another most of the time. A madman is difficult to persuade, not because he doesn't have a set of intrapersonal beliefs and attitudes but because he doesn't "buy" the organizational or interpersonal rules and regulations most persons call reasonable or consistent. He is out of the mainstream and rejected as inconsistent, illogical, or insane. Chapter 5 discusses some of these rules for proceeding.

Cultural or Societal Level

Closely related to the interpersonal tools of analysis are those that relate to the society or culture in which persuasion occurs. In a sense this fourth category is the genus of the third category, but much broader and more generalized. The interpersonal rules or procedures that we accept as logical or consistent are handed down to us as part of a greater set of values and norms our particular culture esteems. In this sense, we are shaped by three forces—our personal experiences with ourselves (the intrapersonal level) our interactions with others (the organizational or interpersonal level) and the milieu in which these operate (our culture or society). In other words, we are susceptible to persuasion because of ourselves, others, and language characteristics; we are also susceptible to certain kinds of persuasion because we have been born and raised in a certain culture.

Western culture, for example, demands that when faced with problems, we search for solutions; other cultures do not place the same demand on their constituents. Suppose that in 1966 someone had suggested that we end the Vietnam war by beginning to blacktop the entire country starting at the 17th parallel and working southward, retreating as we completed the job. Most persons would have said that this idea was unacceptable and unrealistic. Yet on the basis of cost, $35 billion dollars (the approximate annual cost for supporting the war effort at that time) would probably pay for completely blacktopping South Vietnam. On the basis of utility, one could argue that the solution was wise in that it would provide us with the world's largest runway for airplanes. Yet this idea or appeal is not acceptable because, from our

---

[11] Compare the discussions of reasoning in such sources as *Persuasion: A Means of Social Control* by Winston L. Brembeck and William S. Howell (Englewood Cliffs, N.J.: Prentice-Hall, 1952), Donald K. Smith's discussion of topoi in Ch. 5 of *Man Speaking* (New York: Dodd, Mead & Co., 1969), and Ch. 7 in Glen E. Mills's *Reason in Controversy*, 2nd ed. (Boston: Allyn and Bacon, 1968).

cultural or societal frame of reference, we define problem solving as re-moving the cause of ill effects that bother us—in this case, the supposed danger of turning the country of South Vietnam over to North Vietnam. In other words, as persuadees we are culturally programmed to accept certain kinds of information and not to accept other kinds of informa-tion.

The analytical tools for the persuadee, then, include *language char-acteristics*, because language is the most predominant carrier of in-formation in the persuasive process; our own *psychological* or individu-alized frames of reference, because we perceive and act in reference to these; *organizational* or *interpersonal norms*, because social intercourse is rule-governed; and *societal* or *cultural beliefs* or *values*, because they program us as persuadees to accept and reject certain kinds of informa-tion.

A Review and Conclusion

Let us see how far we have traveled in this discussion. First, we live in an information age; we are continually and forcefully overwhelmed with masses of information, some of which is relevant and some of which is not. Second, we spend most of our time processing this information, not producing it. Third, because of the enormity of the problem and the degree to which we act as persuadees instead of persuaders, we must prepare and train ourselves for persuasive appeals by being analytical, aware, and critical when exposed to persuasive messages and appeals. And, finally, the way in which we can receive per-suasion responsibly is by examining it in relation to language, ourselves, our interactional norms, and our cultural values. Given an attempt to be critical in these ways, persuasion can operate ethically and effectively even if the various advocates are not equally skilled or advantaged and even if persuaders operate from hidden agendas.

By means of the four goals or tasks outlined earlier in this chapter, we have taken an initial step toward fulfilling them by examining the context in which persuasion occurs in our society—it is a major in-gredient in a mass society like ours. We have also differentiated per-suasion from other types of communication—particularly those types used in resolving controversy: persuasion is advisory; it suggests what to do while other forms of communication demonstrate validity or seek information. Thus persuasion differs from other forms of influence; it is not coercive (like airplane hijacking, blackmail, or brainwashing). Next, we have defined persuasion as a process that uses symbols to alter frames of reference in achieving desired change in receivers. Finally, this chapter has briefly described the kinds of analytical tools a persuadee can use to evaluate the persuasive messages bombarding him every day. There are at least four kinds of tools: those for analyzing a persuader's style or language; those for analyzing the internal or intrapersonal states of receivers; those for describing the interactional "rules" for persuading; and, finally, those that are culturally inculcated in the other three categories.

As these issues and ideas are investigated in detail in the next few chapters, the student of persuasion should keep in mind that there are many other factors that affect the process of persuasion—factors like the kind of message delivery system used to persuade, the building of persuasive strategy through careful campaigning, and so forth. These factors, however, in one way or another, can be thought of as relating to one or more of the levels of analysis discussed above.

Questions for Further Thought

1. How would you describe the context in which persuasion occurs? (Discuss briefly in a paragraph or two.)

2. Define persuasion as it occurs for you. Compare that definition with the one offered in this chapter. What differences are there?

3. Beginning with the definition of persuasion offered here, attempt to create a model that reflects all of the important elements of the definition. (*Note:* You might begin with a model such as that offered by David K. Berlo in *The Process of Communication* and elaborate on it or make appropriate adaptations.)

4. Identify three different types of persuasion you have received recently (advertisements, speeches, persuasive appeals in discussions with others, or some other type) and analyze each of them according to the definition offered in this chapter (i.e., what are the symbols? what is the persuader's intent? what does the persuasion "say" about the persuadee's probable frame of reference?).

5. Read a contemporary review of problems of a mass society like ours (e.g., Alvin Toffler's *Future Shock*, Philip Slater's *The Pursuit of Loneliness*, or Abbie Hoffman's *Revolution for the Hell of It!*), and attempt to discuss the role of persuasion as noted by the social critic.

6. Compare the three criteria necessary for persuasion in a democracy with the criticisms raised by the person studied in question 5. Given his criticisms of our mass culture, is persuasion possible and likely? Can the three criteria be met? How can each persuadee help assure that these criteria are met?

7. Identify several forms of the various types of communication discussed here (i.e., argumentation, discussion, coercion, and persuasion). How do they differ? What similarities do they have? How would you "translate" one form to another form? (For instance, how would one change your example of argument to coercion, persuasion, or discussion?).

Experiences in Persuasion

1. Write to some institution that engages in persuasion in the nonclassroom world (e.g., the American Civil Liberties Union, the National States Rights Party, the Daughters of the American Revolution, the Black Panther Party, or the National Association for the Advancement of Colored People), and ask for some of its literature. Analyze this literature, searching for its persuasive aspects, its use of symbols, the kind of frame of reference or image of the world to which it appeals, and so forth. In other words, do a review of its persuasiveness.

2. Follow a particular set of persuasive messages focusing on the same specific persuasive goal (e.g., the campaign for election of a certain person or the advertising campaign of a particular product or the debate over a certain issue in your newspapers). Attempt to determine whether the persuader adjusts his messages for various audiences or for various frames of reference.

3. Read an "objective" public report (e.g., the Walker report on the Chicago convention disturbances, the Pentagon Papers, etc.). Identify those parts that are informative. Identify those parts that are argumentative (i.e., those that try to demonstrate proof). Identify the persuasive aspects of the report. Which form of discourse predominates? Speculate as to the document's effect if analyzed as various forms of discourse. Where and why do the distinctions between persuasion and the other discursive forms break down?

Readings for New Dimensions

Andersen, Kenneth E., *Persuasion: Theory and Practice* (Boston: Allyn and Bacon, 1971). See especially Chs. 1, 2, 3. This book is one of the more recent contributions to the study of persuasion. It provides an excellent review of behavioral and traditional research into various aspects of persuasion. Andersen's approach is somewhat source oriented as suggested by the title of the book. Of particular interest at this point are the discussions of problems in defining persuasion, the context in which persuasion occurs, and the role of the persuadee in the persuasive process.

Barnlund, Dean C., "Toward a Meaning Centered Philosophy of Communication," *Journal of Communication, 12* (December 1962), 198–202. Barnlund stresses the difference between message-centered, source-centered, and *meaning* or *receiver*-oriented approaches to the study of communication. This discussion is particularly germane to the perspective used in this book, since the receiver's response is what is attended to and what we wish to focus on.

Brembeck, Winston L., and William S. Howell, *Persuasion: A Means of Social Control* (Englewood Cliffs, N. J.: Prentice-Hall, 1952). This book is one of the early persuasion texts and the perspective it provides is interesting. The authors are extremely perceptive in anticipating the problems of persuasion in the context of mass culture even though the book was written before most homes had television sets and at a time when few of the problems of mass culture were apparent. Though the authors argue that they wish to prepare persuadees for the appeals of an age of advertising, the book focuses on the preparation and presentation of persuasive messages more than on the reception of messages.

Bryant, Donald C., "Rhetoric: Its Function and Its Scope," *Quarterly Journal of Speech, 39,* (December 1953), 401–424. Bryant discusses the distinction between suasory discourse and other forms. It is interesting to note the differences between Bryant's definition of persuasion (rhetorical discourse) and the one presented in this chapter. The review of the concepts used in his definition are of value to the student.

Ehninger, Douglas, "Argument as Method: Its Nature, Its Limitations, and Its Use," *Speech Monographs, 37* (1970), 101–110. Compare Ehninger's discussion of argument as dialogue with that presented in this chapter. Ehninger maintains that marketplace argument is not merely demonstration. However, he observes that formal argument is a method as opposed to an act. In other words, argument is motivated not by a desire to change receivers but to discover "truth."

Fotheringham, Wallace C., *Perspectives on Persuasion* (Boston: Allyn and Bacon, 1966), especially the first two chapters. This book is a good example of the "effects oriented" school of persuasion. Fotheringham defines persuasion as *effect,* as opposed to *intent.*

Gordon, George N., *Persuasion: The Theory and Practice of Manipulative Communication* (New York: Hastings House, 1971), Chs. 1, 3, 5, 6. This book discusses many of the same issues as those discussed in this chapter. Gordon notes that manipulative communication is increasing with frightening intensity. The increase, he notes, is tied closely to technology and electronic media. The chapter titles perhaps best annotate the message of his book: "Communicating Intention," "Mass Culture as Persuasion," "The Making of a Consumer," and "Education, Indoctrination and Training." Gordon maintains that we must understand the manipulative effects and methods of persuasion in a mass culture such as ours. This text also reflects a *source* or *persuader* orientation.

Slater, Philip, *The Pursuit of Loneliness: American Culture at the Breaking Point* (Boston: Beacon Press, 1970). Slater maintains in this book that American culture can no longer cope with the social and the psychological forces at work in our society. In particular he is critical of the competitive life style to which we subject ourselves and of the puritan ethic. Slater would agree with Toffler that these characteristics are intensified in an information age and would argue that we must retreat from this lifestyle if we are to continue to exist in any kind of psychic comfort. His major thrust suggests that persuasion should give way to less manipulative means of controlling people or that people should become more critical of the multitude of persuasion efforts aimed at them.

Toffler, Alvin, *Future Shock* (New York: Bantam Books, 1971). Toffler argues that our present-day mass society is changing so rapidly that human beings have great difficulty adjusting to and responding to this rate of change. Of particular importance is the tremendous overflow of information. This *overflow* and its resulting *overload* on people have particular relevance for the student of persuasion.

2

Language and Persuasion

One of the major factors in describing the context of anything like persuasion involves discussing the raw material from which it is made. So, in accord with the definitional tasks designated in Chapter 1, this chapter centers on the most important and central raw material from which persuasive messages are fashioned—*language*. Now, in discussing anything as complex as language, one has to begin with its origins, and that is our present concern—how and why did man "invent" language? And how does he use it persuasively? Here we will discuss various explanations for the origin of language, focusing on one of these possibilities and considering its importance to the fourth task set forth in Chapter 1—to design tools which we can use to analyze persuasive messages critically.

In particular, we will show that the artistic or symbolic origin of language is the best way to explain the overwhelming interest each of us has in using language.[1] This perspective has important implications; if valid, stylistic analysis can be a potent tool for the persuadee, revealing to him the persuader's artistic and egocentric motivations. These premises are considered in detail later.

Having chosen a perspective from which to analyze language, our next task is to describe the characteristic or salient features of language, focusing on the most important and those most likely to be elaborated upon in developing tools of linguistic or stylistic analysis. Thus, in this

---

[1] There are several discussions of this topic—the symbolic origins of language. See, for example, the preface, Chs. 1 and 2 (Part I) and Chs. 4 and 7 of Part III of Kenneth Burke's *Language as Symbolic Action* (Berkeley: University of California Press, 1966) and the first four chapters of Susanne K. Langer's *Philosophy in a New Key* (New York: Mentor Books, 1951).

chapter, we will look at three important features of language and how they can be used to analyze persuasion.

Finally, we will consider the criteria we ought to use in determining analytical tools in for evaluating messages. To analyze style or language in order to uncover or reveal the persuader's intent or motivation, what sorts of tools ought we to use? What should they be able to show? How else should they be used? And so forth.

In a very real sense, this chapter is based on Seneca's premise that "as a man speaks, so is he." The importance of that premise is demonstrated here by identifying the origins and salient features of human symbolic activity—especially language activity—and then looking at the means for analyzing a persuader's motives as reflected in his language. (Subsequent chapters discuss the tools per se, presenting them and demonstrating how they may be used to evaluate *what* a persuader is saying by examining *how* he says it.)

Thinking about Language and Its Roots

When we think about language and then try to relate it to the idea of persuading someone or being persuaded by someone, several ideas come to mind. First, we are likely to think of examples of what some people call "loaded language" or emotional words, and probably the examples we remember are those in which the persuader is attacking or vilifying some idea or person. In recent times, Spiro Agnew's "nattering nabobs of nihilism" or "effete corps of impudent snobs" are good examples. Then, we are likely to think of instances of language charged with emotion but in a different way—in the way usually referred to as "eloquence." Examples that come to mind are probably dramatic ones like John F. Kennedy's "Ask not what your country can do for you; ask rather what you can do for your country" or Martin Luther King, Jr.'s "I Have a Dream" speech. These instances, like those in which someone is artistically vilified, strike our ears as unique and memorable. Others agree that they are unique and eloquent as demonstrated by the number of times the statements are quoted in books like this one or by other speakers—by the number of times in which they are imitated.[2]

---

[2] Richard M. Nixon, in his acceptance address delivered at the Miami nominating convention in 1968, parodied King's metaphor, saying "I see a day" and then went on, much as King did, to describe various characteristics of the new "day" or "dream." After John F. Kennedy was elected president, many local politicians and commencement-day speakers began to cast their words into the thesis-antithesis

If we think more specifically about language, we are reminded of the admonitions given by some well-meaning teacher of English or speech —vitalize your language, use vivid words, or be clear and concise. We may even think of some assignment in which we were asked to analyze the language of a poem or a short story or an advertisement in order to identify the "good" and "bad" uses of language. For our present purposes we will not focus on "moments of eloquence" or on methods of vitalizing one's language usage, but we will begin with the possible origins of language. There are several ways in which to think about origins of language. For example, we could think about how each individual acquires language as a child, beginning with the babbling and lallation stages of experimentation with voice and articulation and tracing this development on to the discovery of words;[3] or we might think about how languages continually shift and change, looking at how a word like "sincere" developed from Greek and Latin roots until it reached its present form; or we might think about how man first got language, how he "invented" the idea and tool of language. Each of these approaches would result in different answers to the question "What are the roots of language?" simply because they would be looking at language phenomena differently, and it is possible that all three answers could be true or that they all might be false.

Let's look first at what makes man different from animals. Some would argue that man is unique because he is a toolmaker (and, of course, language is his most magnificent tool). Yet this characteristic is shared with certain apes and monkeys. Chimpanzees save tokens which can be traded in for bananas, and it seems reasonable to call these tokens "tools" for the chimp that gets a hankering for a banana. Experiments with apes have demonstrated that it is not unusual for them to fit ferruled sticks together to form a long pole for getting food. Not only do lower animals save objects that can be used as tools, but they also engage, at least primitively, in the act of toolmaking. Making utensils, then, does not distinguish man from the animals.

Some would argue that the ability to communicate with a language that is more than just a series of grunts or growls is man's most unique characteristic. In this view, language is seen as a tool also—an invention made by man to manipulate his environment. But what about the porpoise? Recent studies have demonstrated that this mammal has a complex language system consisting of perhaps over one hundred

---

format. When Nixon was President, there was a tendency to preface vague statements with the Nixonian "Let me make myself perfectly clear . . ." Thus, forms of discourse are imitated—usually because they are viewed by the imitator as effective or eloquent.

[3] A good discussion of this explanation of language origin is found in *Words and Things* by Roger Brown (New York: The Free Press, 1958) and also more compactly in Brown's *Social Psychology* (New York: The Free Press, 1965) in Chs. 6 and 7.

"words" used to communicate a variety of meanings or signs. Even the honeybee has an extremely complex "dance" that communicates the location of flowers, the type of flowers, and the distance from the hive to the flowers. The story is told of a researcher who designed and built an electric bee that could do the honey dance—the problem, it seems, was that the bees in the hive answered the electric bee with a dance of their own—perhaps something like "Okay, we're on the way." The electric bee, however, didn't receive messages—like so many persons, he just sent them and continued his message of "lots of roses, 100 yards northwest of the hive" over and over. The real bees eventually attacked the electric bee and stung it to death. So the communicative process, even in bees, is two way and fairly complex. In fact, we humans could probably learn something from the bee about how to handle compulsive talkers. At any rate, the ability to communicate using a code does not seem to be exclusively human either, though it must be granted that man has developed this attribute to a higher degree than other animals. Nonetheless, animals have "languages" they use in controlling their environments. Some dog and cat owners would argue that their pets can "talk" at a high level of sophistication with a large vocabulary. For the present let us admit the possibility that animals can, perhaps, be trained to use a kind of language, with enough time and enough rewards and punishments. Theirs is probably a language consisting of codes or signals they can convey to other animals or to the environment in general.

We are still left with our problem, however. What does man do that is unique and distinctive? What separates him from animals? Susanne Langer has suggested a characteristic of human behavior that seems to be quite unique, and it is an exciting characteristic from the point of view of persuasion. That characteristic is the ability to *make* symbols, the ability to create *some thing* which stands for *something* else— which symbolizes it.[4] Even the earliest cave dwellings have evidence of this impulse in the hominoid "cavemen." Before the invention of language, people were painting on cave walls and were making charms and amulets to ward off evil or to bring luck. Not only is this characteristic unique, according to Langer, but it is impulsive in humans. That is to say, human beings cannot help but make symbols; the making of artistic things that stand for other things is as necessary to man as breathing, eating, drinking, or sex. You may not accept Langer's proposition, but it is difficult to think of another animal that consciously *makes* symbols.

---

[4] See fn. 1. This notion (man's use of symbols as his most unique characteristic) is also seen in *A Grammar of Motives* and *A Rhetoric of Motives* by Kenneth Burke (Berkeley: University of California Press, 1969) and several other works, such as *The Presence of the Word* by Walter S. Ong, S.J. (New Haven, Conn.: Yale University Press, 1967).

When one considers the range of symbol-making activities—from home decorating to painting to poetry to music to dance—it is difficult to imagine that this activity is "learned" or "trained," as some theorists suggest. Though symbol making can be upgraded by training—the artist can learn about color, the musician about tempo, the home decorator about character in furnishings—the *initial impulse* to decorate cave walls, living rooms, canvases, or silence is seldom directed by others or even by culture. It is this impulsive quality in symbol making that so excites and involves the makers and the viewers of the symbols to which we are constantly exposed.

Those who may still be skeptical about Langer's hypothesis might try to observe a small child in the year-and-a-half to two years before he acquires language. He may only have a few words like "mama," "milk," or "no, no," but they are made to stand for a multitude of things from "mama, I want a cookie" to "the electrical outlet is a 'no no.'" Even without much language, he engages in creative activities, using a few symbols he has to stand for a multitude of meanings. Unlike the *signal* responses the child makes (e.g., crying when uncomfortable, gooing when happy, and so forth), these symbolic acts contain within them the same artistic impulse that led the early man to paint in the gloom of his cave. Once the child reaches a certain level of development, his ability to use language symbolically and his repertoire of symbols both take a quantum leap, and it is as if the power of the linguistic symbol "explodes" from the child. He spends the better part of his day playing with words, naming objects, and experimenting with sentences—much as an artist introduced to a new medium plays with it, trying it in a variety of ways, forms, and textures.[5] Helen Keller dramatically records this explosion of symbol-using power in her biography— the scene she describes is probably one of the most dramatic in the play *The Miracle Worker*, which is based on Miss Keller's life. "As the cool stream gushed over my hand she spelled into the other the word *water*, first slowly, then rapidly. I stood still, my whole attention fixed upon the motion of her fingers. Suddenly I felt a misty consciousness as of something forgotten—a thrill of returning thought; and somehow the mystery of language was revealed to me. I knew then that w-a-t-e-r meant the wonderful cool something that was flowing over my hand. . . . I left the well-house eager to learn. Everything had a name and each name gave birth to a new thought."[6]

---

[5] For a complete discussion of how language development occurs, see *Words and Things* by Roger Brown mentioned in fn. 3; and *The Psychology of Communication* by Jon Eisenson, J. Jeffery Auer, and John V. Irwin (New York: Appleton-Century-Crofts, 1963).

[6] Helen Keller, *The Story of My Life* (New York: Doubleday Doran & Co., 1936), pp. 23–24.

Language Use as Art

What does all this talk about the distinctiveness of symbol making have to do with the roots of language? Let us accept, for the moment, Langer's theory about the uniqueness of symbol making in man and her claim that symbol-making activity is impulsive and artistic. Given these two ideas, imagine yourself as a cave man who has just drawn a picture on a cave wall depicting a hunt in which you managed to kill two deer. Having put the finishing touches on your painting, what is your next impulse? Well, for most people it would probably be to show the symbol to someone, after admiring it at length. It would be a shame to leave your work of art hiding in the gloom of the cave. So you walk outside the cave to where the hominoid you mate with sits eating the remnants of the two deer you have killed. You motion to your mate to follow you into the cave. If the mate refuses, you force him or her to the site of the cave art gallery. Imagine your elation when your mate points to the scraggly drawn deer and then to the chunk of raw meat from the two deer you have killed. You have discovered or perhaps invented a powerful symbol to be used between two people to communicate. What is even more important, you *made* the symbol out of nothing but a few berries and a burnt stick. It is part raw material, but mostly it is you inscribed on the wall.

But most of us say we are not artists; we can't draw very well. Your cave mate might not be able to duplicate your activity even if he or she had seen you in the process of drawing. In that sense the use of the cave painting is limited to "artists"—and is magical. Remembering Langer's proposition, we may feel sorry for the untalented cave painter whose deer look like rocks or whose hunters look like trees, because his impulse for symboling cannot be fulfilled or shared very adequately. He must seek other means to make symbols, and it is probably out of this attempt to find what the psychologist calls "adaptive behavior sets" or other modes of symbol making that such things as music, dance, and ritual evolved.[7] Most important, it is reasonable to suppose that this same seeking for alternate ways of expressing and creating led to language. And what a miraculous invention and discovery that must have been! Here was a symbolic activity that everyone except the mute could engage in to some degree. It is easy to imagine then how the words or symbols used came to have some degree of universal "meaning," first within the family and then the tribe as one family sent symbols to another family.

If Langer's assumptions are at all accurate, then our use of language,

---

[7] See *Philosophy in a New Key* by Susanne K. Langer, Chs. 6 and 7.

and our invention of it, is basically an *artistic* or "making" activity. Embodied in our use of language is the artistic impulse of self-expression—we are our symbols. Interestingly, we still seem to think of it that way, if only at a low level of awareness. We say that a person "makes sense" or that he is "good with words," that his speech is "beautiful," or we ask a person to "give us reasons" (as if what he is about to give is his creation) or to "make an argument" or to "build a case" around a proposition. Rooted in the way we talk about language are clues that language use is essentially artistic or creative—not learned or memorized. And how much more flexible language is—especially when compared with any other artistic activity except perhaps dance. Our language contains over a half a million words (though we only recognize about 60,000 and only use a third of that number). The painter, however, has only a limited number of lines he can use and a limited number of colors or shades; the musician has only a few octaves of sound; and the sculptor is even more restricted. The dancer is limited only by the movements the human body can make. The user of language is limited only by the number of sounds the human central nervous system can produce and process. The number of symbol combinations available with 20,000 words is, practically speaking, infinite (mathematically the limit is found by 20,000 factoral or 20,000 times 19,999 times 19,998 and so on down to zero). Language, then, is the most universal and probably the most flexible art form for making symbols.

Implications of Language as an Art Form

There are some exciting implications associated with artistic activity that should be mentioned before returning to language and persuasion. The reader should be asking himself "So what?" at this point or "What does all this talk of artistic activity and making symbols have to do with speech or persuasion?" The answer to those questions is crucial and difficult. Stated simply, the answer is that artistic activity is highly ego-involving. When a person "makes" something, it is a thing of beauty to him (unless, of course, his creation was a mistake, in which case he wants to destroy it quickly because it is somehow tainted). The product of the creative process contains elements of the creator more than it contains the raw materials with which he worked. The cave man who showed his mate the drawing of the hunt, or the child who shows his parent his scribble, or the wife who shows her husband the dress she has sewn, or the father who shows his children the work he does—all are demonstrating this ego-involvement characteristic of the creative process. The product is theirs, and if they think it is good, they want to reinforce that thought by checking it out with others. And we are pleased and gratified if others think it is good or if our creation has effect. We are trying to show something of ourselves when we create, to communicate something of what we feel and think, and so we put something of ourselves into the creation. In other words, we risk a part of the "self," or ego, when we make symbols.

If language activity is symbolic and creative, it seems reasonable to believe that using language is an ego-involving activity like other creative acts. You have probably had the experience of finding yourself speechless in an argument or discussion only to mull over the argument in your mind, later discovering the key counterargument, phrasing it well, and wishing that there were some way to restage the controversy so that you might "show off" your brilliant logic and word-smithing. You probably say to yourself, "That argument would really kill their position. It would defeat them utterly. If only I can find some way to get it stated." You can see the power of your own symbols, and you want others to appreciate or witness your artistic ability. Even if only one other person were present when you stated your rebuttal argument, that would suffice. In fact, many people, having created a good counterargument too late, go to the trouble to explain the situation to a friend or parent or spouse just so they can demonstrate the now useless counterargument. It is as if the creation must "live" in someone else's eyes before it can be put out of mind. It doesn't really matter whether you have persuaded someone; what matters is that you have *delivered* the work of art—that it has been heard.

What are the basic premises of this discussion of language as it has progressed so far? There are three critical premises or assumptions:

1. Man's most unique characteristic is the impulsive *making* of symbols or creating.
2. Language is rooted in this impulse and serves as the most universal and probably most flexible symbol set.
3. Language use, as a creative activity, is highly ego-involved.

We should also keep in mind that the ego-involvement is risky only when exposed to others and that it is really complete only when it is appreciated by others.

If the above assumptions are at all accurate, the persuadee has a marvelous opportunity for making judgments about the persuasion he is exposed to, on the basis of the language used by the persuader. If the persuader is revealing something of himself in his use of linguistic symbols, the persuadee can analyze what the persuader is up to by listening analytically to the language of the persuasive message. In tuning one's ear to language use, he must be aware of several characteristics of language.

Characteristics of Language

With a perspective for considering language use, let us examine the salient characteristics of language. In trying to identify any of the characteristics of human language, we are bound to overlook some, and we can always question which characteristics are most or least important. The following discussion avoids those terms most of us have come to associate with language study (e.g., syntax, grammar, vividness). Instead we look at three elements or characteristics that reveal more what language *does* than what it means.

Try to think of language as if it were contained within a globe with three axes or six separate poles (see Figure 2–1). Along one axis are the *functional* characteristics of language—*the jobs it can do (naming things and connecting ideas, for instance)*. Along the second axis are the *semantic* or meaning characteristics of language—*the various meanings and shades of meaning that words can represent* (the differences between

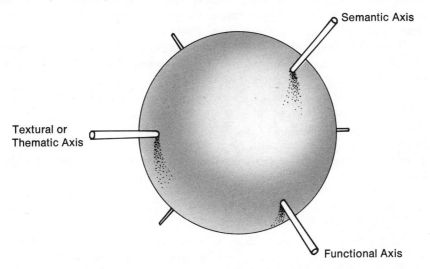

Figure 2–1 This figure is based on a description of a model for meaning suggested by Charles E. Osgood, George J. Suci, and Percy H. Tannenbaum in *The Measurement of Meaning* (Urbana: University of Illinois Press, 1957). They suggest that semantic meaning can be located for any word or concept by charting it in "semantic space" using the Semantic Differential, a tool whereby receivers respond to a word, phrase, or concept along several polar scales. Each end of a scale represents an adjectival description (e. g., "good–bad" or "heavy–light"). The globe here expands such charting to include two other attributes—function and "feel," or motif, of words. An investigator could add other axes to chart the sexuality, the aggressiveness, the dialectical, or other qualities of a particular symbol.

synonyms, for example). And along the third axis are the *thematic* characteristics of language—*the flavor or texture or feeling of various words or combinations of words* (such as the different "flavor" one gets from a slogan like "Stand Up for America," which George Wallace used in his 1968 and 1972 presidential bids, or the one John F. Kennedy used to describe the mission of his presidency—"The New Frontier"). Given this globe, we can chart any given utterance according to its functional, semantic, and thematic characteristics. We might wish to add other axes and poles to our globe representing the Freudian qualities of words or the ideological qualities of words, thus making the locating of utterances even more complex and more meaningful. As a persuadee, you may wish to add axes to this globe, but let us begin with the three shown in Figure 2–1 in a simple example.

During the midterm elections held in 1970, Vice-President Spiro Agnew invented a term, "radiclib." In a sense, it was a meaningless term —it had no real dictionary significance, but it was meant to stand for certain senators and congressmen who claimed to be liberal in ideology. Agnew's argument, however, was that these persons were actually radicals and dangerous ones at that. In his eyes they espoused radical political positions, like withdrawing immediately from Vietnam or that the supersonic transport airplane was a danger to human life and the environment, while calling themselves "liberals."

This term, "radiclib," can be placed within our language globe along the three axes. Along the *function* axis, the word "radiclib" is meant to name some thing or some class of things; it is also meant to modify or explain some other things or classes of things (we could use the word "radiclib" as an adjective, as in "These people are a radiclib bunch"). Along the *semantic* axis, this word was meant to refer to those senators, Republican or Democrat, who were in opposition to President Nixon on a string of issues—the war, nominations to the supreme court, the "no-knock" law, the antiballistic missile system, the SST, and so forth. To various members of the Vice-President's office, the term applied to specific persons—Senator Charles Goodell, Senator Adlai Stevenson III, Senator Wayne Morse, and so on. Thus it would fit into the globe on the meaning pole in two places: first, as a reference to a class of politicians and, second, as a reference to specific members of the class. *Thematically*, the word "radiclib" had negative tones or associations; one wouldn't feel complimented if Agnew called him a "radiclib." Some persons even argued with the use of the word itself, claiming it to be a misrepresentation. The Vice-President, they said, was emphasizing the radical element and understating the liberal part of the word, whereas in reality, the persons referred to were more liberal than radical. Internally, then, the word "radiclib" has a "texture" or "grain" about it. The word could have been "liberad," in which case the accented part of the word would have been *liberal*. But Agnew's invention puts the emphasis on *radical* and not on *liberal.* Further, the word "radiclib" is somehow handier to say than "liberad"—the vocal mechanism seems more comfortable with the Agnew term; it is easier and "more fun" to articulate. Then too, the "clib" part of the word, though a nonsense word, seems to have an unpleasant texture about it, being reminiscent of words like "clod" or "clump" or "clip." We wouldn't feel our stomach juices begin to work if someone told us that the oatmeal was "clibby" this morning. Or we would check in the mirror if he or she told us that our face had a "clib" on it. So internally, as well as externally, there was a texture to this word. Most words are, to some degree, like "radiclib," and they have a flavor or texture or feel to them.

Words or groups of words, then, can be charted or located or identified by at least three characteristics—their *function* (what jobs they do), their *meaning* (what they refer to), and their tone or *texture* (how they feel). Let us look at these characteristics in greater depth.

Functional Axis

Words have jobs they can do. We have traditionally grouped these jobs into grammatical classes—nouns, verbs, adjectives, adverbs, prepositions, conjunctions, interjections, and so on. Every grammar book names and identifies these word classes in objective and clear terms. We have all memorized some of the definitions of these word classes—"a noun is the name of a person, place, thing, or idea." It would be of limited value, however, for a persuadee to diagram the sentences he hears in a persuasive message. Such an analysis might show a pattern of sentence development on the persuader's part or a tendency for him to use certain words or word classes more frequently than others, but such trends are normal for most speakers and really would tell us little about the persuader or his message. What persuadees need is a set of function rules to identify what is happening in a persuasive message. What will help the persuadee is a set of concepts or principles that allows him to answer the question "What are the words *doing* in this message vis-à-vis persuasion?" On this level, he is interested in the *form* of the message, not the content.

When a persuader sends messages, he wants words to *do* one of at least three things: (1) to identify or locate an issue or topic; (2) to assign a cause or a cure for a problem associated with the issue; (3) or to motivate his audience to take purposeful action. These three functions—location, identification of cause, and motivation—are served by language or words.

Let us return to the word "radiclib" for a moment. The word is sometimes used to locate an issue or topic—"I want to talk about those individuals we know as radiclibs." At other times it is used to assign cause—"the radiclibs are ruining this country." And at other times, the same word is used to motivate the audience to action—"unless we do something, the radiclibs will win."

Semantic or Meaning Axis

If the functional axis can be used to answer the question "What are the words doing in this message?" the semantic axis can be used to answer the question "What do the words mean in this message?" Now we move from examination of language function to examination of language content. This second axis looks at why certain words are used instead of others. Take, for example, the slogan of the Kennedy Administration—"The New Frontier." Why is the word "frontier" used? The word "vista" or "future" might have been chosen as well. Asking this question shifts our view of language from function (location of a topic in this case) to the particular meaning of the word. We may find great variance of opinion on the word "frontier," but most would agree that the word suggests challenge, effort, adventure, and discovery. Those synonyms are different from the synonyms suggested for a word like "future." In other words, the semantic or meaning axis can be used to identify the associations or images, or perhaps the "frame of reference," for the words used in a persuasive message (see Chapter 1, pp. 10–11).

Thematic Axis

So far, the persuadee can ask two questions about the language used in the persuasive messages vying for his attention—"What are the words doing?" and "What do they refer to?" There is a third kind of question he can ask—"What commonality exists among the words used in this message and what might that commonality imply?" Answering this question depends on the thematic qualities of language—the flavors or textures of the words used. In a real sense, this characteristic of language is almost mystical and analysis of it relies on intuition or feeling. It's likely we would find only minimal agreement among observers on the "texture" of language, but that is not crucial. Remember, the problem facing the persuadee in our information age is not how to make the *best choice*, or how to come up with the *best solution* to a problem, but how to make a *choice at all* or how to arrive at *any kind* of solution. What is important is that the persuadee become aware of the various thematic qualities of persuasion that may tempt and sway him—and the tone or texture of the language used by the persuader is one the persuadee should be attuned to.

Richard Weaver, in *The Ethics of Rhetoric,* notes that style is a process of accumulation; that is, we really discover the stylistic aspects of a persuader's discourse only after listening to him in a variety of situations or over an extended period of time. In other words, a single word, sentence, or paragraph is not enough to give us the full story. Perhaps one of the most well-known persuaders of the first half of the twentieth century was Winston Churchill. Though many readers will not remember hearing the Prime Minister speak during World War II, they are probably aware of some of his speeches. One of the thematic qualities of Churchill's persuasion was to cast light-dark images,[8] or pictures related to day and night. The Nazis were always pictured as thugs or "gangsters" furtively engaging in monstrous acts in darkened places; on the other hand, the English were pictured as bright, sturdy, and capable of overcoming this "darkness" with the "light of their resolve."

There are many other motifs or families of metaphors and images that persuaders use. For example, Jerry Rubin in his book *Do It!* repeatedly uses images that remind the reader of machinery, particularly of the digital computer. He usually associates education, the courts, and so on with these machines; moreover, these images are associated with semantically negative claims. Throughout the book, there is a condemnation not only explicitly (he condemns modern American culture and society) but implicitly (he associates modern American culture and society with mechanistic images).

As an undergraduate, I once sold *Encyclopedia Americana* door to door. A favorite motif or set of metaphors included in the sales pitch centered around crowding and growth—of schools, of knowledge, of the population, and of libraries. The salesman continually emphasized the impending swarms of children clamoring for books and unable to get to them because of complex and crowded libraries. A similar tactic is used by magazine salesmen who claim to be working for "points" to get a scholarship to one of the crowded and expensive universities or to get a start in business—here the motif is around the individual's attempts to overcome difficulties in the mass society.

Or listen, for example, to the texture of the following remarks by Governor Ronald Reagan following the early stages of the "revolution" on campuses during the late 1960s:

> Consider these words from a campus teacher: "I think we agree that the revolution is necessary and that you don't conduct a revolution by attacking the strongest enemy first. You take care of your business at home first, then you move abroad. Thus we must make the university the home of the revolution."
> From the capture of a police car and negotiations conducted in an

---

[8] For a more detailed discussion and case study of the use of light-dark images, see Michael Osborn's "Archetypal Metaphors in Rhetoric: The Light-Dark Family," *Quarterly Journal of Speech*, 53 (April 1967), 115–126.

atmosphere of intimidation, threats, and fear; we went from free speech to filthy speech.

The movement spread to other campuses. There has been general incitement against properly constituted law-enforcement authorities and general trampling of the will, the rights and freedom of movement of the majority by the organized, militant and highly vocal minority.

Though the causes were cloaked in the dignity of academic and other freedoms, they are—in fact—a lusting for power. Some protesters even marched under banners that ranged from the black flag of anarchy, the red flag of revolution, to the flags of enemies engaged in killing young Americans—the North Vietnamese and the Viet Cong.[9]

Reagan uses words like "filthy," "cloaked," "incitement," "trampling," "lusting," and so forth. These all suggest a negativity, which is clearly intended by the governor, and an insidious kind of conspiracy operating by devious and ingenious means, especially with Reagan's direct reference to these kinds of activities. Thus, there is a thematic aspect to the persuasive language used that we might call the "ruffian" or "villain" metaphor. Cast against these forceful words, there are words later in the speech suggesting quite a different texture:

There is an artificial separation between you, as students and the youth of this State, and what is referred to as the "public interest."

Let me stress that this is an *artificial* separation: It really does not exist.

The majority of Californians want justice—so do you. You want relevance in education as you want relevance and meaning in every other phase of your life. So do the majority of Californians.

You support true academic freedom and oppose anarchy and tyranny. So do the majority of your fellow citizens—of all ages.

You want your campuses free of strife, threats and violence. So do the majority of Californians.

Your interest *is* the public interest.

I wonder if you don't agree, in order to protect true academic freedom and assure the continuation of our heritage, that disorders which disturb or disrupt the work and educational activities of any university or college campus can no longer be tolerated. . . .[10]

Here we find words like "justice," "true academic freedom," "protect," and "majority," with different tones or thematic qualities.

There is, then, a clearly identifiable thematic axis on our sphere of

---

[9] Radio Address by Governor Reagan, December 8, 1968.
[10] *Ibid.*

language use or style. The problem is to devise tools so that we can identify such qualities and make inferences from them. Chapter 3 is devoted to the tools of stylistic analysis and develops a number of devices used in describing this interesting and complex aspect of language.

A Review and Conclusion

Thus far we have been making a case for the necessity of being responsible whenever we are exposed to persuasive messages. In view of the overwhelming number of persuasive stimuli competing for our attention and action, we must choose carefully and wisely. This choosing should be done after careful analysis of the persuasive appeal and by examining how we are persuaded. Language analysis offers us, as receivers of persuasion, one way of being responsible; and it rests on the assumption that language is symbolic and ego-involving. We have also briefly examined language from three perspectives—functions, meanings, and textures or themes. The next step in the process of training ourselves as responsible receivers of persuasion is to systematize language analysis —and that is the focus of our next chapter. For now, though, let's look at some difficulties in analyzing language systematically.

One of the problems in systematically examining the language of persuaders is that there are so many possibilities. On the one hand, there are an infinite number of possible aspects of language a persuadee can examine meaningfully; on the other hand, he is limited by time, his own purposes and motives, and other factors. The persuadee is somewhat at a loss about what to analyze in detail. Even if he decides to look, for example, at the persuader's use of metaphor, how is this task to be completed systematically and equally in all cases? What the persuadee needs is a set of analytical devices that can be used as consistently and as equally as possible. These tools should have certain characteristics:

1. *They should be easily understood.* If they are too complex the persuadee will find himself finishing his analysis long after he can take or oppose the action which the persuader requests.
2. *They should be applicable.* This is not to say that the tools of language analysis must be universal, but they ought to be broad enough that they can be applied in a variety of circumstances and to a variety of persuasive messages.
3. *They must be capable of revealing something about the persuader and his persuasion.*

Suppose persuadees were asked to count the number of pronouns a persuader used in his appeal. This method of analysis would be easily understood—there are only a few pronouns in any language, and they are easily identified. This tool would certainly have applicability and flexibility—it could be applied to television commercials, presidential addresses, or group discussions. It might also be capable of revealing something about the persuader and his intentions; however, this possibility is clearly limited. Thus a "pronoun" tool doesn't fulfill all three characteristics.

We might ask persuadees to use the theories of Freud and search for words with sexual overtones. We would ask him to look for words revealing oral fixation or referring to aspects of the Oedipus complex, and so forth. This kind of analysis would probably be meaningful and applicable, but training ourselves to use it would be difficult. The theories of Sigmund Freud are not easily understood; any tool based on them is likely to be equally difficult.

Persuadees could be asked to analyze the political references or perhaps the loaded words used by persuaders. Both of these aspects of persuasion would be meaningful and easily understood but not all persuaders make political references or use loaded language. In many cases advocates on the same issue vary in their uses of emotion-laden words or political references—so, the applicability of this tool is clearly limited.

The problem is clear. The persuadee must arm himself with analytical tools that are easy to understand and that are flexible in their applicability. They also ought to be meaningful and should reveal to the persuadee something of what the persuader intends and believes. As you consider the tools of analysis presented in the next chapter, keep the criteria outlined above in mind and attempt to relate the tools to these assumptions:

1. Language is symbolic.
2. Symbolic activity is man's most unique characteristic.
3. Language, as a symbol system, is highly ego-involved and thus highly revealing.

Keep in mind, also, that stylistic analysis, or the study of *how* the persuader uses language, is only one of a multitude of potential methods of receiving persuasion critically. Considering the three assumptions laid down in this chapter, however, it can yield abundant results. The persuader is revealing himself, his philosophical assumptions, and most importantly his motives through his "artistic" activity in choosing and combining symbols. He is tipping himself off to his audience, not out of any generosity, but because he is involved in language for what it does *for him* as well as for what it does to *others*. In the words of the behavioral scientist, the persuader engages in language activity for its consummatory effects at least as much as he engages in it for its instrumental effects; it is an end in itself whether it achieves the source's effects or not. (We will discuss the terms *consummatory* and *instrumental* later, but for the present one might think of the term *consummatory* as referring to language for its artistic, cathartic, or expressive uses —for example, when we call someone a name or talk to get something out, as in a confession, or when we try to describe why something is beautiful or ugly. For now, the term *instrumental* refers to language when it is used to manipulate the environment—for example, when we say "Please shovel the snow" or "If you don't let me have the car tonight, it will be the last time I help you with your math assignment." Consummatory language use tends to be more spontaneous and artistic than instrumental language, which tends to be more preplanned and technological—it tries to apply technique, not expression.) This chapter and Chapter 3 in particular deal with ways of "listening" for that consummatory activity. Later we will focus on what the persuader does with language to gain instrumental effects—to affect the environment outside himself rather than the artistic sensibility inside himself.

Questions for Further Thought

1. What is man's most unique characteristic? Give examples of displays of this characteristic from at least four different fields of endeavor.

2. What functions can words perform? Give examples from a daily newspaper's headlines.

3. What is the major texture or theme of Chapter 2? Give examples to prove your point.

4. What are some examples of tools, other than language, that man uses for communication?

5. What methods of symbolic activity (e.g., signs or insignias) can you identify in your immediate environment (home, dorm, or apartment)?

6. Identify two messages that make the same point (e.g., an editorial against war and an antiwar song). What textural differences are evident between the two messages? What semantic differences? What functional differences (e.g., songs may name or identify causes while editorials may propose solutions).

7. Consult an art major or refer to any art history text. What common themes or topics are portrayed by man's earliest symbolic activity? (Consider such things as acts represented, supernatural powers appealed to in the work, and so forth).

Experiences in Persuasion

1. Read parts of Susanne Langer's *Philosophy in a New Key* (e.g., Ch. 5 on "Language" or Chs. 6 and 7 on "Life Symbols"). Identify myths prevalent in our culture or sacraments our culture engages in (e.g., the politician as "a savior" or the reenactment of the revolutionary war on the Fourth of July). Speculate as to their origins. How might a persuader use these symbols to form persuasive premises and messages? What parts of these are metaphorical?

2. Keep a symbology log of your own activities. Some of the things you do, you do out of instinctual needs or drives. Others are responses to knowledge of signs (e.g., you come in from out-of-doors when you hear thunder and lightning). Many things, however, are direct responses *to*, or creation *of*, symbols. If you were to list all of them, you would be writing forever. Instead, record the striking examples of creation of or response to symbols (e.g., giving the peace sign or writing a speech). After logging this activity for a week, review it and answer these questions:

   a. What stimulated the response or creation?

   b. How many persons responded to your response or to the creation?

   c. Which responses or creations were most satisfying (in an ego-trip sense) and why?

   d. How many of the responses were stimulated by language?

   e. How many of the creations utilized language?

3. As you open your mail this week, select a piece of "junk mail," which is essentially a persuasive attempt to get you to behave and/or decide in certain ways. Identify the functional elements in the message or some part of it. Speculate about the semantic elements of the message or parts of it. Identify the thematic or textural qualities of the message or parts of it. Report on these to the class.

4. Identify two or three slogans for a political campaign or for some particular topic (e.g., "Join the Pepsi Generation," or "Happy Days are Here Again," or "In Your Heart You Know He's Right") from a campaign now occurring or that has occurred in the past. Compare the slogans on the three axes described in Chapter 2 discussing functional, semantic, and thematic differences.

5. Using symbols of various kinds (words, pictures, objects, insignias, etc.), create a collage on a sheet of cardboard that expresses some idea or topic. Explain your creation to the class, telling of its function (what it does), its meaning (its semantic qualities), and its theme or texture (its "flavor" or overall tone). Be able to substantiate your contentions by giving examples and by explaining them.

Readings for New Dimensions

Burke, Kenneth, *Language as Symbolic Action* (Berkeley: University of California Press, 1966). See especially Chapter 1 "Definition of Man," which essentially agrees with Langer and with Chapter 2 of this book except that Burke adds that another key characteristic of human beings, as opposed to other animals, is that they invent "the negative," when it fits their purpose. The discussion is delightful and at times tongue-in-cheek. Also interesting is Burke's reversal of "symbol standing for thing" to "things stand for symbols," which again relates to our central theme in this chapter.

Campbell, Karlyn Kohrs, *Critiques of Contemporary Rhetoric* (Belmont, Calif.: Wadsworth Publishing Co., 1972). The first three chapters of this book address the same problems and issues touched on in this chapter. Campbell deals with them more directly and from the perspective of the rhetorical critic; nonetheless, she aims at the same goal described here—to train critical persuadees to examine analytically the discourse aimed at them, utilizing a variety of tools or methods of analysis. Campbell also draws heavily from sources quoted or referred to in this chapter, especially those that view man's symbolic activity as his most essential.

Langer, Susanne K., *Philosophy in a New Key* (New York: Mentor Books, 1951). Langer discusses the problems that philosophy has tried to investigate in the past and points out that any "new" philosophical epoch, such as we are now entering, is typified by new questions—asked in a "new key" so to speak. She suggests that the new key for our present emerging epoch is related to man's artistic nature and in particular to his reliance on the symbol. Her chapters on language, life symbols, myths, and signs and symbols form a core discussion of the essence of this chapter. The book is *must* reading for the serious student, even if not all of it is read.

Ong, Walter, S.J., *The Presence of the Word* (New Haven, Conn.: Yale University Press, 1967). Ong focuses on the importance of verbal symbols in the development of religion and history. The book is most interesting for the light it sheds on scholarly consideration of McLuhanesque speculation and on the almost magical importance of "the word" in culture and religion. With a return to an oral-aural culture, such as we are now experiencing, Ong's insights about the import of sound as opposed to sight in consideration of words are intriguing.

Rubin, Jerry, *Do It!* (New York: Simon and Schuster, 1970). Note especially the introduction to this book, written by Eldridge Cleaver, as an excellent example of the use of language for its consummatory function. Throughout Rubin's book are many striking examples of the use of symbols on the three axes noted in this chapter. These are clear from the comic-strip illustrations, which lend a thematic quality of unreality, to the various tactics used by the political left.

3

Tools for Analysis of Language

Let us assume that you as persuadee have accepted the argument in Chapter 2—that the use of symbols, particularly in language, is both our most unique attribute and one of the most ego-involving and ego-revealing activities in which people engage. Given that assumption, consider the language used in each of the following presidential or campaign slogans or catch phrases:

1960: "The New Frontier" (John F. Kennedy)
1964: "A Great Society" (Lyndon B. Johnson)
1968: "Bring Us Together" (Richard M. Nixon)

How would you go about interpreting each of these slogans? Would you look at what they seem to mean? Would you look at who was the ghost-writer for them? Would you look at the situations that gave rise to them? Or would you look at all of these? The problem is not to decide which method of analysis to choose but to choose one that allows you to proceed somewhat systematically and objectively (i.e., a good portion of observers using the same method would come to the same or similar conclusions). Our purpose in Chapter 3 is to suggest several methods you might use to analyze the style of a persuader in order to "psych him out." But the methods presented are only representative of many that could have been chosen—some of these others will be dealt with later (in Chapter 6, for example, or in Chapters 4 and 5). Your task is to experiment with several of these methods and then to use them or invent your own if you are dissatisfied. Your goal is to take apart the persuasion directed at you and to look behind the words for some indication of what the persuader is like, what he is up to, how it affects you, and why you should be alert and interested in what he says.

Return to the three presidential slogans. What can we say about any of them without the "tools" of Chapter 3? Well, we can first describe their structure and form. The Kennedy slogan is a three-word descriptive phrase consisting of a definite article (the word "The"), an adjective (the word "New"), and a noun (the word "Frontier"). The Johnson slogan has a similar structure—three-word descriptive phrase with an article, adjective, and noun. It differs from the Kennedy slogan in that its article is indefinite (the word "a" depicts one of several, whereas the word "the" refers to the only one). The Nixon phrase is not descriptive —it is an imperative (it gives an order for action, not a description of a situation). It begins with a verb "Bring," followed by a pronoun "Us," and ends with an adverb "Together." Now that the structure of these is clear, so what? There is little we can say, but even this simple action of describing the structure of the three slogans has alerted us to some of their differences. Perhaps the framer of the phrase *"The* New Frontier" will be more *definite* than the framer of *"A* Great Society." Perhaps the Nixon imperative indicates that he will be authoritarian. All of these are, of course, guesses; but they are better than passive reception of the message or conditioned responses to the symbols used by the three Presidents. Clearly, we need to go further and try another tack.

Maybe we could look at the way the words work in each of the slogans. For example, take the adjectives in the Kennedy and Johnson word strings. What does "New" suggest? What kind of word is it? Could other words have been used? Which ones? Initially, I'd say that the word "New" suggests a future orientation, innovation, and progress. There are not many words that could have been substituted for it without a loss of the flavor ("The Innovative Frontier" would not have worked well). It also has links with "The New Deal" of Franklin D. Roosevelt and "The New Freedom" of Woodrow Wilson; in addition to its future orientation it has historical roots. It's an exciting word when we look at it in this context.

What about the word "Great" in Johnson's slogan? It seems more present than future oriented—it describes a state of affairs at hand. It, too, is not very easy to replace. He could have used "grand" perhaps, or "proud," or some other word and have lost less than Kennedy with a replacement for "New," but neither of these two words works well. Then, the word has an egotistical smack to it—I'm great; we're great; isn't it great that we're so great?

What about the nouns in the slogans? Kennedy's "Frontier" could be replaced with "Vista" or "Horizon" with little loss of meaning or texture. It is also future oriented and dramatic—we think of the challenges of the old frontier, the tests of ability, the discoveries, and the heroes. Johnson's word "Society" seems less exciting and less flexible.

You might use "country" or "culture" or some other word, but again it wouldn't have worked well. The word is not exciting and doesn't stir the imagination as the word "Frontier" does. Neither does it call attention to the future—it is a status quo oriented word and fairly ambiguous. (You can "see" a frontier and can imagine it, but a "society" seems more amorphous—less concrete.) Let's draw these word characteristics together:

> *Kennedy:* Definite, future oriented, flexible noun, inflexible adjective, rooted in the past, dramatic
>
> *Johnson:* Indefinite, somewhat inflexible in both adjective and noun, present or status quo oriented, static, perhaps egotistical

Admittedly the cards have been stacked in these two examples but not too unfairly. Members of groups with whom I've tried this out mention these characteristics without coaching. But: Do they signify the man behind them? That is probably a question each receiver has to answer for himself; but as one looks at L. B. J.'s foreign policy there was both an inflexibility about Vietnam and an indefiniteness about what should be done when. The "solutions" never seemed to be future oriented—they focused on present problems. Finally, there is substantial agreement that one of the major problems with foreign and domestic policy was the Johnson ego.[1] Kennedy seemed to be different, if only because of the magnetism of his personality and his youth (though he was really not much younger than L. B. J.). Even considering the meager record of legislative accomplishments of the Kennedy Administration and the criticisms of it, most persons would agree that it was future oriented. It did suggest a repeated sense of the dramatic and historic (the Cuban missile crisis, the Space Race, the response to the Berlin Wall) and often gave the feeling that the Administration was flexible and definite in its aims and programs.[2]

It is probably too early to judge the Administration of Richard M. Nixon, although his three words for the first term in office are certainly different from Kennedy's or Johnson's. As noted earlier, they are imperative—they give an order instead of describing a scene. They consist of a verb, a pronoun, and an adverb. On the semantic axis, they suggest an action that relies upon a man. This man will unite people of varied

---

[1] A good analysis of the Johnson Vietnam policy and its reflection of Lyndon Johnson, the decision maker, is David Halberstam's book *The Best and the Brightest* (New York: Random House, 1972).

[2] There are several good analyses of the Kennedy Administration available. One of the more insightful is Robert Kennedy's on the Cuban Missile Crisis: *Thirteen Days: A Memoir of the Cuban Missile Crisis* (New York: W. W. Norton & Co., 1971). For a more objective study, see Victor Lasky's *J. F. K.: The Myth and the Man* (New York: The Macmillan Co., 1963).

interests; he will, the words suggest, bring orderliness and cohesion to unsettled matters and to confused questions. The phrase is similar to a slang phrase of the times—"Getting It Together"—but it emphasizes communality instead of individuality; there is a corporateness about these words. Though the words were invented by a little girl in Ohio who printed them on a sign she held at a whistle-stop rally, they were embraced by Nixon and became his central theme. Do they reflect the man behind them? Again each receiver needs to make that determination himself, but consider the characteristics we have mentioned: a present orientation, an imperative format (giving of an order), a reliance upon a single individual to be orderly about creating communality, and a suggestion of a corporateness. As one looks at the 1968–1972 term of Richard Nixon, several of these qualities seem to be displayed. There is the reliance upon individuals (on himself even as his own speech writer, or on Henry Kissinger as his foreign affairs expert). There was a desire for a corporate togetherness—the cabinet was called the Nixon "team," and some members of it who did not wish to submit to the President's requests (e.g., Walter J. Hickel, the Secretary of the Interior) were fired or asked to leave at the end of the first term. The words do seem to indicate the man, or vice versa in this case, at least from a limited perspective. The Watergate affair emphasized these attributes.

Some might argue that what has been going on here is a kind of hocus-pocus and amateurish Freudian analysis of presidential slogans. In a sense, the analysis is Freudian in method (i.e., we look beneath the symbolic labels a persuader uses to describe his world in order to infer his psychological motivation), but the persuadee is not looking for psychic problems in the persuader—only for a *hint* as to his motives. As persuadees, we constantly are forced to *seek* persuasion to help us make decisions; at the same time, we are bombarded with persuasion we did not seek but which needs evaluation. We must try to winnow the appeals we need and those we ought to be wary of. Stylistic analysis, such as we have sketched above, is a start at separating the grain from the chaff.

Symbolic Expression

What we have been doing with the three presidential slogans is making a receiver's analysis based on the three language axes described in Chapter 2: We looked at what the words did (their *functions*), what the words meant (their *semantic dimension*), and then we touched on their *texture* (the qualities they had like corporateness, futureness, or static or egotistical qualities). The assumptions delineated in Chapter 2—that language is man's most universal symbolic act; that the symbolic act itself is man's most unique characteristic; and that this act, particularly in language, is ego-revealing and ego-involving—were underlying our limited analysis. Our problem in these initial examinations is that they lack objective and systematic methods of analysis. Aside from the objective grammatical descriptions, the trends observed are general and rely on the individual observer's judgment. We probably would get good agreement on the trends, but not because of any tool we used to code or identify the trends like future orientation or egotistical quality. The rest of Chapter 3 is devoted to explaining and briefly applying tools. The important thing about them is that they are fairly systematic and objective—we still might get some disagreement among various persons using them, but we would expect the various observers to agree more than they could without tools and also be able to use a common "language" in analyzing the words of various persuaders.

Interestingly enough, there is some scientific evidence to support this practice of searching for the motives behind a persuader's words. Recently more and more research and observational evidence supports the notion that a man *is* what he uses for his symbols. He becomes what he symbolizes. The field of psychosomatics (the relation between one's thoughts and words and his physical state) several studies are exciting. For example, research shows that people who often use words related to the digestive system (e.g., "I can't stomach that" or "It's eating me") are likely to develop intestinal problems like ulcers. Their symbols reflect or perhaps even cause their problems and may direct the physical response to these problems.[3] Research into the nature of dying suggests that people can make themselves live for the sake of certain symbols. A higher proportion of elderly persons die in the two months *after* their birthdays than in the two months *before* their birthdays. Thomas Jefferson and John Adams both died *on* the Fourth of July, and Jefferson is reported to have awakened from a comatose-like sleep on the third to ask his doctor if it was the Fourth yet.[4] David Halberstam, in an interview about his book on the Vietnam war, noted that whenever Secretary of Defense Robert McNamara began to lie about troop numbers, manpower requisites, and such, he reflected it in his style—in the way he used his symbols:

> People who were in meetings with him used to say they knew
> when he was lying. His voice would get quicker and more insistent,

---

[3] "Fed Up? It May Lead to an Ulcer," *Chicago Daily News*, 24 November 1972, p. 30. For a more detailed discussion, see Howard Lewis and Martha Lewis, *Psychosomantics: How Your Emotions Can Damage Your Health* (New York: The Viking Press, 1972).

[4] Peter Koenig, "Death Doth Defer," *Psychology Today*, November 1972, p. 83.

more of a chop to it. He would become almost more sure of himself when he was lying.[5]

And we could go on citing cases where this principle seems to hold—a man is what his symbols are and how he uses them. There is good justification for doing stylistic analysis of persuasion—it ought to help the persuadee alert himself to a persuader's motives and intentions.[6]

Tools for the Functional Axis

The functional axis of language deals with what the words do in a particular expression. We have already dealt with this idea at a surface level when we looked at the grammatical qualities of the presidential slogans. A more extensive and definitive kind of tool is needed, however. There are three we can consider here: (1) the "rhetorical aspects of grammatical categories" suggested by Richard Weaver, (2) the ways in which word arrangement or syntax affects persuasion, and (3) how ambiguity helps in persuasion.

Grammatical Categories

Richard Weaver observes that grammatical form may indicate the internal qualities or intentions of a persuader. He argues that sentence structure, for example, may reflect a person's method of combining information and of coming to conclusions. The individual who primarily uses a simple sentence format tends to see the world cast into relatively discrete matter. As Weaver puts it, he ". . . sees the world as a conglomerate of things . . . (and) seeks to present certain things as eminent against a background of matter uniform or flat."[7] This sentence type sets the subject off from the verb and object; it sees the

---

[5] "The Making of Vietnam," *Chicago Tribune,* 26 November 1972, Sec. 1A, p. 1.
[6] For those who wish to explore the relation between symbols and human expression, look at Hugh D. Duncan, *Communication and Social Order* (London: Oxford University Press, 1963); Kenneth Burke, *A Grammar of Motives* (Berkeley: University of California Press, 1970); or Mircia Eliade, *The Myth of the Eternal Return: or Cosmos and History* (Princeton, N. J.: Princeton University Press, 1971).
[7] Richard M. Weaver, *The Ethics of Rhetoric* (Chicago: Henry Regenery Co., 1953), p. 120. For a discussion of the Platonic idealism and political conservatism underlying Weaver's conception of rhetoric, see Richard L. Johannesen, Rennard Strickland, and Ralph T. Eubanks, "Richard M. Weaver on the Nature of Rhetoric," in Johannesen, ed., *Contemporary Theories of Rhetoric* (New York: Harper & Row, 1971), pp. 180–195.

world as having causes that act to have effects upon objects. When a persuader uses this form, the persuadee ought to look at what is being highlighted, at what affects what, and at how action occurs.

The complex sentence does something quite different, according to Weaver. It emphasizes "coexistent" relationships—several causes and several effects at the same time. Weaver says that it ". . . is the utterance of a reflective mind,"[8] which has gone beyond the observational and descriptive process ". . . to express some sort of hierarchy."[9] You could expect a persuader using this kind of sentence to begin to express principles and relationships growing out of those principles. The independent clauses would stand in a higher position than the dependent clauses—the hierarchy noted by Weaver would be expressed by the way the persuader tied the parts of the sentence together. For example, Martin Luther King, Jr., in *Where Do We Go from Here?*, wrote this sentence:

> While this reaction [the Black Power Movement] has often led to negative and unrealistic responses and has frequently brought about intemperate words and actions, one must not overlook the positive value in calling the Negro to a new sense of manhood, to a deep feeling of racial pride, and to an audacious appreciation of his heritage.[10]

The independent and most self-sufficient element in the sentence begins with the words ". . . one must not overlook . . ."—the foremost point in King's mind. We can expect a persuader to put this independent element higher on his ladder of values than the dependent elements introducing the sentence. King's pattern throughout his career is reflected in his words—to value the advances of his opposition in spite of the negative side effects that occurred. He probably would have said that this was one of the principles of his philosophy of life.

To Weaver, the compound sentence tends to set things either in balance (e.g., He ran, and he ran fast.) or in opposition (e.g., He ran, and she walked.); it seems to contain potential for expressing some kind of tension—whether resolved or unresolved. As Weaver notes, it ". . . conveys that completeness and symmetry which the world *ought* to have, and which we manage to get, in some measure, into our most satisfactory explanations of it."[11] Perhaps we could expect persuaders using this sentence type frequently to see the world divided into polarities and similarities—as things operating totally against one another or in concert with one another. The militant who states, "You are either against us,

---

[8] Weaver, p. 121.
[9] *Ibid.*
[10] Robert L. Scott and Wayne Brockriede, *The Rhetoric of Black Power* (New York: Harper & Row, 1969), p. 41.
[11] Weaver, p. 127.

or you are with us!" certainly does this through his words and through his sentence structure. And clearly the compound sentence structure can foster oversimplification.

Weaver also had some observations about types of words and what kinds of persuasive power they had. For example, nouns, since they are thought of as words for things and as labels for naming, are often reacted to *as if they were* the things they name. They ". . . express things whose being is completed, not whose being is in process, or whose being depends upon some other being."[12] Thus when a demonstrator calls a policeman a "pig" he makes that person into an object—a thing. It becomes easier to spit on a "pig" than on a "father of two nice kids who likes to go fishing on weekends with his sons," which he could also have called the same policeman. One of the functions of the noun is to label something as we want it to be. Looking at a persuader's nouns may clue us as to his perception of things, and they may reveal what he intends to do about those things. When you hear a persuader reduce subjects to things or objects—college demonstrators are called "long-haired creeps" —he does it for a reason; he indicates that he wishes to deal with them as things and not as people.

The function of adjectives is to add to the noun, to particularize it in some way. To Weaver, adjectives are second-class citizens. He called them "question-begging" and suggested that they indicated a kind of uncertainty about reality in most cases.[13] If you have to modify a noun, Weaver would say you aren't certain about the noun. This is not the case, in Weaver's opinion, when the adjectives are *dialectical* (good and bad, hot and cold, light and dark). Thus, looking at a persuader's adjectives may reveal what he is uncertain about, what he wants to be sure about, and/or what he sees in opposition to what.

The adverb, to Weaver, is ". . . a word of judgment."[14] Unlike the adjective, it usually represents a community judgment—one with which others can agree and which reflects what the persuader thinks the audience believes. For example, take the judgmental adverbs like "surely," "certainly," "probably," and so forth—each suggests a community of agreement. When a persuader says, "Surely we all know and believe that thus and such is so," he is suggesting that the audience agrees with him and needs only to be reminded of it.

Weaver discusses other word classes, observing that his discussions are, of course, open to debate. Again, the principle is not that we can get universal agreement on how to use a particular analytical tool or on what conclusions are to be drawn from the use of that tool, but rather that we begin using tools to analyze style as well as meaning.

---

[12] *Ibid.*, p. 128.
[13] *Ibid.*, pp. 129–130.
[14] *Ibid.*, p. 133.

Syntax as an Analytical Tool

Another functional characteristic of language is revealed in the way words are ordered. Observing syntax can help the persuadee to be alert to the thoughts and motives of the persuader if he pays heed to the ordering of words and phrases. For example, in the spring of 1970 there were several campus disruptions following the killing of several students at Kent State University. President Nixon chose to respond to these demonstrations some time later in a speech. The story goes that his speech writers wrote something like the following for him: "There is no greater hypocrite than the college student who carries a peace banner in one hand and a Molotov cocktail in the other." Supposedly, Nixon rewrote the sentence to read: "The peace demonstrator who carries a Molotov cocktail in one hand and a peace banner in the other is the kind of hypocrite that . . ." and then went on to elaborate. The original version is called an "aperiodic" structure. It lets the "Molotov cocktail" wait until the end of the sentence; it keeps the audience's attention focused on the end of the sentence where the reason for the hypocrisy is revealed. The rewrite reveals the "hooker" early and focuses on subsequent condemnation of the demonstrator on grounds other than hypocrisy. Syntax, in this case, makes a great deal of difference. Syntax may also reveal what a persuader sees as important. Nixon did not want to use the dramatic structure suggested to him by his speech writers; he felt compelled to reveal the fire bomb early and then to elaborate on a condemnation of the student. He wanted to draw the audience's attention to the potential misdeed and to characterize the demonstrator before the sentence was over, whereas his writers wanted the audience to be led to the conclusion, with the dramatic proof at the end of the sentence. On certain occasions, persuaders create slogans that have great appeal by changing the normal usage, thus shifting the attention of the audience. The normal way of describing political, economic, and legal power for blacks would be to say "the power of black persons." Stokely Carmichael created a dramatic and powerful term by shortening this description and changing the syntactical relationship of the words "power" and "black" into the slogan "Black Power." The impact of this term comes from the semantic qualities of the two words, of course, but it also comes from the way they are arranged.

The persuadee, then, can look at word order to see where a persuader's interests and priorities lie. What does he highlight syntactically? Why does he say "moral decay" instead of "the decay of morals"? Do his qualifiers or modifiers suggest uncertainty? If so, what do these trends suggest about his motives? His program? His potential? All of these questions can be asked when doing syntactical analysis.

Ambiguity as a Stylistic Device

Ambiguity is a tool persuaders often use to ensure maximum identification between themselves and the audience. If we assume that the most effective persuasion is that in which the persuadee himself participates, then the strategy of creating ambiguity and allowing the audience to "fill in the blanks" seems wise. Ambiguity can be created in several ways—syntactically, grammatically, and semantically.

Let's return to the term "Black Power" for a moment. We have pointed out that this is a powerful term, but where does its power come from? Why is it better than "Negro Power" or "Black Strength" or "the Power of Blackness" or some other variation? We can only speculate, but it seems that by allowing "Black" to describe a kind of power instead of using another word like "Negro" makes a difference— a semantic or perhaps a textural or thematic difference. The word order is also important—"Black" predominates more as an adjective than as the object of the proposition in "the Power of Black." The slogan can have many interpretations—economic power for blacks, political power for blacks, the power of blacks to riot, the power of blacks to have pride, and so on. Its very ambiguity is the reason for the term's richness —so many meanings can be ascribed to it. The same thing occurs with the term "moral decay," used by many conservative groups in the 1960s to describe a breakdown in traditional values in society. In this case, the ambiguity seems to arise from a shifting syntax—a structural ambiguity; from a meaning level—a semantic level; and from the "feel" of the positive word "moral" and the negative word "decay"—a textural ambiguity. These three kinds of ambiguity or ways of increasing ambiguity are common. Persuaders shift syntax to create *structural* ambiguity; persuaders use various words to create *semantic* ambiguity; and persuaders use motifs or value-loaded words in unusual combinations to create *textural* ambiguity.

The values of ambiguity are interesting. One of our traditional beliefs has been that it is better to be concrete and definitive as persuaders. Persuaders, viewed from this perspective, are most effective if they state their case clearly, substantiate it well with lots of concrete evidence, and take a definite position. More recently, however, it is becoming clear that audiences react more favorably to persuaders who are less explicit and more vague and who use ambiguous statements and emotion-laden words. In the election of 1968, Richard Nixon elicited a "low-profile" image—he was ambiguous, even to having a "secret" plan to end the Vietnamese war. His opponent was explicit—clearly defined—more concrete. Though Nixon almost lost that election, he was elected and four years later he did not campaign at all—the ultimate in ambiguity—and won by a landslide. We seem to have been conditioned, especially by television advertisements and other electronic media, to respond to vague images, to plotless stories, and to abstract representations. Persuaders are aware of this trend and repeatedly use ambiguity to appeal to their audiences. Persuadees need to look for ambiguity and to try to discover what it indicates, how it is achieved, why the persuader uses it, and whether they consider it unethical.

Tools for the Semantic Axis

The semantic axis of language deals with what words mean—their referents. We have already dealt with this aspect of stylistic analysis to some degree, but again we need a tool to allow persuadees to be objective and systematic about meaning. Of course, whenever we talk about meaning there is bound to be disagreement, but systematizing our discussion of what words mean should help to encourage more objective judgments. We shall consider one tool in particular: the Dramatic Pentad suggested by Kenneth Burke in *A Grammar of Motives*. The Pentad is particularly appropriate for this book, since it focuses on the way in which motives can be labeled and identified from the *way* in which statements are made—Burke intends it for stylistic analysis. Furthermore, the Pentad operates from the assumption that human behavior is seen as inherently dramatic—another assumption of this text.

The Dramatic Pentad

The basic premise put forth by Kenneth Burke, in his description of the Pentad, is that human beings see the world in dramatic terms and that they focus on one of these terms as most important or as most essential. This focus, Burke would say, is reflected in how these persons talk about the world. There are five elements of drama we need to consider—Burke says that the five are comprehensive and include all the possible constituents of dramatic action. You may add other terms, but initially there are these five:

> Scene—or the place where action occurs (perhaps the "rhetorical situation")
>
> Act—or the action which occurs (perhaps plot would be another term that could be used)

Agent—or the actor who acts out the action or plot in the scene

Agency—or tool the actor uses to accomplish his ends

Purpose—or the reason why a person does what he does[15]

Consider the following description of a dramatic situation:

> A young man and a young woman are standing in front of an altar rail in a church. They are dressed for the sacrament of marriage (he in tuxedo, she in a white dress). A young and handsome minister is preparing to conduct the "Repeat after me . . ." portion of the service, when he suddenly turns from the altar rail, walks swiftly back to the altar itself, takes down a massive brass candlestick, and bludgeons the bride to death as the groom smiles.

Which element of this drama is most interesting to you? The inconsistency between the act of murder and the setting of a church? The character of the young minister? The use of a holy object to commit homicide? The reason why the groom does nothing to stop the murder and even smiles about it? Burke would argue that your interest in one particular element over others may reflect how you see the world operating—what you think motivates action and gives meaning. Further, Burke would predict that you would choose to talk about the world according to what struck you as most important; your words would reflect your preference. If you thought that men controlled their own destiny, you would focus on *Agent;* if you felt that circumstances compelled action, you would focus on *Scene;* if you felt that high principles and ideals carried even weak men through trying times, you would focus on *Purpose;* and so on.

Persuaders do the same kind of thing. They center their topic around one of the elements of the Pentad. They choose their evidence in relation to this element, and they devise metaphors drawn from it. Of course, they may draw on the other four terms, but they consistently emphasize one or another term—that is Burke's proposition. Thus, if you are interested in Agent you are different from someone whose focus is on Act, and you will each choose different language to discuss the same problem. Consider the following:

> Over the past few years the image of politics that has taken shape for me is that of an immense journey—the panorama of an endless wagon train, an enormous trek, a multitudinous procession of people larger and more confused than any of the primitive folk migrations.

---

[15] Burke, *A Grammar of Motives* (especially the introduction). See fn. 6.

There—ahead—lies the crest of the ridge, and beyond it perhaps the plateau or the sunlit valley—or danger. The procession stretches out for endless miles, making its way up the tangled slopes through strange new country . . .

Up there, at the head of the advance column, the leaders quarrel bitterly among themselves, as do the people behind. From their heights they have a wider view of the horizon . . .[16]

The Scenic quality of the quotation is clear. The author has a vision of a setting and a background. What is important is the panorama—the view from the ridge—the Scene. He sees the setting as powerful, drawing people and leaders on, forcing them onward, even in ignorance of what lies ahead. Another person might view politics quite differently:

Some wobbly thinkers think that laws will stop you from hating, laws will make you generous. But when I read about street crimes, about hatred with blood, I ask what's happening to the land of the free; what's happened to the principles these men died for? . . . .

. . . and the fault is not only in government, but in us. Ask yourself before going to bed tonight: Did I live today with hate? Did I steal, cheat, hate, take shortcuts? If you answer 'yes,' you haven't been a good American . . .

I deplore those far-out partisans of principles that are trying to tear the American people apart, trying to tear the home apart, trying to assume they can do such things . . .[17]

This persuader (Barry Goldwater) sees the Agent as most important. Consider the number of personal pronouns he uses. He sees problems caused by Agents—"wobbly thinkers" or "partisans of principle." He sees them caused by men acting as individuals who do wrong by cheating, hating, and stealing. He has a secondary focus which is on principle —he sees some important principles as lost or overlooked while there are clever "partisans of principle" who substitute other principles that are ruining the country and its people. Thus there is a focus on Agent and on Purpose. This person will seek solutions in different ways from the Scene-oriented persuader. The Agent persuader will try to bring individual action to bear on problems; the Scene persuader will try to change environments in response to problems; the Purpose persuader may preach repentance.

Consider the following persuasive statement, with a focus on Agency:

Black Power must not be naive about the intentions of white decision makers to yield anything without a struggle and a confron-

---

[16] Theodore H. White, *The Making of the President: 1964* (New York: Atheneum Publishers, 1966), p. v.

[17] *Ibid.*, p. 155.

tation by organized power. Black people will gain only as much as they can win through their ability to organize independent bases of economic and political power—through boycotts, electoral activity, rent strikes, work stoppages, pressure group bargaining . . .[18]

The persuader focuses on the methods or means or tools to achieve ends. He suggests changing traditional agencies for action from demonstrations and nonviolent marches to more aggressive means like rent strikes and so forth. Here the problem is not seen as coming from or being caused by particular individuals—new leadership, so to speak— nor from a change in the scene of action nor in the purpose for acting. Meaningful problems and solutions come from one kind of method or another. Only by altering the methods used will change occur.

The persuader who focuses on Act as a key term is probably a descriptivist. He sketches out what happens for his listeners and perhaps lets them draw their own conclusions. In this sense, his focus is the least "persuasive" of the five. Take, for example, the following description:

> I assume that the proper study of interaction is not the individual and his psychology, but rather the syntactical relations among the acts of different persons mutually present to one another . . . Not, then, men and their moments. Rather, moments and their men.[19]

Notice how this individual's focus is not on the motivations of men or on high purpose. Instead he advocates that the social scientist look only at what he can see and describe. Interestingly, he avoids the use of personal pronouns and instead uses words that describe action—"interaction" or "relations"—and he finally even declares that he thinks we should look at "moments" and not individuals. Though he is trying to be persuasive (i.e., he is advocating a course of action), he is not very aggressive about it.

The Dramatic Pentad of Kenneth Burke can be used in these ways— to discover the persuasive focus and hence the underlying beliefs or key elements of an advocate—and also to discover and to label a persuader's characteristic symbols and rituals. By looking at what a persuader says and at how he uses language (what kinds of words he uses frequently), his underlying symbols and preferences become clear. Let us examine these characteristic "subsymbols" or metaphors more carefully, for they too can reveal the persuader's beliefs and motives to the persuadee.

---

[18] Scott and Brockriede, p. 181.
[19] Erving Goffman, *Interaction Ritual* (Garden City: Doubleday & Co., 1967), from the introduction.

Subsymbols

Depending on one's perspective, there are various ways of labeling the characteristic symbols in a persuader's discourse. If you are Freudian and a persuader makes repeated reference to productivity (e.g., "We have turned out more items this year than in any other—we have made more money than ever before—and we are going to do better"), you might label him as an "anal compulsive," who might have had problems in his toilet training. If you are interested in transactional analysis, you might label the same set of production symbols as being characteristic of someone who feels "Not O.K." and who wants to feel "O.K." and therefore engages in playing a game called "Mine's Better Than Yours."[20] Our perspective is aesthetic and dramatic; that is, focused on the artistic, magical, and dramatic aspects of symbols.

Let us briefly examine one kind of subsymbol: *the rite*. A ritual is an act that is repeatedly performed or one with archetypal and universal elements that are repeated. Its purpose is to enact or reenact some stirring event symbolically in order to involve an audience. It is easy to see how this might relate to persuasion—persuaders can get audiences involved and participating in symbolic ways. Further, it is easy to see how meaning can be carried in the symbolic enactment of the event and how this can be persuasive. A good example of a persuasive ritual is the Pledge of Allegiance. The pledger repeats the "holy" or "magical" words along with others and thus persuades himself that he has allegiance to his country.

One recurring rite is the death ritual or "the rite of kill."[21] We see it in a variety of forms ranging from the burnt offering to the crucifix to the words "Avenge Fred Hampton" and so on. Basically the ritual has four steps. First, a scapegoat is identified. The scapegoat has either neutral, pure, or impure qualities qualifying him to be the sacrifice (the dove is neutral; the lamb is pure; to Hitler, the Jew was impure). The second step is to identify the scapegoat as the carrier of evil (the lamb has sin worked into it through incantation; the Jew in Nazi Germany was repeatedly seen as perverse, money-hungry, and wicked); thus the scapegoat is associated with evil. The third step is to gather power, emotion, and involvement leading to the killing stroke. A good example of this is the elaborate procedures used in killing the sacrificial animal. Also, the ritual for killing Jews in Germany was highly developed and involved such things as moving them to killing centers, labeling them

---

[20] For an easy-to-read discussion of how this transactional focus works in describing communication, see Thomas Harris's *I'm OK—You're OK* (New York: Harper & Row, 1969).

[21] Kenneth Burke, *The Philosophy of Literary Form* (New York: Vintage Books, 1957), pp. 40–43.

with tattooed numbers, dehumanizing them, and so forth. In the final step, the *coup de grâce* is administered, and evil is symbolically removed. In some cases, not only is the evil removed but a positive is accrued—the sacrificer may gain new strength or power from having engaged in the ritual.

The important thing about this ritual is that it can be done *symbolically*—with words. How do we go about doing that? One way is to reduce a scapegoat from the state of being a subject to the state of being an object. When a persuader goes through a fairly elaborate procedure to degrade and denounce a person or a group of persons, he makes them into carriers of evil. He also changes his language when he talks about these scapegoats. For example, consider the following comment about persons who refused to be drafted during the Vietnam war:

> Senator Robert Taft of Ohio is not helping this nation by advocating suspension of the laws regarding the punishment of army deserters, draft dodgers, and shirkers. Nothing will do more to undermine the morale and effectiveness of our fighting forces than to allow these hordes of deserters to pour back into this country. . . . To bring this motley band of scurvy traitors home would betray all of the 55,000 war dead . . . we do not need, nor want this debased mob of deserters . . . ANY form of amnesty for deserters will be opposed by patriots come next election day.[22]

No draft evaders are destroyed in the literal sense here, but look at what happens symbolically. They are reduced from being persons or subjects into being things or objects. They are pictured as shirkers, scurvy, motley, and debased. They "pour" back into the country; they are "hordes," a "mob," and so forth. Symbolically, the scapegoats have been reduced from the status of persons to the status of things. They are filled with attributes of evil; finally, the symbolic kill occurs when the *coup de grâce* is administered. All politicians advocating amnesty will be voted down, thus "killing" any hopes for the draft evaders. In doing this, the source says, people will prove their patriotism. Like the lamb in the religious rituals, the scapegoats take on the collective guilt and evil of society, are debased and defiled to prepare them for the kill, and are symbolically turned into things. All of this results in a kind of redemption or new life for the voters who are now viewed as patriotic, pure, honest, and forthright. The kill rite has several persuasive functions. It unifies those who engage in it; it persuades them, or rather it allows them to persuade themselves; it simplistically identifies the enemy; it

---

[22] *The Thunderbolt*, February 1972, p. 4. This newspaper is printed irregularly by the National States Rights Party, Marietta, Georgia.

makes that enemy easy to deal with, for he is now not a person but a thing; and in destroying the thing, you redeem yourself.

Clearly, the rite of the kill is powerful. When you as a persuadee hear a persuader begin to deride and objectify people, thus making them into scapegoats, you can expect to hear the rest of the steps in the rite of the kill, and you ought to ask yourself, "What is being killed?" "What is the scapegoat like before he is identified?" "What kinds of words are used to defile him, and do they signify anything (e.g., elimination or offal words are aggressive and death oriented)?" "Who are the saviors of the people?" "What are they like?" Important meaning is revealed in the ritualism of causes or issues, particularly in the rite of the kill.

There is an often-heard counter to the rite of the kill; it sometimes links us with or merges with the rite of the kill. You could call it "the rite of salvation" or "the rite of conversion." It has a simple plot: The people concerned have gone astray but can make amends by having a conversion and returning to a pure and good existence. The decision to convert parallels the *coup de grâce*, in that it guarantees salvation. We are probably most familiar with it in the revivalist tradition—for example, in the persuasive attempts of Billy Graham or Oral Roberts. Here the sinner is depicted as having gone astray; there is a minor scapegoat in the figure of the devil, but he is less to blame than the "weakness of the flesh." The problem is that the sinner needs to cleanse himself in some symbolic and powerful way. He needs to get back on the track—on the right road—and the way for him to do this is to have a conversion experience. In most revival meetings this conversion is dramatic, with the sinner walking up to the front of the meeting and overtly renouncing his former ways.

The same procedure operates in other conversion-type groups like Alcoholics Anonymous. This rite was used to persuade the Congress to enact prohibition in the 1920s. And it is used by political persuaders today—George McGovern talked in his campaign about "coming home" to the good old way. To get off the path that led to Vietnam, McGovern suggested a conversion act—to vote and work for him. The sinner could get rid of his guilt by voting for McGovern. This same strategy is sometimes used in advertising. The consumer is depicted as having fallen off the track in the past—he may have started smoking filter cigarettes or purchasing foreign autos—and he can get "saved" by coming back or by converting in some dramatic way. Thus the salvation or life rite is also a subsymbol often used by persuaders. And there are others.

In this section, we have touched on only a few ways to examine the semantic qualities of persuasion. As a persuadee, you may use these tools of analysis or you may look for others. The important thing, once again, is that you do not passively accept the persuasion directed at you but that you examine it as closely and as objectively as you can, all the while seeking revelation of the persuader's motives.

Tools for the Thematic Axis

The thematic axis of language refers to a quality that is not really functional (syntactic) or semantic. It is not concerned with word order or the referent for particular words. Rather, it refers to the "texture" of the language. A classic example is shown when we try to rewrite Lincoln's Gettysburg Address—"Eighty-seven years ago the signers of the Declaration of Independence started a new country designed to have liberty and equality for everyone. . . ." We find a semantic correspondence between this set of words and Lincoln's version, but there are obvious thematic differences.

Sometimes thematic differences come from a repeated sound. (Burke argues, for example, that his childhood prayer: "God loving me/Guard me in sleep/Guide me to Thee" relies on a G—d or "God" form.) Sound repetition is one of the textural qualities of language. Onomatopoeia (or phonetic sounds that resemble their referents—e.g., "swish" or "rustle") is another example. We will now look at three thematic or textural tools in some detail: (1) the use of motifs and metaphors, (2) the development of God and Devil terms, and (3) the pragmatic versus the unifying style. Beyond these, there are other tools you may want to explore.

Motifs and Metaphors

Persuaders can establish a great deal of their message by setting the mood for the persuadees. They can depict a setting appropriate for the message by repeatedly using certain sounds and certain images. In a study on the use of archetypal metaphors (or universal and primal images consistent within and even across cultures), in particular the light-dark comparison, Michael Osborn maintains that, traditionally, we identify light with the sun, warmth, growth, comfort, and so on; while we see dark associated with mystery, night, cold, and other uncomfortable and troubling things. Osborn points out that persuaders often use repeated reference to this dichotomy.[23] John F. Kennedy, in his first Inaugural Address, used this archetypal metaphor when he talked about passing a torch from one generation to another and predicting that the light from this symbolic torch could illuminate the

---

[23] Michael Osborn, "Archetypal Metaphor in Rhetoric: The Light-Dark Family," *Quarterly Journal of Speech*, 53 (April 1967), 115–126. See also Douglas Ehninger and Michael Osborn, "The Metaphor in Public Address, *Speech Monographs*, 29 (August 1962), 223–234.

world for freedom—the light was viewed as good, warm, friendly, and virtuous. Elsewhere the world was filled with darkness and poverty and misdeeds.

There are probably other archetypal metaphors. For example, in many sources there is a recurrent reference to the power of the sea, and often holy or magical powers are given to water (e.g., the fountain of youth or baptism). Mircia Eliade is convinced that there is an archetypal metaphor of "the center." We repeatedly look for a central point—a symbolic navel for our world. For some groups it is a specific place (Mecca for Moslems, Munich for Nazism, Jerusalem for Jews and Christians, or Chicago for the New Left).[24] For some students, a certain place on campus may be the symbolic center—their dorm room, the student center, or a fraternity house. On some campuses there is a "free-speech area," often a focal point for antiwar speeches or other protest gatherings. The White House is a sacred center for many persons.

Associated with these motifs or repeated references to images that set the stage for persuasion, we also seem to have a strong attraction for myths or dramatic metaphors. A good example is the American fascination with the "savior." During the peace negotiations in 1972, Henry Kissinger observed in an interview that Americans admire the lone cowboy who comes into a town and cleans it up single-handedly or who leads the wagon train through all sorts of danger. Persuaders often use this image of the "savior" or man of power. Take, for example, the television advertisements for "The Man from Glad" who swoops down out of the sky to save the day by bringing a package of Glad Bags to the lady in distress. The thought of it is ludicrous; yet people are persuaded by this image. The savior comes in various versions: Mrs. Olson must have saved hundreds of young marriages from the divorce courts by whipping out her ever present can of Folgers; the Mission Impossible team saved the world week after week, using ingenuity and mechanical wizardry in the nick of time; and in other cases, actual wizards or genie-type characters arrive on the scene to save the day (e.g., the Mr. Clean figure). There are other "archetypal" dramatic metaphors that set the stage for persuasion or embody universal values and beliefs that can be used as persuasive premises. As a persuadee, you may want to explore in depth some of the metaphors or images described here or to identify and describe others. Some mythological patterns that seem to recur are the search, or the hunt; the ritual of passage or initiation; the wisdom of the rustic; the trial by fire; the power of the machine; and the sacrifice. Each has its own characteristics, and each may be used in various ways and places—advertising, political persuasion (see Chapter 6), or interpersonal communication. We all use

---

[24] Eliade, as cited in fn. 6.

these universal molds at one time or another, but we are reluctant to recognize and label them as tactics in the persuasion of others.

God and Devil Terms

Another thematic or textural characteristic of style—often used in persuasion—is the development of families of terms. Persuaders, like the rest of us, like to see the world as divided into neat easily labeled, categories. They also use these categories to try to persuade others and are often successful. One of these category sets is the creation of "God terms" and "Devil terms," as suggested by Richard Weaver. Weaver notes that terms or labels are really only parts of propositions, but they are often linked together with other terms or labels to shape a persuasive message or a persuasive sense. He defines "God terms" as an expression ". . . about which all other expressions are ranked as subordinate and serving dominations and powers. Its force imparts to the others their lesser degree of force . . ." Weaver sees a God term as an unchallenged term that demands sacrifice or obedience in its name.[25] He uses three terms as examples of God terms: *progress, fact,* and *science.* Though these were God terms for the 1950s when Weaver described them, they have changed considerably. We do not now attach highly positive values to "progress"—counter terms have identified it with waste, war, pollution, and a series of other ills. Science has lost some of its credibility, for the scientist also designed the atomic bomb and other awesome instruments of war. In the 1970s several other God terms seem to have emerged—individuality, forthrightness, concern, communality, and others. Over time, they, too, will probably fall out of vogue. The important thing is that persuaders and persuadees have an attachment for families of related terms, and that each persuader designs his discourse to highlight those terms he sees as having high value. For example, the human-potential movement uses the following God terms: tenderness, loving, openness, trust, letting go, acceptance, touching, love, and together. In many cases, these terms may have negative value to certain persons (some persons see "touch" as a bad thing), but for the human-potential movement they are God terms. They set the mood or the motif for a persuasive message—be yourself, tell others that you love them, don't worry about the future, and be open with yourself and others.

At the same time that a persuader devises God terms, he may also devise sets of terms expressing negative values—Devil terms. Weaver defines Devil terms as "terms of repulsion," which group together and

---

[25] Weaver, pp. 211, 212, and 214.

have great potential in arousing emotions. Weaver says that though ". . . they defy any real analysis . . . they generate [a] peculiar force of repudiation. One only recognizes them as publicly agreed-upon Devil terms." As examples, he uses the terms "prejudice," "communist," and "ignorance." Again, though in vogue during the 1950s, these terms seem to have lost some of their potency. But we have replaced them with terms like "military industrial complex," "restrictive," "establishment," or "waste," all of which have negative connotations. Each of them might have a series of minor synonyms that make up a Devil family (e.g., *waste* is something that *depletes* resources and causes *pollution* and *exploitation* by the *haves*).

In an interview concerning the problems facing blacks in the 1970s, Reverend Jesse Jackson of Operation PUSH said:

> It is futile for us to think about ending racism; that is a psychological problem that seems beyond our attempts to affect it. We are fighting to end colonialism—oppression and exploitation. That requires power. The civil rights movement is a lifetime struggle for power. A man who is impotent, no matter how courteous and pleasant looking he is, is told to wait in the lobby. But if you have power, you can be an illiterate boor with tobacco juice running down your face and they will open the door for you.[26]

Notice the development of a set of Devil terms that come into opposition with one God term. "Racism," "colonialism," "oppression," and "exploitation" all form the Devil family, which is met by the single potent God term—"power"—which is capable of surmounting the combined effects of the entire Devil family. Notice that there is a minor Devil family here also; it is associated with the "Uncle Tom" image: "courteous," "impotent," and "pleasant," all describe qualities that will get you nowhere. Again, "power" is in opposition to these words. In a sense, the development of these terms is a miniature drama in itself—the two sets of terms do battle, and one emerges victorious.

Weaver points out that, on occasion, terms with a decidedly positive or negative quality can be turned around and reverse their connotation. His example is the value placed on "killing" terms used by soldiers. Words formerly associated symbolically with death or killing (e.g., defecation words or words referring in one way or another to the sex act or to sexual perversion) take on acceptable values to the soldier associated with a lifestyle that emphasizes death. The draftee returning from boot camp finds that he says at the dinner table, "Please pass the f------ peas," and he associates a negative aggressive symbol with the life symbol of food, which makes the contrast even more emphatic. The propensity

---

[26] *Playboy*, November 1969, p. 108.

of the New Left in the 1960s to use profanity may well have been a response to the death-oriented culture they perceived associated with the
Vietnam war. There are other occasions where terms have their value
reversals. "Military" seems to be in disrepute (though in the 1950s it
was a God term), as does "status quo" or "progress" or "Negro," while
other previously negative terms have assumed positive values—"Black,"
"intimate," and others.

Weaver describes another kind of term that does not seem to have
the same ideological sense of goodness or badness as God or Devil terms.
He calls it the "charismatic term," or ". . . term(s) of considerable
potency whose referents it is virtually impossible to discover . . . Their
meaning seems inexplicable unless we accept the hypothesis that their
content proceeds out of a popular will that they *shall* mean something."[27]
His example is the word "freedom," which has no direct referents but
which seems, even twenty years after Weaver wrote about it, to have at-
tractiveness for persons from various political positions. Another might
be the word "power" which, though it has positive connotations at times,
may have negative connotations at other times (e.g., the New Lefter ad-
mires student power but objects to military power). Power, too, seems
to have no real referents but derives its meaning from the consent of a
certain group of persons.

The development of sets of words with high positive or negative value
loadings for their user—God and Devil terms—is one of the tactics used
by persuaders to lend texture or a thematic quality to their discourse.
Things seem to be consistent and to "go" with one another. The persuadee can learn much from identifying a persuader's sets of positive
and negative terms, for they signal the kinds of relationships he sees
operating in the world—what he sees in opposition to what.

Pragmatic versus Unifying Style

A final characteristic that builds a thematic wholeness or
gives a kind of texture to persuasion is the reliance of a persuader on
one of two kinds of styles—the pragmatic style or the unifying style.[28]
These styles can be thought of as signifying two separate strategies; and
persuaders can utilize the tactics of either strategy, or they can choose
some tactics of both extremes.

A pragmatic persuader is usually in the position of having listeners
who do not necessarily support his position. As a result, he must try
to change their minds, as opposed to reinforcing their beliefs, and must

---

27 Weaver, p. 227.
28 For examples of speeches illustrating these styles, see Wil A. Linkugel, R. R.
Allen, and Richard L. Johannesen, eds., *Contemporary American Speeches*, 3rd ed.
(Belmont, Calif.: Wadsworth Publishing Co., 1972).

choose appropriate tactics. The unifying persuader is faced with a much more comfortable position. He is talking to persons who, in large measure, already believe what he is going to say. He doesn't need to change their minds; he only needs to reinforce their beliefs—to whip up their enthusiasm or to give them encouragement and dedication. These two styles demonstrate two opposing situations, and they describe the problems facing the persuader in these situations. The problems for the pragmatic persuader are very practical—he must change opinion before he can expect action. The unifying persuader can be much more idealistic —he can be more bombastic and probably not offend his audience. He can be more emotional and less objective than the persuader faced with a questioning audience. What are the stylistic devices of these extremes?

The unifying persuader, because he can afford to be idealistic, will focus much of what he says on the "then and there"—on the future or on the past where things were ideal or where they can become ideal. His position is that things look better in the future, particularly if we compare them with the present. His language choice, since his audience will fill in the blanks, can be abstract. It is usually poetic and filled with imagery; these attributes (imagery and abstractness) excite the imagination of his audience. Though there may be little that is intellectually stimulating (or that requires careful logical examination) about what he says, there is much that is emotionally stimulating to the audience. The words and images offered by the persuader are precisely the words his listeners believe they would have said if they were the one talking. The unifying persuader is thus the mouthpiece or sounding board for the entire group. His abstractions provide the others with the cues, but not the details, of the message. They can participate with the persuader in the creation of the message; in fact, they sometimes actively participate by yelling encouragement to the unifying persuader or by repeating shibboleths to underscore his words—"Right on" or "Amen, Brother" or "Tell it like it is."

The pragmatic persuader, on the other hand, because he must win an audience, cannot afford to take the risk of appealing to abstract ideals. He must be concrete, focusing on facts instead of images, emphasizing that which cannot be disputed or interpreted so easily. He will not try to depict an ideal situation in subjective "there and then" terms; instead he will have to focus on real aspects of immediate problems familiar to audience—problems of the "here and now," which are realistic, not idealistic. His orientation is toward the present instead of the future. Since the pragmatic persuader is forced into a position where he must be concrete and realistic, his language is concrete and prosaic. Lofty sentiments are of little value, especially if they are expressed in equally lofty words. He tends to focus on facts and statistics instead of imagery.

Clearly, these two extremes are not an either-or proposition—persuaders may, on occasion, utilize the tactics of both perspectives. When this happens you can be pretty sure that they pick the tactics carefully or that the audience is not what it seems to be. It is either more doubting than it seems or more favorable to the persuader's position. Here are examples of these two persuasive types. First, the *unifying style:*

> Occasionally there comes a time when profound and far-reaching events command a break with tradition. This is such a time . . . The moment has arrived to harness the vast energies and abundance of this land to the creation of a New American experience, an experience richer and deeper and more truly a reflection of the goodness and grace of the human spirit. The seventies will be a time of new beginnings, a time of exploring both on the earth and in the heavens, a time of discovery . . . Our land, this land that is ours together, is a great and good land. It is also an unfinished land and the challenge of perfecting it is the summons of the seventies.[29]

This is from the early portions of the 1970 State of the Union Address by Richard Nixon. Though the congressional and television audience may disagree with the President when he evaluates his own accomplishments or when he suggests new programs in a state of the union address, most listeners are not disperse in their beliefs about the greatness of the country. Thus at least for his beginning and his conclusion, a President may appropriately be unifying in style as Nixon is here. Note the attention to the future of the country, in the repeated references to the seventies and the break from the present and the past. Nixon uses numerous abstract images—the harnessing of energy, the creation of a new kind of American experience, the reference to a good and graceful spirit, and the summons of the future. None of these images could be visualized in concrete terms by groups of persons; they are appeals to each person's individual imagination. There are few facts here, and the language is certainly poetic as opposed to prosaic. The example fits all of the characteristics of the unifying style.

Now, let's look at a *pragmatic* example:

> Yes, you know power rates are too high, gas rates are too high, telephone rates are too high. Pick up your telephone book and see if you can find how much it costs to call Phoenix City, or Mobile, or Dothan, or Huntsville. Because it costs more to call Fort Paine, Alabama than it does Chattanooga. It costs more to call Dalton, Alabama than it does Panama City. It costs more to call Mobile than it does Pascagoula, Mississippi. And that has come from the pockets of every citizen in this state . . .[30]

---

[29] Richard M. Nixon, "State of the Union Address, 1970," as quoted in L. Patrick Devlin, *Contemporary Political Speaking* (Belmont, Calif.: Wadsworth Publishing Co., 1971), p. 66.
[30] George C. Wallace, "Gubernatorial Campaign Address," Birmingham, Alabama, April 10, 1970, as quoted in Devlin, pp. 83–84 (see fn. 29).

This speech is one delivered by George C. Wallace when he ran for governor of Alabama in 1970. The examples used cannot be described as abstract. The language is concrete and oriented to the "here and now" and not to any future or past ideal—it is realistic. Even an audience polarized against Governor Wallace would have difficulty dismissing his evidence. Nothing—because of the concreteness of the evidence—is left open to interpretation. Finally, there is a prosaic, everyday quality to the language—in no sense is it lofty.

Both of these politicians have utilized both the unifying and the pragmatic styles at one time or another—often even in the same speech. The point is that they choose them to fit what they believe the audience is like—the persuaders adapt their style to their own perceptions of the audience. These adaptations can give us a clue to what the persuader's own image of the world is like. At that time, Nixon seems to have believed that the nation was unified in favor of his program and his view of the future. Wallace seems to have thought that his audience felt exploited.

Tuning One's Ear for Cues

Persuadees—to be aware and critical—ought to tune their ears for the various clues to style and motives already discussed. What are some ways in which one can tune his ear? Consideration of these tools is one. If you have seriously considered these tools, if Langer's theory about self-revelation through symbols has sparked your imagination, or if you have tried to apply these tools to the persuasion around you, you have already started the tuning process. Applying the study questions at the end of this and other chapters is another good way to continue the process. There are at least three other things you might do to make yourself more critical of style and to "read" or "psych out" persuaders:

·   1. *Role play the persuader.* Assume that you are the persuader or a member of a group with a persuasive cause. How would you have shaped the persuasion you hear? If you were Nixon, would you have used the Kennedy-like theme of a "New Frontier" in your State of the Union Address? How would you have changed it? In other words, try to act as if you were the persuader writing out the manuscript for the persuasion about to be delivered. Seek the differences between your version and the one the persuader himself used. Once you have done this, compare your version with what he says and look for differences. Then ask yourself what these differences might indicate about the persuader and about his view of the world compared with yours. This method of listening for stylistic features forces you to consider carefully the words chosen by the persuader and the way in which he links them together. You might want to use the tools suggested in this chapter to analyze what he has done. You might want to seek other analytical tools.[31]

2. *Restate a persuasive message numerous times.* Instead of pretending that you are the ghostwriter for the persuader, just try to restate what he has said in several different ways. Ask yourself what his options were (as we did sketchily with the three presidential slogans at the beginning of this chapter). Then try to determine how these options would have changed the intent of the message and its ultimate effects. This process should lead you to drawing some conclusions about the persuader's intent. You might want to determine what the persuader's Pentadic emphasis was and then try to restate the persuasion from the viewpoint of the other four elements of the Pentad. You might want to use methods of criticism drawn from other chapters in this book or from other books. (For example, how do small-group theories relate to persuasion? Could you use part or all of what you have learned about small groups to interpret persuasion?[32]) You might choose analytical tools from other disciplines or from popular literature. (For example, how might the terms of Eric Berne's *Games People Play* or Thomas Harris's *I'm OK—You're OK* be used to describe style?)

3. *Attend to language features in discourse.* Don't allow yourself passively to "buy into" any persuasive suggestion that is being hawked. Instead, get into the habit of looking at the stylistic features of persuasive messages. Analyze billboards, television spots, the language used by your parents in a discussion with you, the wording on packages you purchase (a student once wrote a brilliant paper on the language used on the package for a product called "Screaming Yellow Zonkers"), or on the discussion between you and your friends, enemies, girlfriends, boyfriends, or salesmen. In other words, start listening not only to *ideas*— the thrust of the messages aimed at you—but to *words* or the packaging of those ideas. Try it on me. What kind of words do I use? Why? What do you think I'm like. How does my style differ from Richard Johannesen's (see Chapter 9)? From other persuasion textbook writers? From the way you would have said it? By attending to these features in

---

[31] There are numerous critical tools that might be used. See, for example, the various analyses in the Devlin reader cited above or some of those in Karlyn Kohrs Campbell, *Critiques of Contemporary Rhetoric* (Belmont, Calif.: Wadsworth Publishing Co., 1971). For a discussion of various methods of criticism, look at some of the suggestions in Robert L. Scott and Bernard L. Brock, *Methods of Rhetorical Criticism: A Twentieth Century Perspective* (New York: Harper & Row, 1972).

[32] A good example of this kind of criticism is Ernest G. Bormann's "Fantasy, Rhetoric, and Social Reality: A Dramatistic Approach to Communication and Rhetorical Criticism," *Quarterly Journal of Speech, 58* (December 1972), 396–407.

as many places as possible, you will develop an intriguing pastime in being a kind of amateur psychoanalyst or political commentator. Further, you will develop an ear for stylistic tipoffs which is immensely valuable in your interpersonal relations with others—it allows you to predict and respond to the communication of others.

A Review and Conclusion

In conjunction with Susanne Langer's suggestion that artistic activity is man's most unique characteristic and that language as a symbol system offers most persons their entry into artistic activity, this chapter has tried to present several tools for analyzing the stylistic aspects of language activity.

There are at least three stylistic axes we can look at: the functional characteristics of style, the semantic aspects of style, and the thematic or textural qualities of style. Though there are numerous tools one might use to critique these elements of style, Weaver's use of word classes, syntactical characteristics, and the nature of ambiguity all relate to the functional axis. At the same time, persuadees can explore the semantic nature of persuasion by using the Dramatic Pentad suggested by Kenneth Burke, as well as subsymbols or metaphors, such as the rite of the kill, that emerge when one looks at the dramatic qualities of persuasion. Finally, we can attempt to get a notion of the textural or thematic trends in persuasion by looking for families of God and Devil terms, by exploring motifs and metaphors, and by looking at the unifying as opposed to pragmatic characteristics of the persuasion.

All of these critical devices are, of course, enhanced in their potential by role playing, restating, and developing awareness of the words and style as well as the ideas in a persuasive message, be it a speech, a television documentary, a film, a candidate, a social movement, a package designed to sell a product, or a friend's entreaty.

Questions for Further Thought

1. What are the three axes of language activity? Give examples of them from your own writing or speaking. Give examples from the speaking or writing of a parent or friend.

2. What functional tools might be used for studying style? Take a popular song and transcribe the lyrics. Now analyze them according to the functional tools presented here. Is there a preference for a certain word type? A certain sentence structure? What does the syntactical pattern of the lyrics tell you? Is the message ambiguous or concrete? Explain.

3. What are the semantic tools suggested here? What do you think is the Pentadic perspective of the author of this book? Why? Give examples. What do you think is the Pentadic favorite of your instructor? (Does he see persuasion as a thing of situations, men, actions, means, or principles? What might that tell you about how you should write papers for him? What might it tell you about his politics?)

4. What kinds of rituals do you go through in a given day? Give examples (e.g., in eating, in sleeping, in relating to roommates or classmates or teachers). Are they symbolic? In what ways? What are you trying to communicate?

5. Find some examples of the ritual of the kill in popular persuasion occurring on your campus. Discuss it in a group in class. Offer an analysis of this discussion to your class.

6. What are the tools for a thematic or textural analysis of language? Use some of these to analyze the persuasion occurring in a recent political campaign. What do these analyses tell you about the candidate? Explain.

7. What are the God terms held in esteem by your parents? What are the Devil terms? Shape a request for something from your parents, expressed in terms similar to their God terms. Now do the same thing with Devil terms. Try them both out as an experiment.

8. How does a unifying persuader differ from a pragmatic one? Find examples of each type of persuader in your class, in some persuasive attempts of the past, or in some persuasive issue being discussed on campus or in your community. Are there other differences between these two types? What are they? What kinds of persons are they?

9. What are three ways to tune your ear to the symbolic and ego-revealing aspects of language use? Give an example of where you have done this. Make a prediction about a persuader, based on your analysis of him using the tools of this chapter and the three suggestions offered at the end of the chapter. Present the reasons for your prediction in an essay or speech.

Experiences in Persuasion

1. Attend a film with a persuasive message (i.e., one which does more than merely tell a story). Analyze the words of one or more of its characters, using the tools of this chapter. Do you think the tools work in other symbolic media like film? Why or why not? Why is the film persuasive to you? Analyze your own reasons for saying that it is or is not persuasive. What in the film made you react that way? Was that thing a scenic phenomenon, or did it focus on actions, agents, principles, or methods (e.g., someone might say that Hitler's propaganda film *Triumph of the Will* was persuasive

because of the spectacle it presented—tens of thousands of people, huge flags, etc.—all scenic items, while someone else may have found *Dr. Zhivago* persuasive because of the power and charisma of Omar Sharif).

2. Analyze the persuasive impact of a particular show on television—it may be a talk show or a dramatic show. Does its persuasiveness come from a particular part of the Pentad? Which one? Give examples. Now look at each of the characters in the episode. Explain how each of them tries to persuade others. Refer to the kinds of words they use, the sentence structures they use, and so on; use the tools of this chapter.

3. Get a copy of L. Patrick Devlin's *Contemporary Political Speaking* (Belmont, Calif.: Wadsworth Publishing Co., 1971) and find examples of speakers or parts of speeches that are drawn from or that rely on each element of the Pentad. Present these examples in a paper. Do the same thing looking for pragmatic or unifying speeches. Try to dig deeper into the situation surrounding these speeches and discover what kind of audience was addressed, what the speaker said in other situations, and so on. Compare these with your analysis. Does your analysis allow you to predict what the speaker might do in another case? How?

4. Catalog the uses of obscenity you find in popular literature or reported as being used by persuaders for certain causes. What word classes are they (see the discussion by Weaver)? Which element of the Pentad do they represent? Why are they called profane? Who gets bothered by these words? What are they responding to in the words? Refer to tools of this chapter. (For example, in the January 1973 issue of *Playboy* magazine, Germaine Greer reports that people find the word "rape" acceptable but reject its four-letter synonym as obscene because the one suggests forced intercourse while the other suggests willing submission—a focus on act as opposed to purpose.)

5. If you have ever been interviewed for a job or if you are in the process of interviewing for a job, attempt to discover the interviewer's "key term" on the Pentad, from what he says and how he says it. Shape your messages accordingly, and report the results to the class. (*Note:* On most campuses you can sign up for an interview at the placement bureau quite easily, or you might for the sake of the project respond to a newspaper advertisement.)

6. Compare the advertisements for vacations in the travel section of a major newspaper (usually on Sundays). What different aspects of the Pentad are emphasized by what kinds of vacation spots? (For example, do some seem to emphasize that certain types of Agents go there, while others focus on the grandeur or power of the Scene?) Rewrite the copy for these ads, using another element of the Pentad. Identify the sets of God terms highlighted by these spas (e.g., "sun," "fun," "freedom," and "relaxation" might be the positive terms for Florida). Design a new set of terms for one of the advertisements.

7. Go to a local television station and ask for old commercials. (Stations usually have multiple 16mm copies of the 20- and 30-second spots used on the air and are more than willing to part with them since they usually throw them away.) Combine the spots into a 2- or 3-minute "film" or series of clips (this might take 10 or 15 television spots) demonstrating a single Pentadic focus (e.g., all on Scene, all on Act, or all on Agent). An alter-

native might be to show separate clips that focus on various elements of the Pentad in advertisement of the same kind of product (e.g., soap commercials often focus on the situation—they also might focus on Purpose or Agent); find a variety. Show your production to the class and explain how the "film" demonstrates what you feel it demonstrates. You may wish to do this project as a group.

8. Get copies of several speeches by different speakers on the same topic (speeches on the Vietnam war by antiwar protestors, a Secretary of Defense, a past President involved in the war, congressional doves or hawks, etc.). How do these speeches differ stylistically? Present this variation to the class or discuss it in a paper showing how style shifts according to a person's perspective (e.g., you would expect persons favoring the Vietnam war to talk about Purpose and those who oppose it might shift to the horror of war or the Scene).

Readings for New Dimensions

Alexander, Hubert G., *Meaning in Language* (Glenview, Ill.: Scott, Foresman and Co., 1969). This book would be an excellent one with which to begin consideration of language characteristics. Alexander discusses such topics as signs and symbols, connotation and denotation, meaning, tonal and contextual aspects of meaning and style, sentence types, and syntactic meaning. All of these are considered in much more detail than in Chapter 3, but the discussion relies less on the aesthetic perspective used here.

Blankenship, Jane, *A Sense of Style: An Introduction to Style for the Public Speaker* (Encino, Calif.: Dickenson Publishing Co., 1968). This is an excellent introduction to the notion of style. Though somewhat traditional in parts of the discussion, Blankenship's observations about identification through word choice, her discussion of the resources of language, and her definition of style are insightful and exciting. Students may wish to contrast and compare her discussion of semantic meaning and structural meaning with the discussion of semantic qualities and functional qualities of language included in this chapter. The references to the works of various linguists, particularly Noam Chomsky, should provide additional perspective for the study of style presented here. Several tools for analysis of style can be derived from this book or by combining some of Blankenship's suggestions with those offered in this chapter. See especially the suggestions for training oneself in the use of style. Note that Blankenship focuses on style from the source's point of view, while this book looks at style from the receiver's perspective.

Burke, Kenneth, *A Grammar of Motives* (Berkeley: University of California Press, 1970). The first 15 pages of this book would be of immense help in applying and understanding the Dramatic Pentad. They are fairly difficult, but clear. Students may want to look at Burke's discussion of the four master tropes. Much of the rest of the book is probably inappropriate and confusing for study at this point.

Burke, Kenneth, *The Philosophy of Literary Form* (New York: Vintage Books, 1957). This collection of several works by Burke is a good way to extend knowledge of analytical tools beyond those discussed in this chapter. An especially good selection demonstrating how stylistic analysis can work is "The Rhetoric of Hitler's Battle." Burke analyzes Hitler via his book *Mein Kampf.* Burke's analysis is especially insightful when one considers that he made the predictions and judgments before the fact in the 1930s. There are several other suggestions that might excite readers interested in doing detailed stylistic analyses. His discussions of magic and religion, associated clusters, the rite of the kill, and scapegoats are all clear and applicable. Some of the book may be confusing, so selectivity is advised.

Crable, R. E., and John J. Makay, "Kenneth Burke's Concept of Motives in Rhetorical Theory," *Today's Speech, 20* (Winter 1972), 11–18. For those particularly interested in the discussion of Burke's Pentad, this article should be helpful. The authors argue that instead of using Burke to identify *what* persuaders say, we ought instead to use Burke to identify *how* persuaders say their message. They discuss George Wallace's "Speech in the Schoolhouse Door," in which he refused James Meredith entry to the administration building of the University of Alabama. The analysis uses Burke's Pentad, providing an excellent example of how stylistic analysis via Burke can reveal motive.

Eliade, Mircia, *The Myth of the Eternal Return: or Cosmos and History* (Princeton, N. J.: Princeton University Press, 1954). This book focuses on the whole notion of ritual and mythical metaphor by investigating themes or myths that seem to be found in all cultures. The periodic destruction myth is a metaphor that Eliade discusses at length, for example. This theme is one persuaders repeatedly use (e.g., Hitler's building the Third Reich out of ashes). The book is anthropological in its perspective, but it can provide interesting and provoking models applicable to persuasion.

Hagen, Michael R., "Kenneth Burke and Generative Criticism of Speeches," *Central States Speech Journal, 22* (Winter 1971), 252–257. Hagen discusses the values of using Burke to analyze speeches. He also suggests rewriting speeches in Burkean terms and the notion of dramatism, in order to discuss and to identify the characteristic God and Devil terms used by persuaders. The article fits well with suggestions offered in this book.

Osborn, Michael, "Archetypal Metaphor in Rhetoric: The Light-Dark Family," *Quarterly Journal of Speech, 53* (April 1967), 115–126. This article is one most often referred to when critics begin to discuss metaphor as an analytical tool. Osborn argues that there is a set of metaphors consistent from culture to culture; and that the light-dark family is one of these. He suggests the need to look for others. Readers may want to see what Osborn has done with the light-dark family and then compare that with other archetypes that emerge in the persuasion to which they are exposed. Compare this source with the Eliade discussion of the eternal return and the symbolism of the center as archetypes.

Richards, I. A., *The Philosophy of Rhetoric* (New York: Oxford University Press, 1936). Richards's discussion of metaphor, though highly philosophical, is clear and useful, especially in considering characteristics of style. Richards's notion that thought is metaphorical and, hence, all language is metaphorical is provoking and could serve as the theme of excellent group or individual projects.

Sanders, Keith R., and Robert P. Newman, "John A. Stormer and the Hofstadter Hypothesis," *Central States Speech Journal, 22* (Winter 1971), 218–227. This is a quantitative analysis of a stylistic tool—Richard Hofstadter's notion of the "Conspiracy Argument" (mentioned in Chapter 6). The article is of special interest in that it empirically tests a critical tool used in stylistic analysis. Though the results show that Hofstadter's hypothesis does not test out in right-wing literature, the method used is worth exploring.

Weaver, Richard M., *The Ethics of Rhetoric* (Chicago: Henry Regenery Co., 1953). This book is a collection of several essays by Weaver concerning the use of language and how it indicates a persuader's view of the world, his habitual ways of perceiving cause and effect, and his motives. Weaver also investigates the nature of language and its reflection of political philosophy. See especially the chapters on the rhetorical functions of grammatical categories, the rhetorical characteristics of social science writing, the discussion of ultimate terms in contemporary persuasion, and his examples of how various types of arguments were habitually used by Abraham Lincoln and Edmund Burke. The book is difficult, but well worth the effort.

Winterowd, W. Ross, "The Uses of Grammar," *Today's Speech, 20* (Winter 1972), 3–10. This article is interesting for the perspective it offers on Chomsky's notions about generating sentences. The discussion should be of particular interest in connection with the initial discussions of presidential slogans offered in this chapter. The discussion of the "generative metaphor" should also be interesting to compare with the discussion of metaphor offered here. Along with the references made by Winterowd to B. F. Skinner's *Beyond Freedom and Dignity*, these discussions can give the reader some notion of the almost terrifying power of metaphor in any age, but particularly in a technological age.

4

Process Premises for Persuasion

          In Chapters 2 and 3, we have been discussing the mode of persuasive discourse—symbolic transmission of information for consummatory purposes, or for the purpose of revealing self-expression. In his role as artist, the persuader is communicating with himself. In a sense, we have been looking at the "channel" element, which appears on most models of communication,[1] and perhaps even at what McLuhan and others refer to as "media." However, as already noted, communication is both consummatory and instrumental. In this chapter and the next, we will focus on the instrumental uses of persuasion, with the persuader in the role of manipulator, making his appeals to others.

    No one can deny that language is used to achieve effect. When I say "please pass the peas" at the dinner table, I fully suspect and hope to have an effect—that someone at the table will pass the peas. This is an instrumental use of language—it is an instrument or tool we use to control, manipulate, or influence the environment outside ourselves. Of course, we can use language for both consummatory and instrumental purposes at the same time. We can say to our enemy, "Get the living hell out of my front yard or so help me I'll shoot your head off the top of your lousy body!" At the same time that we reveal our ego-involvement at a consummatory level (i.e., spontaneous and expressive), we also hope and fully suspect that what we say will have instrumental (i.e., manipu-

---

[1] See David K. Berlo's model in *The Process of Communication* (New York: Holt, Rinehart and Winston, 1960) and "A Transactional Model of Communication" by Dean C. Barnlund in *Language Behavior: A Book of Readings* (The Hague: Mouton Publishers, 1970).

lative) results on the environment around us—in this case, the presence or absence of a person we dislike. Let's look at the way persuasion uses language instrumentally to control and manipulate the world.

Content and Process Premises

All persuasion is built on premises in one way or another. Perhaps I say, "Believe my advice and follow my direction because I am a good and wonderful human being," or perhaps I say, "Do thus and so in order to avoid being killed by your enemies," or perhaps I say, "You need to do comparison shopping to avoid being overcharged on a per unit basis at your local supermarket." In all these cases, I am trying to persuade you to take a certain course of action. In the first case, my credibility is a kind of premise on which you as persuadee can decide and rely; in the second, fear of death is a kind of premise that can be used to motivate persuadees; and in the third, the reasonableness of avoiding being overcharged serves as a premise for persuasion. Premises that might be used to persuade you can generally be divided into two classes—*process premises*, or those that usually involve some psychological or cultural set of procedures which most persons follow (e.g., they try to escape death or danger if possible); and *content premises*, or those that rely on the consistency of information and evidence supporting or substantiating the advice or direction being given. One might call the process premises on which persuasion is built the psychological (they are logical to the psyche) and the content premises the rational (they are reasonable to the intellect). In Chapter 4 we will be examining some of the process premises persuaders appeal to or rely on whenever they frame messages intended to produce changes in the beliefs, behaviors, or attitudes of their audiences. Again, we ought to approach these process premises as persuadees—alerting ourselves to their occurrence and responding to them. Sometimes it is these premises that force us to seek out persuasive messages and persuasive individuals who will help us to make decisions. But there are many messages we do not seek out—messages that are trying to manipulate our behavior; and we ought to be aware of what happens to us and be alert to the persuader's premises and goals.

Whether the persuader utilizes process premises or content premises to achieve his effects, he generally follows the same steps. First, the persuader analyzes the persuadee to discover his emotional and rational states of belief. Given this information, the persuader is able to identify certain notions or premises the persuadee is likely to consider important. (Sometimes the premises are process premises, and sometimes they are content premises.) Next, the persuader uses these notions as building blocks on which to construct his arguments and persuasive appeals. When the premises already believed by the persuaders are coupled with appeals that rely on them, the persuadees are persuaded in two ways: first, by hearing or reading the persuader's message and, second, by participating in the decision because of their own beliefs. In other words, the persuasion that occurs is a process of co-creating on the part of both persuader and persuadee.[2] The process or content premises already held by the persuadee serve as one part of the persuasion; the arguments and appeals made by the persuader form another part.

Premises: A Political Example

For an example, let us suppose that we are the strategy planners for a politician who is planning to run a series of television advertisements in his campaign for election. He gathers information about his constituents and discovers that they are basically middle- and lower middle-class working people. They tend to have large families. They are more likely to go fishing or hunting than to the golf course. Most of them have three bedroom homes with high mortgages. They tend to be churchgoers and usually belong to some kind of fraternal order or veterans organization. Clearly, such an audience has certain beliefs and values, which they tenaciously maintain and which could serve as content or process premises to be utilized in persuasion. The persuader can appeal to these drives and beliefs.

What might some of these values be, and what messages would we as strategists construct to utilize them as premises in persuasion? Of course, there are several answers to this question. First, these people are probably interested in economic security. At one time or another, they have been laid off their jobs; and even when they work steadily, they never have an overabundance of money. We might then suggest to our hypothetical politician that he deliver some television messages stressing concern with inflation and a stable economy. The members of the audience may value education. They probably want their children to be educated so that they can get good and secure jobs. Our politician might want to suggest that, if elected, he would support legislation which subsidized colleges and technical schools—hoping to appeal to this audience-held value or belief. In these cases, the listeners would be supplying at least half of the persuasion. Obviously, if they didn't value educa-

---

[2] See Gary Cronkhite, "Logic, Emotion, and the Paradigm of Persuasion," *Quarterly Journal of Speech, 50* (February 1964), 13–18.

tion or security (process premises), they would say "So What?" to our well-planned campaign messages. Their responses will probably be dictated by their beliefs, however. They may respond, for instance, to the message about subsidizing education something like this: "Hmm. He wants to subsidize the costs of educating kids at college and tech school. That's not a bad idea. Hell, that's what I've been saying all along. People like me just can't send all four kids off to college and still keep bread on the table. And everyone knows these days, you just can't start from the ground and work your way up like I did. Yup, they need education all right. Well, this politician has at least one good idea, which is more than I can say for most of those crooks."

Notice that the persuadee *restates* the case here. He doesn't take what the persuader has said as the truth verbatim. Rather, he restates it from his own situation and experiences. Inevitably, this restatement leads to some distortion of the original message. For example, the politician suggested subsidizing colleges and trade schools. This solution doesn't necessarily mean that the cost of educating our blue-collar worker's four children will go down. It may very well remain the same or even rise, in spite of subsidies, because of increased costs. But the persuadee sees it slightly differently. He sees the suggested legislation in personal terms. He participates in his own persuasion by building arguments based on his own values after hearing the persuader's original message. He couples the premises inside his own mind with the suggestions offered by the persuader and comes to a conclusion, which is a hybrid of the two.

Assumption of Similitude

There is an interesting principle operating here—one that underlies the persuasive use of internal premises whether they are used in small groups, in front of large audiences, or over the mass media. This principle is the *assumption of similitude*. Human beings like to believe that they are not alone; that there are other human beings who are like themselves—who think the way they do; who believe the things that they believe; and who value the same things they value. Furthermore, most humans want their values, beliefs, and opinions to be esteemed by others; and when they find another person thinking and evaluating as they do, they feel gratified. Thus the persuader serves the function of telling others that they are right. He verifies, to some degree, what they have always believed to be true. He may do this vaguely or in abstract ways, but since we assume that others are or at least ought to be similar to us —the assumption of similitude—we can take what the persuader says and fit it into our own scheme of things. We may even distort what he says to make it fit our own beliefs or needs. We can couple what the persuader says with our internal premises easily, as long as what the persuader says is not too different from our own beliefs. During presidential elections, it is interesting to listen to what people say about the various candidates. In most cases, people find that the candidate thinks as they do on a wide variety of issues, or that he has merely stolen some of his "good" ideas from other candidates, or that the candidate is so far removed from reality that he doesn't deserve to be elected to the most lowly position in government. In other words, with the *assumption of similitude* operating, we quickly sift out those pieces of information that are similar to our own premises in any message and then identify with those pieces of information. If we happen to discover that the source of that information is someone we dislike, we swiftly rationalize this discrepancy by saying that the information was lifted from someone we do admire. Either way, we are participating in our own persuasion.

Inherent Dangers

There is a danger in this, however. Unless persuadees are aware of their own part in the persuasive process, they can be led astray by clever and manipulative persuaders who use the beliefs, opinions, values, and thought processes of audiences in persuading them of undesirable ideas or actions. Hitler, for example, relied on deep-seated values and beliefs in the German people. They, like most people, wanted to hold themselves in esteem and wanted to think that their country was important and honored. Hitler promised them a "place in the sun," and, in this way, they as citizens would also be honored and valued. Using this desire for self-respect and several other factors, such as the economic deprivation of the depression, the Jew as a scapegoat, and the demands of the Treaty of Versailles, Hitler was able to establish a dictatorship with broad powers. Had these citizens been critically aware of their own values, prejudices, and desires, they might still have been persuaded by the Führer but not without forethought. Their actions would have been less naive and more aware.[3]

Again the persuadee finds himself at a disadvantage. He is bombarded daily with persuasive messages that appeal to his own internal premises. How can he wisely choose to react to some of these and to reject others? By this time the answer to this question should be clear—he must be *aware* of the premises persuaders can rely on, just as he needs to be aware of the persuader's use of language. Once again he must watch himself being persuaded; he must examine himself in an attempt to discover

---

[3] For a more detailed description of how Hitler succeeded in persuading an entire nation, see "The Rhetoric of Hitler's 'Battle'" in *The Philosophy of Literary Form* (Baton Rouge: Louisiana State University Press, 1941); or Jesse G. Delia, "Rhetoric in the Nazi Mind: Hitler's Theory of Persuasion," *Southern Speech Communication Journal*, 37 (Winter 1971), 136–150.

the "givens" he carries with him (and which many others carry within themselves) and that serve as the starting points for persuasion. And once again the question is the same: What tools of analysis can the persuadee use to receive—critically—the persuasive messages being sent to him?

Let us proceed by looking at two of the most fundamental and essential human process premises—the premise within us that relates to how we feel and fulfill physical and psychic needs and the premise that relates to our desire to experience a consistency between what we believe to be true and right about the world and what the world actually is like. Some might argue that these two kinds of premises begin from different beliefs about the nature of man—premises operating on the assumption that man is filled with drives continually needing satisfaction and premises resting on the assumption that man is most happy when he has homeostasis or when he is not in conflict over drives or beliefs—when he is at rest. These positions are probably not as contradictory as they seem. Man has impulses for satisfaction; that satisfaction can be physical (i.e., he needs and gets food or sexual outlet), or it may be psychic (i.e., he needs to see the world as a set of consistent and balanced pieces of information).

Needs: The First Intrapersonal Premise

Human beings are like other organisms. They have needs —some weak, some strong—that must be at least partially fulfilled at various times for satisfaction in life. The problem is to identify these needs systematically, for they often serve as the first premises in persuasive arguments. For example, if a man is dying of thirst in the desert, he can probably be easily persuaded to take drastic action in order to get to water to fulfill his need for liquid. The need for H_2O is an important premise in persuading him.

Maslow's Pyramid

Abraham Maslow, a noted psychologist, offers us a starting point for examining and identifying gross need levels in man.[4] He notes that men have various kinds of needs which emerge and reemerge

---

[4] Abraham Maslow, *Motivation and Personality* (New York: Harper & Row, 1954). See also Abraham Maslow, *Toward a Psychology of Being* (New York: Van Nostrand–Reinhold Co., 1962). For criticism of Maslow's explanation of motivation, see Chapter 13, "Self Actualization and Related Concepts," in *Motivation: Theory and Research*, ed. Charles N. Cofer and Mortimer H. Appley (New York: John Wiley & Sons, 1964).

as they are unfulfilled. For example, the need for food or drink alternately emerges and then recedes as this need is fulfilled or unfulfilled. Maslow argues that these needs have a "prepotency"—that is, they are interrelated in their strength in such a way that weaker needs, like self-respect, emerge only after stronger needs, like the need for food, have been fulfilled. We probably couldn't persuade our man in the desert that he ought to clean up a little and be presentable before going to the well; we had better fulfill his need for H_2O first. The need to slake his thirst is prepotent. Until that is fulfilled, it is literally impossible for him to consider persuasive proposals relating to topics other than "thirst slaking." Maslow arranges the various needs in a clear and understandable model. He says that needs are arranged in pyramid fashion, with lower levels representing the stronger needs and higher levels representing the weaker needs (Figure 4–1). Remember that the pyramid is only a representation

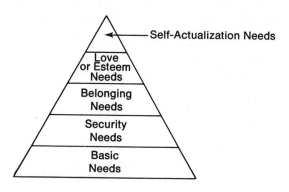

Figure 4–1

and that the lines between needs are not as distinct as the picture suggests. It should also be noted that the "higher" needs are not any "better" or more valuable than lower ones; they are just different and, in all likelihood, weaker and less likely to emerge until stronger needs are fulfilled.

Basic Needs   On the bottom level of the pyramid are the strongest and most prepotent needs man has—*basic needs*. These are the physiological needs each human being experiences. He needs regular fulfillment of needs for air, food, water, sex, sleep, and elimination of wastes. Until these needs are fulfilled, the individual cannot concern himself with other kinds of needs. The basic needs are too strong and essential to be forgotten, except on rare occasions, in favor of other needs.

Security Needs   The second level of Maslow's pyramid is the need for *security*. There are several ways one might look at the need for security. We may want to feel secure in our ability to get basic needs fulfilled. In this way, the man who feels that his job may end shortly experiences a strong need to establish security. He may want to get another more "secure" job. Or he might want to save money for that time when he will not be earning money. This is one kind of *security need* experience. At the same time we might look at this need level in another light. Let us suppose that the worker establishes job security—his boss assures him that he will be the last to be let go if the company experiences rough times. This individual may still feel insecure because of the rising crime rates in his neighborhood, and he may be willing to take rather drastic action to ward off thieves. He might, for example, install a burglar alarm system, or he may sleep with a loaded pistol under his pillow. Even when he feels secure about his home, he may still experience insecurity about world politics. He may feel that his country needs more nuclear missiles or antimissile missiles. In other words, this need for security emerges and reemerges as various aspects of the "security issue" become clear and need to be fulfilled. Once the need is fulfilled, it does not cease to be important—it redefines itself in other terms or from other perspectives and thus is always present to some degree.

Belonging Needs   Once the individual's immediate security needs are at least partially fulfilled (he knows he will have a job in the future and that criminals will have difficulty robbing him), other needs on the third level of Maslow's hierarchy are likely to emerge. These are *belonging* needs. The individual who feels fairly secure, like the horse who looks longingly at the field of clover across the road, looks to other things which he feels in need of—in this case, the need to associate with others and to be able to identify with them and have them identify with him. He again has a number of options open to him in fulfilling this need for association. He may, for instance, choose to fulfill these needs in his immediate family. We all know of individuals who have no reference group other than their job and family. This kind of fulfillment of basic needs is the exception rather than the rule, however. Usually the individual seeks various groups with which to fill this socialization need. Suburbia is filled with persons who seem to have an insatiable need for belonging—they are the joiners of our society. They become members of dozens of groups like the PTA, bowling leagues, church organizations, golf clubs, or service groups. Usually we keep the number of groups we join to a minimum and, though we may be members of a number of organizations, we are active members in only a few. Regardless of how many groups an individual joins or of how active he is in any of them, the individual, by associating with others, is seeking fulfillment of his belonging needs. He will continue to join and associate with groups throughout his life, for this need is also a reemerging one.

Love or Esteem Needs   Once the individual has partially satisfied his belonging needs, he will, according to Maslow's predictions, feel the emergence of other needs, represented on level four of Maslow's pyramid as the need for *love or esteem*. Once one has become part of a group, he wants to feel that the group—be it his family, his lodge, or his bowling team—values him as a member. Unless he does feel this sense of worth, in all likelihood the individual will drop the group in some way. As human beings we want to feel wanted and valued. Just as the caveman was elated when his mate demonstrated an understanding of his cave painting, we are elated when our families show understanding and admiration of the things we do. This need for love or esteem is, like the other need levels, a reemerging need. That is, if we find that we are needed and esteemed and loved by our family, the need for esteem does not immediately disappear. Instead, it becomes partially fulfilled, but its focus shifts. We want now to feel needed and loved or esteemed by our coworkers or our boss or by our friends. Discovering this kind of esteem, the need becomes more satisfied, but in all likelihood it is never fully satisfied and we continually seek other circumstances in which we can achieve status and rank that will add to our need for love and esteem by others.

Self-Actualization   At the top of Maslow's pyramid is the need for *self-actualization*. Stated in another way, this need might be called "the need to live up to what I think is my own true self-potential." The wealthy, secure, and esteemed businessman who gives up his business position to enter politics is probably demonstrating fulfillment of the self-actualization need. Although this need is weaker than the other need levels, there are cases where lower needs on the pyramid are displaced to fulfill the need for self-actualization. We have all heard of individuals who starve just so they can continue painting or composing music or some other creative and self-actualizing activity. In all likelihood, such cases are unusual in that the individual has defined his self-actualization level as a basic need. To the artist, painting is as basic as breathing or eating or sleeping. As W. H. Auden describes it, this is genius—the man who wants to do what he must do. For our purposes, though, this need is not a strong one, and its emergence depends on at least partial fulfillment of lower and more prepotent needs. Again, the need for self-actualization is a reemerging one and even when partially fulfilled becomes emergent in other areas. One good example of this reemergence of self-actualization needs is revealed by what happens to any ex-President of the United States. Clearly, once out of office, the ex-President has fulfilled and satisfied most needs on Maslow's pyramid. Now what is he to do? He has achieved the highest office in the land. There just isn't much more esteem available. He has also probably done his utmost at living up to his own potential. In many cases, ex-Presidents decide to self-actualize by writing their memoirs and by assembling libraries. In some cases, they do guest lecturing, and on occasion they engage in political power broking. At any rate, their self-actualization needs do not just go away once they have been fulfilled in as important a post as President of the United States. This need, like the others, is a reemerging one; we continually set up new self-actualizing goals.

Some Uses and Conclusions

Thus, one "given" at the process level is the organism's need state. A persuader may capitalize on the whole notion of human need levels; that is, he knows that the audience or persuadee has certain needs or drives that must be fulfilled. Relying on this process, the persuader shapes messages directed at particular needs. The idea of a need state is like a premise in an argument; the argument runs like this: "Since you have within you a need for x, I will show you how to get x. You will get x by following my advice." A persuader's success depends in large degree upon his ability to assess the persuadee's need state accurately.

We may wish to relabel our needs in terms other than Maslow's, but the pyramid of prepotent needs serves as a good general descriptive device of human needs. As persuadees, we ought to consider the requests persuaders make of us from the perspective of our own need states. For example, if a persuader asks us to use a new brand of soap because it pollutes less, we ought to ask if our security is really threatened to the degree that we ought to change brands of soap at the cost of extra money and with only an uncertain assurance of its reducing pollution.

As persuaders, we ought to examine the current needs of those we wish to influence. If we do that, we are not only more likely to succeed in our persuasion, but we are also more likely to do our audience a service by providing them with a means to satisfy their needs.

A good way to train yourself from this critical perspective—as persuadee or persuader—is to try to restate existing pieces of persuasion, such as television commercials, while considering the five need levels of Maslow's hierarchy.

Take for example, an advertisement for mouthwash. The ad suggests that if your breath is bad, you will not have a happy love life. Clearly, the ad attempts to present a threat to your esteem or love needs, but it has potency at other levels, too. The critical persuader-persuadee will restate this request in other terms. He may say, for instance, that "the mouthwash for lovers" will also make it easier to belong to certain identifiable groups, thus making the ad appeal to the belonging need. This kind of testing of appeals and playing with variations of appeals encourages a critical awareness on the part of the persuadee. He is able to observe and identify various persuasive techniques—an ability that ought to serve him in his various roles as persuader trying to sway the opinions and actions of others or as persuadee attempting to make a wise decision in the face of various persuaders. Maslow's pyramid can be used in many everyday persuasive opportunities—when one wants to persuade his teacher that a certain grade or method of evaluation is unfair, he must analyze what kinds of needs the professor has. Is he likely to feel insecure? Is he in need of esteem? Is he trying to self-actualize? Or suppose you were trying to persuade your roommate to take a trip to Florida with you instead of working over the break period. You would want to know what kinds of needs were being fulfilled by the potential trip or by the plan for work during the vacation. Many marital quarrels are rooted in differing motivations—a wife may want to take a trip to Washington, D.C., for the vacation while a husband is interested in going to fishing country, with each trying to fulfill different needs. Ultimately, either coercion or persuasion will occur and one side or the other will agree to give up his or her plans. The insurance salesmen who plague college students offering "special" rates are also appealing to needs (probably security needs) they assume operate in the student.

In conclusion, we can say that people are motivated by the assumption of similitude (they assume the world behaves in accordance with their own perceptions of it) and by their own particular need states. An organization called the National Institute for Straight Thinking states it interestingly. This organization believes that people are motivated by two things: (1) the possibility that they might lose something they now have or (2) the possibility that they might get something which they don't already have. Drew Pearson, in his novels *The Senator* and *The President*, has his main character, Benjamin Hannaford, plan a whole political career around this principle. He calls it the "Creative Use of Greed." In essence, Pearson's character and the National Institute for Straight Thinking have similar beliefs. They both feel that people are basically self-centered or egocentric in their need fulfillment. In a sense, this notion is a simplified version of most theories of motivation. As we have seen, Maslow's pyramid expresses levels of needs that persons try to satisfy for their own comfort or fulfillment. Similarly, B. F. Skinner's theory of reinforcement schedules would predict that humans, like rats, seek to alleviate personal deprivations. In all likelihood, there are real need premises in each of us—humans all have needs they wish to fulfill. These needs emerge and reemerge for us in our roles as parent, child, sibling, lover, student, and friend. As persuader and persuadee, we need to be aware of need states.

Consistency: The Second Intrapersonal Premise

All human existence probably revolves around successful adaptation to situations. For example, take the person who enters a new and unfamiliar environment—a new college freshman perhaps. He is not aware of all that is going on around him—the confusion of registration, grades, book buying, using the library, finding various buildings on campus, and other variables affect his lifestyle for at least a semester and for perhaps a number of years to come. What does this initiate do in response to this unknown and hostile atmosphere? Simply stated, he observes and searches for patterns and information which will allow him to *adapt* to the unknown (e.g., that you can study at the library without interruption, or that dorm food is fattening, or that parking is available before but not after 10:00 A.M.). Adaptation is more or less successful depending on the individual's ability to predict his world. In other words, neither you nor I can live very successfully anywhere unless the world behaves in accordance with our predictions of it.

Likewise, for a teacher who can cope with his class and the students in it only in accordance with his predictions. Unless the lectures he prepares generate the kind of discussion or feedback he predicts, he will abandon them and substitute something else. Unless the students relate to the class in meaningful ways (i.e., they absorb and apply the concepts he teaches instead of sleeping their way through the class), the instructor will be forced to change the class or leave it.

Not long ago a student persisted in riding a bicycle up and down the aisles of a lecture hall during an anthropology class. The situation became intolerable, not only for the instructor but for the students, who finally "persuaded" the cyclist to practice elsewhere.

These examples demonstrate the basis for the second intrapersonal premise humans respond to—the need for balance or homeostasis or predictability. Essentially this premise relates to the feeling of psychological comfort one has when his predictions about the world are reasonably accurate. Human beings want a resolution of psychological and interpersonal conflict and have difficulty tolerating incongruous elements in their worlds. This desire for resolution provides a potent process premise to which persuaders may appeal.

Two ways of looking at this problem of resolution of incongruity are found in Fritz Heider's Balance Theory[5] and Leon Festinger's Theory of Cognitive Dissonance.[6]

---

[5] Fritz Heider, "Attitudes and Cognitive Organization," *Journal of Psychology*, 21 (January 1946), 107–112.

[6] Leon Festinger, *A Theory of Cognitive Dissonance* (Stanford, Calif.: Stanford University Press, 1962).

Heider's Model: Balance/Imbalance

Heider's theory is relatively simple. It reduces potential incongruity to its simplest instance—one person talking to another person about a single topic or idea. Attitudes between the two persons (we could call one a persuader and the other a persuadee) can be represented by positive (+) signs or by negative (−) signs. Thus, the two communicators could like (+) or dislike (−) one another; they could agree that the idea they are dealing with has negative (−) or positive (+) values; or they might disagree with one another so that one felt positive (+) toward the topic while the other felt negative (−) toward it (see Figure 4–2). Notice that both the receiver and the source are

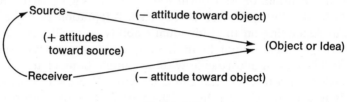

Figure 4–2

positively oriented toward the source of information. Since they agree on the topic and relate positively toward one another, the receiver (persuadee) experiences psychological comfort or in Heider's words "balance."

There are three possible ways in which a person can experience this psychological balance:

1. The source and receiver can both have a negative attitude toward the object or idea and can have a positive attitudinal set toward one another, as in Figure 4–2.

2. The source and receiver both have a positive attitude toward the object or idea and can have a positive attitudinal set toward one another. (You and I can like the same idea or object and like one another, thus experiencing comfort or balance.)

3. The source and receiver can have differing attitudes toward an idea or object and can dislike one another or experience a negative attitudinal set toward one another. (Since you and I are not alike and since we dislike one another, it is comforting to know that we disagree about the values of certain things or ideas.)

The underlying principle here is that we like to have our symbolic representations and beliefs about the world confirmed. In the words of one professor: "We like to have the world wired the way we think it ought to be wired." It is comforting to know that those we respect and like have the same values and ideas as we do, and it is also comforting to know that those we *dislike* disagree with us.

The persuader who tries to strengthen preexisting beliefs in an audience can do so by strategically creating a "balanced" or psychologically comfortable situation for his receivers, whether or not they hold the persuader in high or low esteem. As persuadees, we need to be aware of this strategy. When a persuader deals with you on a face-to-face basis and confirms your beliefs (e.g., that living in a suburb is bad, that the price of food is skyrocketing, that you are a wise and intelligent person, that your choice of make for your new automobile was wise), you ought to realize that he is utilizing the strategy of creating balance—a strategy that will undergird your existing beliefs and make them stronger.

Suppose that the persuader finds himself in a position where he wants to change beliefs and attitudes, not to strengthen existing beliefs. It will be foolish for him to try to create balance for his audience. Instead, he will try to throw their view of the world out of whack by creating an imbalanced situation—one in which their beliefs are not confirmed but rather are negated (consider Figure 4–3). In this case, someone whom

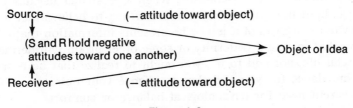

Figure 4–3

I do not respect dislikes the same things which I dislike. I am bound to feel uncomfortable or in a state of "imbalance" in such a situation.

Suppose you wanted to persuade your parents to let you go to Europe this summer and to help subsidize your trip. You might already know that they feel the trip might be dangerous or that they are afraid you might smoke pot or that in some other way you will be "led astray." Further, they probably feel that they cannot afford to pay your way and will feel the pinch of your not earning your own keep for the summer. Obviously, you will not get much persuasive mileage by telling them that it is none of their business if you experiment with drugs and that you are grown up enough to handle yourself. Instead, you need to create imbalance in their beliefs. You might observe that the probability of getting involved with drugs is higher at home when people are bored than it is while they are getting college credit on a European art tour. Or you might point out that you have performed well in the past when given independence and that you will travel with a trustworthy friend. Or you might remind them that there will be no cost for food or entertainment while you are not at home. All of these tactics aim at creating *imbalance* in order to change minds, not at creating balance to strengthen existing beliefs.

There are probably only two ways in which to create imbalance in persuasive situations:

1. If the source and receiver hold favorable attitudes toward one another but disagree about an object or idea, imbalance will be experienced.
2. If the source and receiver hold unfavorable attitudes toward one another but agree with one another on attitudes toward an object or idea, imbalance will be experienced.

Again, the same underlying principle operates. As receivers we want the world to live up to our expectations of it. If it does not, we experience imbalance; if it does, we experience balance.

The persuader who wants to get his receivers to change their minds about a particular idea or object can do so by creating feelings of psychological imbalance or discomfort. When a persuader negates your beliefs (e.g., he demonstrates why you are wrong to believe that a college degree will assure you of a job or he presents information that attempts to prove that joining a fraternity or some other group will detract from your social life, not add to it), you ought to realize that he is trying to create imbalance for you and thus to change your opinions, relying on your inherent need for psychological balance or comfort.

Festinger's Model: Consonance/Dissonance

Heider's theory is, of course, fairly limited. Not often do people hold beliefs that are easily identifiable as positive or negative. Beliefs have magnitude as well as direction, and we can have strongly positive opinions toward a certain topic or only slightly positive feelings toward another person or highly negative or slightly negative attitudes toward a certain topic—and there are other problems with Heider's theory. The theory proposed by Leon Festinger in his book *A Theory of Cognitive Dissonance* attempts to deal with some of Heider's shortcomings. Festinger calls imbalance "dissonance,"[7] which he defines as a feel-

---

[7] See Festinger, and "Consonance and Dissonance: A Model"—a paper presented by Charles U. Larson at the International Communication Association, Minneapolis, 1970. See also *Cognitive Consistency*, ed. Shel Feldman (New York: Academic Press, 1966).

ing resulting from the existence of two nonfitting pieces of knowledge about the world: ". . . considering the two alone, the obverse of one element would follow from the other."[8] "Consonance," Festinger's pair term for balance, exists when ". . . considering a pair of elements either one does follow from the other."[9] The degree to which one of these pieces of knowledge or elements may or may not follow from one another is variable, unlike balance theory. Thus, though I may greatly dislike door-to-door salesmen as a group, my slightly positive feelings toward a particular salesman may create only slight feelings of dissonance or imbalance. Let us try to represent this type of instance, using Festinger's theory.

As in balance theory, there are situations in which things fit or "go together." This is what Festinger calls *consonance*, or, in its Latin derivation, "sounds with one another." Festinger would maintain that any two cognitions, images, or beliefs could be expressed as two lines superimposed or overlaid on one another (see Figure 4–4). The solid line repre-

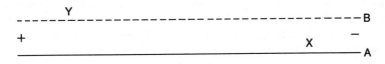

Figure 4–4

sents cognition A, and the X on the line marks an individual's attitude or values toward that cognition or belief. The broken line represents another cognition or other information about cognition A. The Y on this line represents the individual's position on the new information or on a "new" cognition, which we might call cognition B. The *distance* between these two cognitions represents the *amount of dissonance* an individual experiences when the two cognitions (points X and Y) are not congruent. The person feels psychic discomfort—the world isn't behaving as it should. The problem of the uncomfortable feeling arising from the dissonant cognitions must be reduced, and this is the basis for a number of speculations. Some persons predict that the individual experiencing dissonance will change his attitudes or cognitions until they are more approximately congruent (points X and Y are both moved closer to one another); others predict that the individual will "rationalize" his problem away by discrediting the source of one of his cognitions; and yet others predict that the individual will escape from his feelings of dissonance by the process of "selective perception," "selective retention," or "selective exposure." In other words, he will choose to forget or not

[8] Festinger, p. 13.
[9] *Ibid.*, p. 15.

to receive/perceive or not to expose himself to the dissonance-producing situations or information.

Let's look at a real case. Suppose that you smoke cigarettes—assume, for the sake of argument, a pack or so a day. Now assume that you hear that the odds of contracting lung cancer is 70 times greater now that you smoke. Under Festinger's theory, you will experience psychological discomfort because of these two cognitions (your smoking habits and the information relating to the danger of these habits). You may choose to do several things to reduce this discomfort. You might cut down to 15 cigarettes a day; you might quit altogether; you might ignore the information and switch to some other more comfortable message; or you might rationalize the dissonance away (e.g., hope for a cancer cure soon, discredit the source of the message).

Return for a moment to Figure 4–4. There is a problem with this model. The only time you or I do not experience dissonance to some degree is when points X and Y are absolutely congruent. Mathematically speaking, the probability of not experiencing dissonance is $(1/\infty)$—one divided by infinity, or in other words, *never*. If everything is dissonant, then there is no need to consider consonance. Yet you and I know that there are times when we experience a great deal of comfort or "consonance." In these cases, we do not seek to *reduce* the differences that may exist between our cognitions; instead we seek to exploit them or use this information about our "rightness" to give ourselves a pat on the back. We bolster our own beliefs. For instance, suppose you think you have discovered how a certain game of chance operates (you have "learned" the tricks or tactics of poker). If you test out this cognition in the real world by playing and winning at the game, your beliefs are strengthened, and you continue to follow your "winning" strategy, believing it to be "good," "predictable," and essentially comforting to your perception of the world.

To visualize how both dissonance and consonance work, consider Figures 4–5 and 4–6. In Figure 4–5 we have not only represented the magnitude and type of attitude a receiver has initially, but we have also

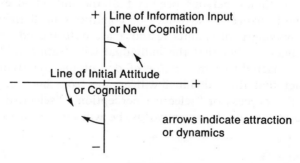

Figure 4–5

allowed for two different experiences by adding the arrows indicating that "likes attract" or that having positive initial feelings, one is most attracted by positive inputs or inputs that create balance—consonance (the upper-right and lower-left quadrants represent consonant possibilities). The arrows also suggest that there is tension in a situation where the individual gets information input or cognitions counter to his initial attitude, thus creating imbalance or dissonance (in the upper-left and lower-right quadrants. In Figure 4–6, a hypothetical case, based on

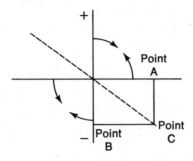

Figure 4–6

this model of consonance and dissonance, is depicted. Suppose that you had positive feelings toward taking a job with IBM because of what you had heard about salary, innovative opportunities, and so forth. You begin on the initial attitude or cognition line at point A. Now suppose that you happen to meet someone who worked for IBM and begin to hear negative information—IBM can move you overnight; they just say on a Friday that starting Monday you won't be reporting in Baltimore anymore but in Dallas. In fact, your acquaintance informs you there is a standing joke among IBM employees that the call letters of the company do not really stand for International Business Machines but for "I've Been Moved." Furthermore, he points out that there are strict and rigidly dogmatic rules for behaving if you work for IBM. For example, when you go out in the evening with a fellow employee it's husbands in the front seat, wives in the back. If you have a cocktail at lunch, don't come back for the rest of the day. And be sure to wear knee-high socks and wing-tipped shoes. All of this strikes you as negative information. The input is at point B, causing dissonance at point C (Figure 4–6).

Psychological discomfort is caused by the inconsistency or incongruity of your initial position, the desire to get information that would confirm that original position, and the input of information running counter to your initial stance. The tension created must be relieved in some way, and Festinger and others have suggested several ways in which persons try to reduce dissonance or even to resolve it:

1. The receiver may devalue his initial beliefs—he is persuaded and changes his positive feelings about IBM either to less positive ones or to negative ones.

2. The person may devalue the information by labeling it as biased, unproven, untrue, or part of the game of being in big business.

3. The person may perceive the input as a hatchet job. Researchers have called this method of relieving dissonance the method of selective perception—seeing what you want to see.

4. The person may try to forget about the new information. This is called selective retention or selective remembering and forgetting. (Parents are good at this one sometimes.)

5. The person may rationalize by saying something like "Oh well, things are like that all over."

In some cases, a person may do more than one at the same time—he may change his attitude about IBM in general while devaluing the information and rationalizing. This combination is familiar among smokers who, after hearing of the dangers of smoking and its links to fatal diseases, may cut down on their own intake, devalue the research studies as incomplete and not really conclusive, and may rationalize that you have to die of something anyway. At any rate, the type of experience depicted in Figure 4–6 is common, and persuaders often try to create dissonance for their auditors—to get them to feel psychologically uncomfortable and thus to nudge them to change their attitudes.

Though Festinger doesn't deal with the notion of consonance very deeply in his book, it seems clear that most persons engage in a great deal of communication, as receiver and source, that is not dissonance producing. We listen to the candidate of our choice, not very often to the man we dislike. A good deal of research indicates that we expose ourselves to information that is consistent with our beliefs and that we avoid information that is counter to our beliefs. Conservative persons read conservative newspapers; liberal persons read liberal ones. Figure 4–7 depicts what happens in a consonant situation where, for example, a receiver initially has negative attitudes toward religious conversion (point X). Now suppose he sees a film like *Marjoe*, which tells the story of a child evangelist who was coached by his parents to deliver revival sermons at the age of seven, responding on cues from his mother like "Praise the Lord," which might have meant that it was time to take up the collection or to ask for the penitent to come forward and make a commitment to the Lord. This information input (point Y) is consistent or consonant with the persuadee's initial belief, so he experiences psychological comfort or consonance at point Z. These feelings confirm what he always knew; they are related to the assumption of similitude mentioned earlier—we like to have our view of the world confirmed by other persons and by other information.

In Figure 4–7 there is no need to resolve any inconsistency or any

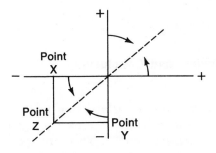

Figure 4–7

psychic discomfort, but there is a different kind of pressure. It is out-ward, away from the center, as if point Z were being squeezed away from the center because of increased negative information. This experience is common; we find information confirming our position, and that makes our belief stronger. There are various responses we can take as feelings of consonance:

1. The receiver can revalue his initial beliefs, making them stronger in all likelihood—now he knows for sure that revival conversions are faked.
2. He can revalue the source of information input. He may view the story of Marjoe as a typical and highly unbiased documentary.
3. He may perceive the information as stronger than it actually is and focus on the strongest parts of it.
4. He may remember the most negative parts of it and choose to highlight those that best support his belief.
5. He may repeatedly expose himself to other antirevivalist informa-tion by reading novels like *Elmer Gantry* or newspaper exposés.
6. He may do several of the above at the same time, increasing his negativity towards conversion, highly evaluating the source and content of *Marjoe*, and exposing himself to other debunkers of re-vivalism.

The tactic of creating consonance, then, is used to create stronger attitudes, to undergird existing cognitions, and to increase one's source credibility. The creation of consonance and its power to cause revalua-tion of the source of new inputs negates the old saying that "flattery gets you nowhere" and turns it around to "flattery gets you everywhere."

A Review and Conclusion

Returning to our early notion in this chapter, the need to avoid feelings of dissonance and to seek feelings of consonance are premises that operate intrapersonally. They are the "givens" on which persuaders can build arguments. Like the other needs mentioned earlier (basic needs, security needs, etc.), the persuader can utilize the tendency to seek balance or consonance in persuading others. He can also use the reverse side of this coin. He can utilize people's desire to avoid imbalance or dissonance as a building block of persuasion.

In polarized audiences—where members feel similarly toward a particular topic—the creation of balance or consonance is probably the best strategy. With such auditors, the persuader wants to strengthen beliefs. The degree to which a person will experience dissonance or consonance will, of course, interact with a number of other variables such as his ego-involvement, his personality, or his prior exposure to various types of information in support of or counter to our beliefs.[10] Consonance and dissonance are both heightened and affected by our past experiences; and sometimes we are open to persuasion vis-à-vis these past experiences. In other cases like the "true believer," whom Eric Hoffer talks about, we encounter persons who are rather impervious to persuasion that does not agree with their beliefs. The persuader probably cannot change their minds; he can only strengthen them. This explains why mass rallies usually are for people who already hold strong beliefs. No minds are changed; no persuasion to "my" or "your" side occurs. In nonpolarized audiences, or audiences with more open-minded members, the creation of imbalance or dissonance may be the best persuasive strategy— particularly if the persuader hopes to change attitudes in his audience. Such persons are not closed-minded and when presented with dissonant information or that causes imbalance, there is a good chance these persons will change their minds about topic X or person Y. The role of the

[10] For a good review of the effects of various elements of personality on persuasion, see *Personality and Persuasibility*, ed. Carl I. Hovland and Irving L. Janis (New Haven, Conn.: Yale University Press, 1959). For a more specific discussion of ego-involvement and persuasion, see the discussion of latitudes of acceptance and rejection in Ch. 2 and of ego-involvement in Ch. 3 of *Attitude and Attitude Change: The Social Judgment Involvement Approach* by Carolyn W. Sherif, Muzafer Sherif, and Roger E. Nebergall (Philadelphia: W. B. Saunders Co., 1965). See J. E. Brinton and L. N. McKown, "Effects of Newspaper Reading on Knowledge and Attitude," *Journalism Quarterly 38* (Spring 1961), 187–195; or Ben Cherrington and L. W. Miller, "Changes in Attitudes as the Result of a Lecture and of Reading Similar Materials," *Journal of Social Psychology, 4* (November 1933), 479–484.

persuader is to choose the appropriate strategy at the appropriate time. The role of the persuadee is to be aware of which strategy a persuader takes and to determine whether or not he, the persuadee, wishes to respond to this choice.

Whatever the case—arguments that cause dissonance and imbalance or arguments that cause consonance or balance—the persuadee is responding to a need that is as strong as any of the needs cited on the Maslow pyramid—his need to feel that the world is behaving according to predictions. Like the needs identified by Maslow, this need can also provide the necessary "first premise" upon which persuaders can build.

Whenever one tries to go inside another person's skin and make statements about what motivates that other person or about what that person "feels" at any given moment, he is taking a risk. We can never know for sure what motivates others. On the intrapersonal level of persuasion as persuaders, we are only guessing at best. We probably operate under the assumption of similitude that, since we are motivated in a certain way, others must be motivated in that way also. As receivers of persuasion, however, we can be more sure of what is happening, at least within our own skins. Here you and I *can* make statements about what motivates us or about what we feel motivates us.

As persuadees in an information age, it is our responsibility and in our own self-interest to ask questions like "What need am I now experiencing?" and "In what ways am I psychologically vulnerable to persuasion at this moment?" Asking such questions will help make each persuadee more critical and choosy about the information he utilizes in his decision making, and about the information he chooses to reject in his decision making.

This chapter has presented three "tools" for analyzing how we act and why we act and respond to certain kinds of appeals: Maslow's hierarchy of needs, Heider's balance theory, and Festinger's dissonance-consonance theory. These three are only a beginning. The persuadee who wants to *learn to be persuaded*, must go further and continually seek other models, theories, and paradigms to clarify his own intrapersonal reactions to appeals and to information. Only in this way will successful and responsible reception of information be continually a part of each receiver's approach. Vance Packard's book *The Hidden Persuaders* (mentioned in Chapter 1) revealed to many consumers the kinds of appeals being made to their subconscious nature. Once known and publicized, these techniques lost appeal and effect and were changed or discarded in favor of other more successful methods. The persuadee who wants to be critical and aware as he processes persuasive information, must "keep up with his homework" and continually seek new and more complex explanations for his behavior and for the new packages in which persuasion is presented to him.

Questions for Further Thought

1. What other needs (aside from those listed in Maslow's hierarchy) do humans experience? Which of them could be translated into Maslow's terms? How? Give examples.

2. What is the difference between a *process premise* and a *content premise?* Cite several examples where these have operated in your life recently.

3. When a demonstrator yells "Off the pig!" into a policeman's face during a march, is he engaging in language for its consummatory function? Its instrumental function? Or both? Discuss and defend your decision.

4. When the policeman responds to the demonstrator, saying "Go home, little boy—before you get hurt—know what I mean?" is he engaging in language for its consummatory effects? Its instrumental effects? Or both? What if he responds by hitting the demonstrator with a club? Is this instrumental or consummatory expression, or both? Is it symbolic expression?

5. A person disliking Mayor Richard Daley of Chicago and authoritarian-type "law and order" and hearing of Daley's order to "shoot to kill or maim" during the disturbances following the assassination of Martin Luther King, Jr., would experience what (consonance or dissonance)? In what quadrant of the model (page 90) would you place him? What attractions or dynamics are operating in this case? What might this person do in reference to his initial beliefs and/or the credibility of the information he receives? Why? Explain.

6. If a person likes Mayor Daley and hears the same information but would not support shooting to kill, how would his reaction differ from the person in question 5? Would he experience consonance or dissonance? What could he do about it, with his beliefs or based on the information he hears?

7. Cite examples of the following methods of reducing dissonance:

   a. Devalue the source of inputs or information causing the dissonance

   b. Selectively expose oneself to nondissonance-producing information

   c. Selectively forget information that causes dissonance

   d. Selectively remember information that reduces dissonance

   e. Change attitudes or beliefs

   f. Selectively perceive the world in order to reduce dissonance

   You may wish to follow a single case through these methods of reducing dissonance (e.g., your parents facing a dissonance-producing problem, such as letting their "baby" have an apartment off campus), or you may cite several different examples.

8. Cite examples of the following methods of increasing the feelings of psychological comfort experienced in consonance; follow the directions given for question 7:

   a. Revaluing the source of the consonance-producing source

b. Selectively exposing oneself to consonance-producing information

c. Selectively remembering consonance-producing information

d. Selectively perceiving things which are consonance producing

e. Changing one's attitudes or beliefs

f. Selectively forgetting things which do not lend themselves to feelings of consonance

Experiences in Persuasion

1. Select newspaper and magazine advertisements for a certain product or type of product (deodorant, for example). When you have a good selection (10 to 20), analyze them according to the needs on Maslow's hierarchy to which they appeal. The ads may be doing several things at once and may appeal to more than one level. Discuss this concomitance of appeal. Argue for the effectiveness or ineffectiveness of one of the ads in particular (the ads for Volkswagen have been favorites of students in some classes).

2. Write a letter to the editor of your campus paper or your local paper, couching it so that it would appeal to the *security* level of Maslow's hierarchy. Rewrite it so that it appeals to the *belonging* level; the *esteem* level; the *self-actualization* level. Determine which of the four ways would be the best; discuss how and why it might be the best. (If you do this as a group, one person might write the message aimed at *security*, another at *belonging*, and so on; then the group would determine which was most effective.)

3. Trace the history of research concerning dissonance (try speech communication journals such as *Quarterly Journal of Speech* and *Speech Monographs*, as well as journals in other fields such as the *Journal of Abnormal and Social Psychology*) and report to the class on your findings. What do we know about dissonance? Self-persuasion? Belief discrepancy?

4. Do the "letter to the editor" assignment (see number 2), but this time write a letter answering an editorial in the paper. Do it once in a way that will cause dissonance for the editorial writer and then write it in a way to cause consonance. Submit both letters using your own name on one and the name of another person on the other if he is agreeable. What happened? Explain to the class what you did and what were the results.

Readings for New Dimensions

Beisecker, Thomas D., and Donn W. Parson, *The Process of Social Influence: Readings in Persuasion* (Englewood Cliffs, N. J.: Prentice-Hall, 1972). This collection of readings should be of value to the student of persuasion. The book groups research reports related to persuasion as well as theoretical speculation about persuasion into the following categories: "The Psychological Context," "The Source: Properties of Speaker Credibility," "Characteristics of the Message," and "The Effects of Persuasion." The first section is especially related to this chapter. Other sections relate to other parts of this book. See especially the selections in "Section I: The Psychological Context" authored by Katz, Kelman, Zajonc, Sears and Freedman, and Sherif, Sherif and Nebergall.

Brown, Charles T., and Charles Van Riper, *Speech and Man* (Englewood Cliffs, N. J.: Prentice-Hall, 1966). Van Riper and Brown, operating from the perspective of the speech scholar and pathologist, discuss what we have referred to in Chapter 4 as the distinction between consummatory and instrumental effects of language. The discussion of consummatory uses occurs in the chapters on speech and emotional expression, identity, and "The Pleasures of Speech"; and on the instrumental uses of language in chapters focusing on the uses of speech as an instrument for communication, control, and thought. The first chapter of the book also has an exciting discussion of the enormity and wonder of speech; every student of human communication ought to read it.

Cronkhite, Gary. *Persuasion: Speech and Behavioral Change* (Indianapolis: Bobbs-Merrill Co., 1969). This book has the most compact and thorough discussion of the history of research and philosophy in persuasion that I have seen. Note especially the discussions of balance theory and dissonance theory. Cronkhite's paradigm for persuasion is also closely related to the notion discussed here—that the persuadee has within him certain "premises" or notions, which serve as the building blocks of persuasion. The book also has excellent bibliographies, which can serve as good starting points for any student interested in investigating concepts discussed in this book to a more complete degree.

Hovland, Carl I., and Irving L. Janis, *Personality and Persuasibility* (New Haven, Conn.: Yale University Press, 1959). The book is a collection of research reports that investigate the relationship between such personality characteristics as self-esteem and emotional disorder and the likelihood of being persuaded. This research centers on the nature of the "premises" held by the receiver. These variables are extensions of the needs for specific fulfillments mentioned here and the need for balance or dissonance and other *internal* premises upon which persuaders rely.

Miller, Gerald R. *Speech Communication: A Behavioral Approach* (Indianapolis: Bobbs-Merrill Co., 1966). Though Miller is discussing communication in general, many of the elements discussed in the book are closely related to issues raised in this chapter. The discussion of models as well as the nature of *process* relate to the receiver orientation of this book and to our discussion of "process premises," or premises that rely on some psychological internal process.

Sereno, Kenneth K., and C. David Mortensen, *Foundations of Communication Theory* (New York: Harper & Row, 1970). Though there is some overlap between this book and the Beisecker and Parson book, both are worth adding to one's persuasion library. Again, information relevant to material in this and other chapters of this book is grouped into various sections, each containing research reports and/or theoretical speculation about communication. See especially the introduction to the book and Part I, both of which provide a frame of reference from which to judge persuasion theory in relation to communication theory. The introduction to Part III directly addresses the problems receivers face and the characteristics they display. Like other items either footnoted in this chapter or mentioned in this bibliography, Sereno and Mortensen are concerned with the recipient of information and his ability to decide. Some selections directly discuss items covered in this chapter, such as dissonance theory and psychological variables in communication.

5

Content Premises in Persuasion

In Chapter 4, we drew a distinction between the consummatory and the instrumental uses of language and pointed out that although we engage in language use for pure pleasure—to satisfy our aesthetic *self*—we also attempt to use language to manipulate the environment around us. We try to make the world around us behave in ways that are comfortable and pleasing to us.[1] The persuader who is alert and sophisticated often relies on our propensity to use language instrumentally. He does this by appealing to process premises, or psychological processes within each of us, that we utilize to exist in the world around us (e.g., he appeals to our need for consistency by telling us that cigarette smoking is bad for our health and costs money that could be used for other things). These *process premises* serve as the building blocks in persuasive messages, and the alert persuadee observes the appeals made to his psychological processes. He notes the appeals made to his security or esteem needs; he records the attempts made by persuaders to his need for balance; and with all these observations in mind, he decides whether or not he will respond to the persuasion.

---

[1] For a good discussion of the distinction between these two functions of language and of the tendency to use language instrumentally, see Leon Festinger's "Informal Social Communication," in *Psychological Review*, 57 (1950), 271–282. The discussion of "emotional expression" in that article suggests that consummatory functions of language are most likely the result of emotional motivation and situations, while instrumental functions of language are useful in achieving balance or consonance (see Ch. 4). Our position in this book is that consummatory language usage is first and foremost artistic—it may be emotional or nonemotional, while instrumental language usage is primarily technical and used as a tool (or an instrument) to achieve the completion of some task. Unlike consummatory use, instrumental use of linguistic symbols is never for pure pleasure; it always has an end, other than its own performance, as its objective.

The persuader, however, has a number of other tools at his disposal, and we need to explore these as we did the process premises. These are also entwined with man's symbolic impulses and his language-using behavior. This chapter centers on one other set of premises that are often used by persuaders: *content premises*, which rely on universally or nearly universally accepted modes of responding to information instead of the highly individualized psychological states upon which process premises rely.

In appealing to *content premises*, the persuader has a much greater likelihood of predicting the success or failure of his appeal. He is aiming at premises that are quite verifiable and that would be acceptable to a majority of persons as "reasonable" or "rational" or "consistent" in some way.

One problem with content premises is that any discussion of them needs to be carefully structured and organized—and there are several ways of structuring this discussion. For our purposes, we will approach this problem by discussing these topics and questions:

1. *The nature of content and proof:* What causes us to believe or not believe a persuader who is appealing to our intellect? Why do we sometimes believe with very little evidence presented and at other times demand much detailed evidence? How much proof is enough?

2. *The nature of evidence and reasoning:* What is evidence? What is reasoning? What are the basic modes of drawing conclusions or of linking information to action?

3. *Strategic and tactical levels of content premises:* What is the difference between the *overall* organization of content-oriented persuasive messages and the *internal* steps used to get agreement with this overall thrust of the message? Are there easy ways to describe and analyze both levels?

4. *Proving a point:* Does *self-persuasion* operate in all persuasion? If so how? Is one kind of *evidence* better than another for the purposes of proof? Is one kind of *proof* better than another? Why do some methods seem more successful than others? Why is emotional or empathic evidence so persuasive?

With these questions and others in mind let's look at persuasion as it occurs around us—on television, in the newspaper, in the classroom, on campus, and in our homes. We know that we are persuaded many times each day and that we need to be persuaded in order to make choices in this confusing and complex world. But *how* are we persuaded?

What Is Content?

Suppose someone came up to you in the street and said, "You must leave this area at once!" You would probably ask for a reason; you would want to know why the person wanted you to leave, even though he or she seemed agitated and excited. What you would be asking for would be reasons, or *content premises*. Now at times the kind of content required by you would be minimal (e.g., if the person's face were bloodied and his eyes were filled with fear or if some sort of scenic detail caught your eye—like several demonstrators being chased toward you by a group of police). At other times the kind of content you require would be demanding (e.g., suppose you are in the middle of a discussion with someone whom you want very much to date, and you are about to get to that point where both of you are ready to make an agreement as to time, place, and occasion). In some cases, you might not be persuadable by any kind of content (e.g., you may have vowed never again to leave your post of duty as a traffic controller at the local school playground after being responsible for an auto accident which killed a young child; or you may have decided that it is time to say your piece regardless of the consequences, and no authority figures or threatening personages will change your mind). Notice what we have been seeing in these examples. The persuadee is not appealed to on the basis of his internal state—he may respond because he is afraid or because he seeks gratification of some need—but the initial appeal in each case (e.g., the danger of being involved in a police-demonstrator confrontation) is directed at some "rational" or universally accepted relationship. In this case, the relationship is between danger and a dislike of potential damage resulting from the danger. Thus, the appeal is not made on the basis of some psychological mechanism, which *may* or *may not* be operant inside your skin, but to some "stuff" that most persons would buy as reasonable.

What Is Proof?

Clearly, then, in some cases a certain amount and kind of content will persuade you to do some particular thing, while in other cases a different kind and type of content will cause you to follow the same advice. The point at which enough of the right kind of content is presented to elicit the desired behavior, be it "leaving the area at once," "burning your draft card," or "buy the quart-sized bottle of Pepsi-Cola," is also the point at which a *proof* has been demonstrated. What then constitutes *proof?*

Most theorists ultimately are reduced to simplifying the matter of proof and end up saying something like "Proof is the result of reasoning plus evidence."[2] Well and good, but how does this help the persuadee who is faced with reams of evidence, much of it contradictory (e.g., buy product "A," since it has *more* of the cleaning power of hexachlorophene, and buy product "B," because it has *less* hexachlorophene that is harmful to eyes and skin)? What the persuadee needs again, as with the process premises and language-usage level of persuasive analysis, is a set of models or tools to allow him to look carefully at the persuasive messages bombarding him each day.

For our purposes, let us now define *proof* simply but more discretely and concretely than "reasoning plus evidence." *Proof is a consistency between the action requested and the reasons given for taking that action that is sufficient to elicit the action after it has been considered in reference to other options.* Of course, such proof is bound to be closely tied to the style in which it is presented, so the concepts of Chapters 2 and 3 also relate here. Notice that this definition of proof is not contingent upon a somewhat vague relationship between evidence and reasoning. Instead, what we have said is that there is a threshold point at which the reasons given "add up" so that the persuadee will follow the advised course of action. These reasons are made up of evidence plus reasoning, but they also interact with the severity of the action requested. Thus, *proof* has at least three components: (1) the kind of action suggested or requested by the persuader; (2) the amount and kind of evidence offered to compel such action; and (3) the strength of the intellectual linkages between the request made and the reasons given (how realistic or negotiable the linkage is).

To summarize, content premises do not rely upon the discrete and individualized motivational states of persuadees in the audience but upon more universally accepted standards that "most" persons would buy and, thus, are more predictable and less dependent upon discrete analysis of specific audiences.

---

[2] For example, see the discussion of reasoned discourse in such texts as *Persuasion: A Means of Social Control* by Winston L. Brembeck and William S. Howell (Englewood Cliffs, N. J.: Prentice-Hall, 1952), pp. 187–212; *The Art of Persuasion*, 2nd ed., by Wayne C. Minnick (Boston: Houghton Mifflin Co., 1968), pp. 119–145; or *Evidence* by Robert P. Newman and Dale R. Newman (Boston: Houghton Mifflin Co., 1969).

Evidence and Reasoning

Instead of looking at traditional descriptions of evidence and reasoning, Chapter 5 will view these two concepts from this perspective: The way in which information is linked (i.e., reasoned out) is the strategic element in discourse using content premises; and the information that is combined and the choice of it (i.e., evidence) are the tactical elements in content premise persuasion. We are interested in *strategic* effect. By examining what the persuader does—how he operates—we can infer motives and discover what he is ultimately up to. For example, suppose I wished to persuade you that smoking causes lung cancer. The thrust of my message—the strategy of it, so to speak—is to create a cause-effect argument. I want to prove to you that a given effect—lung cancer—has a given cause—cigarette smoking. Along the way I might engage in a variety of *tactics* (e.g., I might show slides of infested body cells; I might give vivid testimony of the pain and suffering involved in cancer deaths; I might offer statistical correlations; or I might do a variety of other things), but they are all related to my general strategy, belief, motive, or intention. These *tactics* are the "stuff" from which proof will ultimately emerge for you as persuadee; somewhere along the line, I will reach the threshold for you and will have "proved" to you that you must stop smoking. In other cases, other elements will persuade you to stop—the key may not even be planned by a persuader but can still be the threshold for change.

By looking at the traditional rule-governed ideas about evidence and reasoning as the *strategic* level of persuasion, we are able to consider various kinds of "proof," ranging from direct experience to emotional description to intellectual consideration of data and statistics—all under the label *tactics* or evidence. When coupled with the notion of a threshold for persuasion, the set of terms suggested here for analysis offers the persuadee a maximum amount of flexibility in examining not only what kinds of content premises a persuader utilizes in his persuasive attempts but also the ways in which he presents these. The rationale behind these moves can indicate motive or intent and can again provide the persuadee with a powerful tool for critically examining and reviewing persuasive information prior to making a decision. Instead of describing a persuader's action in terms such as "He used conditional (if–then) reasoning supported by statistical evidence, all of which led to a cause-effect argument that violence was caused by harassment," the persuadee can say something like "His strategy seemed to be to couple situational evidence and examples with fearful potential effects to lead to the conclusion that 'if you don't leave us alone, we will burn your house down.' He used a lot of dramatic examples to demonstrate this pattern, and they all seemed to have the same kinds of details."

Motivation is more evident when using the second analysis than when using the first. Let us proceed to the strategic level and examine the raw materials of content premises.

Types of Evidence

Earlier, brief reference was made to the varying strengths of bits of evidence: in some cases statistics are strong; in other cases pictoral evidence is most powerful; and in yet other cases experience is the best evidence. In all of these instances, persuasion relies on an assumption that one can learn and act on the basis of information gained indirectly and vicariously.[3] Even experiential evidence relies on the assumption that the same experience need be enacted only once to have persuasive potency. For example, the jury of men and women who listened to the trial of Adolf Eichmann, the architect of Hitler's mass extermination of Jews, heard Eichmann say that he had never committed murder but that he had "exterminated" and "relocated" Jews. Having heard this pronouncement once, the jury did not need to repeat that experience to realize that *renaming* an activity changed it in the Nazi brain. From that point on, words from Eichmann's mouth became much more important and double-edged than before. When he talked about words like "solution," "experiment," or "protection camp," they knew that the words did not mean what they might normally mean.[4]

Given this assumption of vicarious learning, the problem for the persuader is to determine how best to get his audience to change or to "learn" new activities, and it is here that the nature of evidence becomes important. What kind of evidence is most effective and efficient in retraining persuadees? How much evidence is enough? How much is too much? How should the evidence be presented? All of these questions face the persuader as he prepares his messages. Generally, evidence falls into two categories: the emotionally laden, which appeals dramatistically to the imagination and emotions of the persuadee, and the rule-governed,

---

[3] A good discussion of this premise (that we learn much of our knowledge vicariously) is presented in Mark Abrahamson's *Interpersonal Accommodation* (New York: Van Nostrand-Reinhold Co., 1966).

[4] Hannah Arendt, *Eichmann in Jerusalum: A Report on the Banality of Evil* (New York: The Viking Press, 1964). See especially p. 22, where Eichmann is quoted as saying ". . . I never killed a Jew or a non-Jew, for that matter I never killed any human being"; and p. 84, where Arendt cites some of the "code names" for extermination, such as "evacuation," "special treatment," and "resettlement," and discusses the "language rules" of the Third Reich.

which appeals to the intellect. Let us look at these types more carefully. Actually, they are two of the ancient categories—pathos and logos—now viewed as parts of content premises.

The Dramatistically Oriented Imagine the following situation in your class: a student stands and announces that he is going to give a speech on abortion. As an introduction to this speech, he turns on a cassette tape recorder, and you begin to hear an interview with a young girl who is dying in a hospital as a result of an illegal abortion. The testimony is being taken by a hardened policeman, and the young girl is weakly gasping for breath. Her voice rattles in her throat as she recounts the abortion scene, the amount of money paid, the instruments used, and so forth. She is clearly in pain, as indicated by her voice, and she is also obviously frightened and in need of comfort. As the details unfold, you feel yourself becoming sick to your stomach. When recorded this way, the bare facts are almost unbearable.[5] The persuader is utilizing what most persons would call "emotionally laden" proof—some call it psychologically oriented. Clearly aimed at deep-set fears and dislikes, its purpose is to cause revulsion in the listener—and to persuade him that illegal abortions are horrible. Although the evidence is emotionally oriented, it is certainly not "illogical" to conclude, as a result of it, that illegal abortions are not desirable; in fact, it is *totally* logical to draw such a conclusion. Instead of labeling this evidence and reasoning as "irrational," "nonrational," "illogical," or "nonlogical," we call it *dramatistically oriented* evidence.

The point is that emotional responses to problems are often as logical as intellectual responses. One doesn't need to sift systematically through mounds of statistics on abortion. The conclusion isn't based on intellectual ability but on human emotional response. This reality has been one of the points made by advocates for the counterculture—that we don't respond emotionally often enough, that we rely too often on "intellectualized responses" to problems, thus neglecting human situations and feelings in favor of hard cold facts. Perhaps a single example of illegal abortion *is* enough evidence to convince any *reasonable* person that legalization of abortion is needed to prevent human suffering. If the evidence is dramatic or emotional enough, persuadees will not ask for more; they will not engage in philosophical discussions about first premises relating to the sanctity of human life. Instead, by vicariously suffering with the victim of the illegal abortion, the persuadees become convinced.

---

[5] This example is a real one that happened in one of the author's own classes. After listening to the tape, which was used to serve as an introduction to an in-class debate over abortion laws, the negative side asked to be allowed to concede. It was evident that a major portion of the class audience had been persuaded by the raw realism of the data.

Perhaps it is that word "dramatic" that really is important here. *Dramatistically oriented evidence invites and encourages vicarious experience on the part of the persuadee in an attempt to persuade him to a certain course of action.*[6] Such persuasion relies upon the persuadee's ability to project himself into a context or situation described by the persuader—to "feel" what others feel, to live the problem vicariously.

If one were to look at historic persuasive speeches or at highly successful speeches of the present, he would undoubtedly find a great deal of emotionally oriented and dramatic evidence. The persuader presents a dramatic situation to his audience and then "invites" his listeners to participate in the drama—in their imaginations, to become actors themselves.[7] There is no intellectualizing here; at the same time, one would be hard put to say that the audiences reacted "illogically" or "irrationally." They merely responded to dramatic evidence. This type of evidence encourages the persuadee to co-create proof with the persuader. The result is powerful persuasion, which is probably long lasting.

The Intellectually Oriented In our discussion of dramatistically oriented evidence, we used the example of a speech with a highly dramatic and involving piece of evidence: a tape recording of a deathbed statement from a young girl dying as the result of an illegal abortion. Now imagine that the same student stands up in class and announces that he is going to give a speech favoring abortion reform. He proceeds to point out that there are over 60,000 deaths annually due to abortions, more deaths than occurred to the American forces in Vietnam in all the years of the war. He cites examples of testimony from prominent gynecologists, all of whom observe that abortions are safe and simple if performed in clinically controlled and sterile operating rooms. He notes that in the state of New York, which has legalized abortion, the rate of death due to illegal abortions has dropped

---

[6] Several good discussions of the importance of the dramatic structure can be found in literature from various fields. For example, Kenneth Burke, operating from the perspective of literary criticism, notes the power of the dramatic to cause identification (persuasion) in *A Grammar of Motives* (Berkeley: University of California Press, 1970). Robert Bales, a sociologist, observes the same power of the dramatic in his research concerning the sociology of groups in *Personality and Interpersonal Behavior* (New York: Holt, Rinehart and Winston, 1970)—see especially Ch. 7, "Describing Fantasy Themes", pp. 136–155. Ernest G. Bormann, borrowing from both of these perspectives, suggests that there is a power to create an entire "rhetorical vision" in the utilization of dramatic instances—see "Fantasy, Rhetoric, and Social Reality: A Dramatistic Approach to Communication and Rhetorical Criticism," *Quarterly Journal of Speech, 58* (December 1972), 396–407.

[7] Good examples of the use of dramatistic invitations can be found in a number of speeches in recent times as well as in the history of public speaking. Some examples are George McGovern's acceptance address, wherein he repeatedly invited his audience to "come home"; Clarence Darrow's defense of joy killers Loeb and Leopold, which "invites" the judge to join in the high drama of humanitarian change; John F. Kennedy's Inaugural address, which invites the listeners to do something for their country; and William Jennings Bryan's "Cross of Gold" speech, which invited participation in populism.

dramatically and observes that this trend is similar in other states and countries that condone therapeutic abortions. Finally, he addresses himself to the moral question—whether anyone can make a decision about another person's life—and quotes documents from every religious group one can think of, all of which imply that such decisions are of individual and not institutional origin. In this case, the persuader arouses no one to feel sick to his stomach; he does not dramatically draw a gory picture of the problem and then invite the audience to share in the drama. Instead, he rather systematically answers several related questions:

1. Is there a problem?
2. How bad are things?
3. Can they be changed?
4. How?
5. What are the benefits of the change in comparison to the detriments?
6. Are there philosophical reasons for following the advice given by the persuader?

All his evidence is objective and representative, not of particular cases but of general trends. Let us further suppose that persons listening to this speech become committed to supporting efforts to legalize abortion nationwide. In other words, as in the case involving dramatic evidence, persuasion occurs and the audience becomes committed to action. In all likelihood, both audiences would exhibit some of the same behaviors as a result of the persuasion to which they had been exposed. They would both probably be excited about the issue; they might try to persuade other persons to support efforts to legalize therapeutic abortion; they also might try to effect change by writing to congressmen or by making donations.

It would be foolish to label this second case study in persuasion "logical," as opposed to the emotional nature of our first case. Instead, it seems more reasonable to say that the first case appealed in large part to emotional biases and responses (perhaps the ability to *specify*), while the second example appealed to the intellect and the ability to *generalize*. In other words, *dramatistically oriented* persuasion appeals to the ability to be subjective, to empathize, and to experience vicariously particular, specific events, whereas *intellectually oriented* persuasion *appeals to the ability to synthesize, generalize, and categorize and to draw conclusions from the generalizations and trends that are usually acceptable to most persons.*

Neither mode is "illogical" in any sense—they are both logical but in different ways. Intellectually oriented evidence has its greatest use and impact in formal situations that are highly rule-governed (e.g., in the courtroom, or during serious political debate, such as in the speeches of Henry Clay during the debates over the compromise of 1850, or during considerations over a family budget). This approach, though not as widely used in public persuasion, probably has the longer lasting effect— the person persuaded by dramatic evidence has difficulty "reliving" the experience many times, and each time the experience is relived it becomes less exciting and involving. The intellectually persuaded person is detached and doesn't experience this "wearing out" process. He can run the facts and figures over and over again, and if powerful enough in the first place they will continue to add up.

Nonetheless, it would be senseless and unproductive to think of one of these methods as "better" or "worse" than the other. They both "work"—that is the important point. At times we may want to make a particular choice as a result of dramatic evidence; at other times we may wish to respond in cool, intellectual, and rule-governed ways.

Types of Reasoning

In our discussion of evidence types, we have touched on reasoning to some degree. Whenever we begin to talk about "reason" or "rational" processes, we inevitably talk about the kinds of ways in which people *link* the conclusions they make to the evidence given and to other conclusions or courses of advised action. Consider this example: Suppose I come up to you on the street and say that it would be worth your while to prepare to meet your Maker since the world was about to end and that I would therefore suggest that you sell all you have, give it away, and go to a church and pray. If you don't dismiss me out of hand as another religious fanatic, you might ask me why I thought the world was about to end and perhaps even why giving away possessions made any sense in the face of impending doom. What you would be doing would be asking me for evidence to support my request or advice. Now suppose I answer, "Why, the world will end because I dreamt that it would, and I also had a car accident on the way to school today and an upset stomach when I got up." If you were patient with me, you still might not totally dismiss me as a lunatic, and you might ask what those three things possibly had to do with the end of the world. What you would be asking for is the *relationship* or *linkage* between my proof and my conclusions. How in the world does a car accident or an upset stomach have anything to do with doomsday? A dream about the end of the world is at least related to the claim that tomorrow is the end of time, but accidents and gastrointestinal problems seem at best to be totally unrelated to my request. Until I can demonstrate the relationship to you adequately, you would not, in all probability, sell off your belongings or go to church to pray. In other words, until some *reasoning* could be demonstrated, persuasion would not occur. You would have been an astute and aware persuadee in choosing not to follow unsupported or undemonstrated advice. In this case, the choice *not to follow* advice would be easy; at other times it is more complex and less clear. Let us look at the ways in which linkages or reasons for following advice work. First, we need to examine the problem of consistency between evidence and conclusions; then, we need to see the ways linkages can be formed; and, finally, we need to study the basic factors in rational linkages. In a sense, we need to look at the raw material of reasoned persuasion (consistency between evidence and conclusions), at the method of reasoned persuasion (the ways in which linkages are crafted), and at the end product—the linkage itself.

Consistency between Evidence and Conclusions Let us return for a moment to the argument concerning the end of the world—on the surface of the argument or advice to sell all your belongings and prepare to meet the end, there seems to be little consistency between the evidence offered (dream fantasy, bad driving luck, and stomach problems). Even so, there is a sort of "evidence hierarchy" at work. Clearly, the dream is the most powerful bit of evidence offered; the bad omen associated with the car accident is probably the next most powerful piece of evidence; and the upset stomach is probably the weakest evidence for the advice being given. Interestingly though, even with this clearly foolish and ridiculous argument, there is a shred of consistency between at least two of the pieces of evidence and the action requested. If one were mystical, he could see a reason to pray in the face of disaster on the basis of the dream fantasy about the end of the world. Even if he were not particularly mystical, he might be partially persuaded by this piece of evidence if we could demonstrate that I have a good track record on dreams—that I am psychic. The persuadee in this argument might be even more persuaded if it were also demonstrated that every time the psychic dream was followed by a bad omen and an upset stomach, the dream came true. In other words, as the consistency between evidence and conclusion increases, receivers begin to label the argument as more and more "logical," "reasonable," or "rational." It has currency and can be cashed—we "buy" what the persuader is saying.

Rational Linkages Having looked at what evidence and reasoning are, at the types of evidence one can use, and at the nature of rational or reasoned discourse, we find the next most logical question to be "What are the ways in which one can link evidence to conclusions?" Stated in another way: "How do persuaders try to get compliance with their advice vis-à-vis reasoned argument?" The ancient rhetoricians talked about the *topoi* of argument, or "topics" that could be argued or "seats of arguments." What they were looking at were the kinds of linkages a persuader might employ in a persuasive attempt.[8] Behavioral scientists have investigated the same kind of issue from different perspectives by looking at such things as primacy versus recency[9] or the presence of emotional arguments as opposed to rational arguments.[10] Though we shall investigate both of these perspectives in more detail later, it should be noted that the findings or theories of both groups of communication scholars deal with what we have been talking about—"What makes some pieces of persuasion work while others don't?" or "Where do persuaders find the stuff of persuasion?"

There are probably only three types of linkages: (1) *cause and effect* linkages, (2) *correlational* linkages, and (3) *congruency* linkages. As we examine each of these types, keep them in mind for later discussion since, on both the strategic level of reasoned persuasive communication and on the tactical level, these three categories can serve to link evidence to conclusions.

Cause and effect linkages rely on a *temporal* relationship between two phenomena. We could, using Burke's terms (see Chapter 3), call these two phenomena "the act" and "the agent" (actor) if we were willing to allow agents to be more than persons. The cause and effect linkage appeals to a temporal frame of reference (i.e., you see the cause as coming *before* and sometimes *with* the effect). For example, we could argue that Senator George McGovern lost in his bid to become the President of the United States because, in early 1972, he committed himself to such controversial issues as legalization of abortion and pot, amnesty for draft resisters and conscientious objectors, and full civil rights for homosexuals. In this argument, we are assuming that some action (here, statements referring to these issues) had unobserved results (change in attitude against McGovern), which ultimately led to the observed effect of loss of the election by nearly a 60–40 percent vote difference. Moreover, that happened in a year when the opposition candidate, President Nixon, was vulnerable on a number of important issues like the war in Southeast Asia, the lackluster economy, unemployment, and governmental disregard for minorities and individual rights.

---

[8] Aristotle, *The Rhetoric*, trans. by Lane Cooper (New York: Appleton-Century-Crofts, 1932), pp. xxiv, xliii, and 159–176.

[9] The most complete discussion of the primacy-recency issue available under a single cover is *The Order of Presentation in Persuasion*, ed. Carl I. Hovland (New Haven: Yale University Press, 1957). See also Ralph L. Rosnow, "Whatever Happened to the 'Law of Primacy'?" *Journal of Communication, 16* (March 1966), 10–31.

[10] See, for example, the discussion included in Gary Cronkhite's *Persuasion: Speech and Behavioral Change* (New York: Bobbs-Merrill Publishing Co., 1969), pp. 40–43; Edward Z. Rowell, "The Conviction-Persuasion Duality," *Quarterly Journal of Speech, 20* (November 1934), 469–482; Gary Cronkite, "The Relation of Scholastic Aptitude to Logical Argument and Emotional Appeal," Master's thesis, Illinois State University, 1961; and Gary Cronkhite, "Logic, Emotion, and the Paradigm of Persuasion," *Quarterly Journal of Speech, 50* (February 1964), 13–18.

Correlational linkages do not rely on time sequences or the "before-after" mode of connecting ideas; instead, they deal with *association*. For instance, suppose I were to try to persuade you to purchase a small economy car. I would probably tell you how much less pollution is emitted by the small car engine, and I might point out to you the economy of repairs and the decreased likelihood of getting into an accident because of increased maneuverability. In all of these arguments, I try to *correlate* two things: owning a small economy car and certain advantages (savings, safety, ecological values, etc.). In other words, I say that the two phenomena are associated with one another—that they occur together—that they are "symptoms" of one another. Although this example is fairly simple and straightforward, most correlational linkages are not nearly that simple and clean. They usually are more complex and difficult to analyze. For instance, a correlational linkage that relates to political persuasion might be something like "Since he is in favor of Gay Liberation and women's rights, he is clearly some kind of queer, or if not a queer then at least a revolutionary!" This kind of comment is not unusual. Of course, there is little evidence backing it up aside from the known facts about a person's support of certain issues; nonetheless, the logic or linkage underlying it is precisely like that underlying the small car arguments. Support of controversial and radical issues is usually associated with revolutionary thought, and persons who work for issues like Gay Liberation tend to be homosexuals themselves. "The one is symptomatic of the other" is what the underlying correlational linkage says.

Congruency or analogical linkages are not concerned with a time scheme (before–after) nor with an associational model (characteristic A is associated with or symptomatic of characteristic B); instead, they rely on a model that shows the extent and limit of *similarities and differences* between two phenomena. In a sense, this method of linking conclusions and evidence is like what we have traditionally thought of as the analogy. In the analogy, two different objects, phenomena, or ideas are compared with one another in an attempt to persuade the audience that what is characteristic of the one is also characteristic of the other (e.g., government is like a spider web—dangerous, delicate, and complex). Several theorists have argued that this form of proof is not very effective and that it is vulnerable,[11] while others argue that it is at the

---

[11] The belief in syllogistic reasoning as the appropriate format and the belief that analogy is a weak form of argument can be repeatedly seen in Elton Abernathy, *The Advocate: A Manual of Persuasion* (New York: David McKay Co., 1964), pp. 48, 49, 64, 86, 112; Glen E. Mills, *Reason in Controversy*, 2nd ed. (Boston: Allyn and Bacon, 1968), pp. 173–184, 194; Wayne C. Minnick, *The Art of Persuasion*, 2nd ed. (Boston: Houghton Mifflin Co., 1968), pp. 136–140; and Henry Lee Ewbank and J. Jeffery Auer, *Discussion and Debate: Tools of a Democracy* (New York: F. S. Crofts Co., 1946), p. 164.

root of human thought and human symbolic activity[12] and is therefore the strongest method of linking proof to conclusions. This method of linking evidence and advice is typified by this hypothetical argument:

> The problems with getting along at school this year are like the problems of getting along there last year—dorm costs are rising; the price of food is skyrocketing if you cook for yourself; books are incredible; and there seems to be an ever shrinking job market.

Notice that several pieces of evidence are offered for the conclusion or premise that last year resembles this year (e.g., price trends, etc). The assumption underlying the argument is that since a number of the limits or characteristics of one are also characteristic of the other, then the two instances are similar in other ways and can be understood in reference to one another. In a classic case of analogy, A is an analog for B and is therefore predictive of B. Some argue that this form of linkage is vulnerable, because there are other characteristics that may be different. For example, in the preceding example, it is possible that this year there are more scholarships or better summer job opportunities.

In any case, the congruency argument differs from both the correlational and the causal linkages in that it is not dependent upon association or time but rather operates on a *spatial* kind of level. That is, the argument depends on the degree to which one incident or case is *congruent* with another, or the degree to which a boundary of one matches up with a similar boundary of the other. In all likelihood, this is the way we learn—by matching situations and attempting to predict. Persuadees ought to ask themselves whether congruency linkages reflect all possible factors and whether the situations being compared have fully congruent parameters.

Content Premises: The Strategic Level

Having considered the theoretical nature of proof, evidence, and reasoning, we now face the task of seeing how these operate in practice. We will do that by looking at content premises on two levels:

---

[12] See the discussion on human understanding and the importance of analogical methods of learning in David Hume, "Enquiry Concerning Human Understanding," in *Eighteenth Century Philosophy*, ed. Lewis White Beck (New York: The Macmillan Co., 1966), p. 96. See also *The Philosophy of Rhetoric* by I. A. Richards (New York: Oxford University Press, 1965), especially the chapters on metaphor.

(1) the overall thematic level, or *strategic level*, and (2) the more particular and specific, concrete level, or *tactical level*. In so doing, we must continually take the notions offered here and compare them with the persuasion presented to us every day. We ought to look for the strategic moves made by persuaders in editorials in the campus newspaper, in advertisements on television, or by politicians trying to capture our support.

Again, we assume that the way a man uses symbols is indicative of his world view, his likely intentions, and his probable actions. This assumption applies not only to language use (see Chapters 2 and 3) and to how those language choices are organized and put together—but also to our interest here. One way to look at the strategic level of content premises is through the use of the syllogism as an organizational device; another is through the system for argument analysis proposed by Stephen Toulmin—both systems are discussed in the next section.

Types of Syllogisms

To begin with, there are three major syllogistic formats: (1) the *conditional* (if A, then B), (2) the *disjunctive* (either A or B), and (3) the *categorical* (since A is a member of category X and B is part of A, then B is also part of X). Each of these formats have a number of varieties or hybrids and can appear and operate in several forms. At the root of these hybrids, however, a basic form predominates and forms the skeletal and strategic structure of argument.

The Conditional   The *conditional* syllogism has as its basic form "If A is true, then B is also true." This is the *major premise* of the syllogism, and it makes a statement about a relationship assumed to exist in the world (e.g., if you add water to Kool-Aid, you will get a refreshing cool drink"). Now we might argue about the truth of these relational statements, but we assume that if proven "true" they will accurately describe a situation in the world. The next stage or step in the conditional strategy is to present data that relates to or makes a statement about some part of the major premise—or, tactically speaking, to present evidence. The following sentence is an example of a *minor premise:* "A is known to be true by all world experts." When put together with the relational major premise, a *conclusion* (in this case, that B is also true) can be drawn. In the example cited, one could pour water into Kool-Aid powder or state that he had done so. Given these pieces of "truth," the persuadee and the persuader together draw the conclusion that a cool, refreshing drink is at hand.

In both of these cases, by affirming or stating the truth of the "if" part of the major premise (sometimes called the "antecedent"), we can then also affirm the "then" part of the statement (sometimes called the "consequent"). One of the combination rules for the conditional syllogism is the "affirm antecedent–affirm consequent" form. Another form is the "deny consequent–deny antecedent" variation (e.g., there is no refreshing drink around, so obviously no one poured water into Kool-Aid powder). These are the only two "valid" combinations that can be made with the conditional form.

Remember, however, that many persuaders successfully use *invalid* combinations to achieve their goals. For example, one invalid form is affirming the consequent and thereby affirming the antecedent (i.e., because B is true, then A must also be true—there is a refreshing drink available; therefore, someone must have added water to Kool-Aid powder). This form is invalid because a third and unseen factor may have caused the observed effect (e.g., someone could have poured water into lemon concentrate). Yet advertisers often use this form as a strategy and argue that because one feels better the morning after eating cold tablets, then those tablets cured him. It is possible that the sleep, the hot toddy, or the penicillin injection had something to do with the cure. Likewise, with the other possible variation on the conditional syllogism—deny the antecedent and deny the consequent. The flaw here is like the flaw in the other invalid line of proof—there may very well be an interceding and outside third factor or combination of factors that may cause the consequent, since we have no rational reason to consider the antecedent as the one and only cause of the consequent. Nonetheless, this "invalid" form is often used by persuaders (e.g., if McGovern had renounced his economic policy and tax program, then he would have won the election—he didn't renounce it and because of that he lost the election; but his stands on a number of issues as well as his problems with his running mate Senator Eagleton, and so on, may have been the actual causes for the loss of the election). The persuadee who finds this strategy employed ought to search for other explanations and, in fact, will find that he is better able to engage in counterargument if he does look at syllogistic strategies in this way—searching for validity and truth and answering in accord with what he finds. The conditional syllogism is, as you have probably noticed, similar to the cause-effect linkage described earlier.

The Disjunctive   The *disjunctive* syllogism has as its basic form "Either A is true or B is true." This sentence is the major premise of a disjunctive syllogism and is usually accompanied by some set of proof or evidence that suggests the probable presence of A or B, or the probable absence of A or B. The conclusion is then drawn on the basis of these probabilities. For example, during the late 1960s and early 1970s, many patriotic citizens began to display flags and signs. Among them was a bumper sticker with "America" printed on it, followed by a statement that people ought to "Love It or Leave It." If you had stopped to talk to one of the persons displaying this sticker, you probably would have found that he would have provided you with some sort of "minor premise," such as "Why this is the greatest country in the history of the world. Where else can you have so much opportunity?" or "It's just like at home; you either take the food and shelter and other advantages that your parents are willing to give, or you take a powder and forget about freeloading anymore." In both cases he is trying to show, in the minor premise, something about the supposed truth or falsehood of the antecedent or consequent. The flaw in this type of reasoning is usually easy to sense but harder to identify specifically. Usually, though, the flaw lies in the fact that one rarely finds a situation in which a neat and perfect dichotomy like "either A or B" exists. More likely, we find situations in which there are many variables and possibilities. The answering sticker sometimes read: "America—Love It or Leave It or Change It or Ignore It," or some other variation of answering the "either–or" dichotomy with an appropriate search for third, fourth, or more possibilities. The task of the persuadee, when faced with a strategy based on the disjunctive syllogism, is to do what the bumper sticker did—point out to others and oneself that there are probably more than two possibilities. At times, the disjunctive syllogism is similar to the congruency linkage and at times resembles the correlational linkage.

The Categorical   The *categorical* syllogism is a "spatial" kind of reasoning. The persuader considers the world as divided into separate spaces or sets and subsets, to use modern math terms. That is, every phenomenon is either a part of a larger kind or class of phenomena or the genus of some smaller set of species of phenomena. Thus, the major and minor premises in this form can be expressed in the sentence "All of A is included in category B." For example, a recent letter to the editor of *Playboy* magazine addressed itself to the debate about the legalization of abortion on demand. The writer stated: "I keep hearing about right-to-life groups. I presume these are the people working to abolish the death penalty."[13] The letter was a facetious jibe at the groups working to prevent legalization of abortion—groups like SOUL (Save Our Unwanted Lives), the Catholic church, and others. These groups, at least in the letter writer's mind, were also likely to favor the conservative position of retaining capital punishment while promoting the equally conservative position of outlawing abortion. To the letter writer, there was an inconsistency in the two positions, best expressed in categorical terms: (1) Persons who want to protect capital punishment are

---

[13] *Playboy*, June 1972, p. 68.

not in the category of people who want to preserve human life; (2) persons who want to outlaw abortion are in the category of persons who want to preserve life; (3) therefore, persons who disavow abortion must also disavow capital punishment.

This kind of argument smacks of "guilt by association" or "you must be bad because you keep bad company." This kind of reasoning is often used in public persuasion dealing with political issues (e.g., "since you look like a hippie, you must be a Commie because hippies tend to be Commies") as well as persuasion dealing with more mundane issues (e.g., "join the Pepsi generation—and you will be going strong since members of the Pepsi generation all go strong"). Lewis Carroll used it even more cleverly in his descriptions of Alice in Wonderland—the pigeon tells Alice that she must be some kind of snake since she eats eggs and that is just what snakes do too.[14] All of these examples have the same characteristic flaw—because one possesses *some* characteristics of a group does not mean that he possesses *all* characteristics of that group.

Persuaders use and persuadees respond to the *invalid* "guilt by association" form of this strategy. The responsible persuadee must ask himself, when he finds the categorical syllogism operating as a skeletal structure in an argument, whether the categories are accurately represented. He must seek to discover whether the membership in one category necessarily implies full membership in another. (Because one is a member of the category of persons with long hair and beard, does this necessarily imply membership in the category of "left-wing Communist sympathizer?") In this way, the categorical syllogism is like the congruency linkage described earlier.

Truth and Validity

As we can see from our brief investigation into syllogistic reasoning, there are some knotty problems here. First, true (empirically verifiable) statements can be linked logically or validly, but the same true statements can mislead the persuadee when they are joined in illogical or invalid ways. At the same time, untrue (empirically unverifiable) statements can be linked in logical and valid ways or in illogical and invalid ways. Furthermore, we seldom encounter clearcut syllogisms in our everyday lives. Few persuaders, be they politicians, advertisers, peers, subordinates, or superiors, run around saying "If A then B" or "Either A is true or B is true but not both and at least one" or "All A's are B's and all C's are A's; therefore all C's are also B's." Instead, we

---

[14] Lewis Carroll, *Alice in Wonderland* (New York: Lancer Books, 1968), p. 58.

find that persuaders arrange more extended pieces of persuasion, such as entire speeches or campaigns or complete advertisements, into syllogistic patterns. A classic example is the standard toothpaste, mouthwash, or deodorant advertisement saying that a person has bad luck on a date because he has forgotten to get his teeth shiny or his breath sweet or his underarms dry. Ten minutes after he has used the advertised product, he is pictured in a church wedding scene. The syllogism is an "if–then" conditional one. (If you use Toothbrite toothpaste, you will have a lover's mouth and get the girl. He brushed with Toothbrite. Conclusion?) Perhaps the best each persuadee can do is to outline, formally or informally, the general point of the persuasion he is exposed to and then to search for the relationships the persuader is attempting to "sell." Having discovered these, the persuadee can look for the traces of syllogistic reasoning in the arguments and relationships.

Content Premises: The Tactical Level

As already noted, we seldom hear syllogisms formally stated and used by persuaders. Instead, they underlie larger pieces of persuasion. What do we typically hear in real-life situations? Typically, we hear statements of one of these categories or types:

1. Those that advise action or state conclusions
2. Those that present bits of evidence to support conclusions or courses of action
3. Those that explain why the evidence is related to courses of action or conclusions (The "linkages" described earlier are good examples.)

These three kinds of statements make up what we hear on the *tactical level* of persuasion—they are the *stuff* of which persuasion is made. A British philosopher and logician, Stephen Toulmin, has identified and labeled these three elements as the *data*, the *warrant*, and the *claim*. The assumption is that persuaders present data or evidence, which is linked by warrants or reasons, to claims or conclusions. The sample argument, as diagramed in Figure 5–1, uses the Toulmin system.[15]

---

[15] Stephen Toulmin, *The Uses of Argument* (Cambridge: Cambridge University Press, 1969). See Ch. 3, "The Layout of Arguments," pp. 94–145.

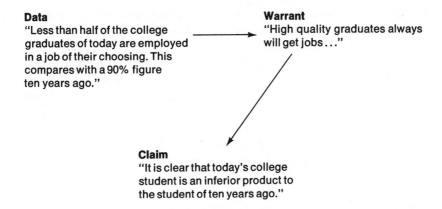

Data
"Less than half of the college graduates of today are employed in a job of their choosing. This compares with a 90% figure ten years ago."

Warrant
"High quality graduates always will get jobs..."

Claim
"It is clear that today's college student is an inferior product to the student of ten years ago."

Figure 5–1

Your first response may be something like "Hey, that's not the whole story; there are other reasons for a bad job market—inflation, slowed government spending, and so on." On the tactical level, you don't have to search for underlying strategies. You are readily confronted with the real, immediate, and concrete elements of persuasion. You respond almost instinctively to them and have a sense for what ought to be said in response to the persuasive message. That is the point. We tend to respond to the smaller elements in persuasion rather quickly and automatically, but that is where the problem arises. Unless we, as persuadees, have first examined the strategy underlying the tactics, and unless we respond to the tactics we hear in more sophisticated ways, we are likely to come off as naive, argumentative, and sometimes stupid. You are probably all too familiar, for example, with those time-worn phrases parents use: "When you get a little real experience, then you'll see what I mean," or "Oh, all that baloney they teach you kids at college, it just isn't able to hold water," or "Well, that's just what you think."

Toulmin's system does afford us some opportunity to approach this tactical level of persuasion more specifically and systematically. So, let's look more closely at how the typical interpersonal attempt at persuasion flows or operates and then apply Toulmin's system to it.

Claim

Suppose that you want to persuade an authority figure that he is overlooking important information that could affect his decisions, which in turn affect you. Let's say that you want to persuade your persuasion teacher that he ought not give you an open-book midterm examination. You begin by raising your hand and saying something like "Why do we have to take an open-book test? Why not just have a take-home test? It's the same thing." What you have done, in Toulmin's terms, is make a *claim*—that take-home tests and open-book tests are essentially the same. You hope he will draw the conclusion that there is no need for a test in persuasion class, that another paper will serve the purpose. Let's assume that your teacher listens and seriously considers your claim. He then has three options. He may, if you have been persuasive enough, agree to accept your claim as it stands and permit you to write up a take-home exam instead of an open-book one. Another option for him is to reject your claim out of hand; he might say, "Well, I run the class and I have scheduled the exam into the syllabus and have it made up already. We'll take the open-book test." His third option is to ask you to demonstrate further the reasonableness of your claim. He might say something like "Well, you may have something there and then again you may not. How do you know that these two kinds of tests are essentially the same kind of activity? What proof have you?"

Data

In Toulmin's terms, you are faced with a request for the *data* supporting your *claim*. Of the teacher's three responses, the first two typify immediate and spontaneous responses to persuasive tactics. The third response is closer to the critical and aware persuadee's response, at least on the content level of persuasion. Instead of making a snap *yes* or *no* judgment, the persuadee explores the issue further (in this case, the teacher decides to look into the comparison between two different types of examination) and suspends judgment. Unfortunately, most persuadees respond most of the time in the first two ways and not nearly often enough in the critical and reserved manner suggested by option three.

Warrant

Let's continue this interpersonal exchange. Suppose you happen to be taking a course in tests and measurements the same term that you study persuasion, and you have access to information about open-book and take-home methods. Your sources say that identical sets of subjects repeatedly scored essentially the same on take-home and open-book exams in an experiment conducted at several colleges. You tell this to your open-minded persuasion instructor, and he considers your evidence. Again, he has three options. He can accept your evidence as supporting your claim and agree to let your class have a take-home exam, or he may reject your data out of hand, saying something like

"Well, if they are the same, then I may as well give the open-book exam as I had originally planned," or he might again follow the third option (remember he is a very open-minded instructor) and ask for more proof. In this case, however, he asks you to tell him *why* that evidence leads to the conclusion that you should have a take-home exam instead of the regularly scheduled test. In Toulmin's terms, he is asking for a *warrant* to link the *data* you have presented in support of your *claim.* The flow then goes from claim to data to the warrant, where the real philosophical elements in the issue are likely to arise.

Let's see what you will do next. Suppose you say in response to the instructor's request for a warrant:

> I assume that the most valuable asset we have as students and teachers is learning time together. Now the scheduled exam will take one entire class session and part of another in the critiquing process. We only have thirty class sessions together, and some of them are already eliminated by vacation days, convocations, and other matters. We can't afford not to have a take-home exam, since it is equivalent to the open-book test now scheduled.

That is pretty sound reasoning, and it seems to fit with your data and claim. The instructor may consider this sufficient evidence and agree to cancel his exam. He may want you to modify your request and agree to an open-book final exam if the midterm is a take-home, or he may be stubborn and refuse to reschedule or change his plans. In any case, he has the same three options—agree, disagree, or ask for more (in this case, for concessions in your request). If the issue is not as simple as this one, the persuadee may argue about the philosophical position inherent in the warrant. The interaction could then continue, but on issues central to the question and not on whether the experiments comparing take-home exams with open-book exams were carefully conducted. You would be discussing implication, not facts; and after all, facts are usually not very debatable.

Substantiating Elements

Toulmin's system has a number of secondary terms. For example, in the preceding case, the concession in the claim is called the *qualifier.* (Usually it is a simple qualifier—something like saying *"In most cases,"* or *"Probably* we don't have to take an open-book test," or *"It is likely* that open-book and take-home exams are parallel.") The point is that the term or concession "qualifies" or limits the claim; it allows for the possibility that this is not an "Either A or B" type of argument. The claim is *probably* acceptable and true, but there is the *possibility* that another factor may enter in and affect the final outcome. To continue our example, the qualifier to the claim would probably be something like "Open-book exams and take-home exams are *essentially the same kind of test, at least on the basis* of evidence now available."

Another minor term in Toulmin's system is the *reservation*, a statement attached to or related to the warrant. For instance, suppose, in the argument over examinations, it became clear that the instructor did not consider examination time to be an inferior learning activity but rather one that was just different from regular classroom activity. The warrant would then probably evolve into something like *"Unless there is reason to believe* that exams are a learning experience and not an evaluation experience, then class learning time between teacher and student is the most important asset which we have." Notice that the reservation states the conditions under which the assumptions and philosophical bases of the argument operate. This aspect of the reservation is often overlooked by persuaders and persuadees alike—they assume that both parties begin from the same point, from the same "frame of reference"—to use the terms of our definition of persuasion (see Chapter 1). Only when we begin at the same point or when we make allowances (such as reservations) for these differences, can we really progress in any persuasive transaction. Coupled with the qualifier, the reservation allows for great flexibility in persuasion because both terms allow dialogue to occur; both provide the persuadee with the opportunity to object or agree to part but not all of the persuasion. As persuaders, we need to include these elements of flexibility in our persuasion. As persuadees, we need to request them of the persuaders who are attempting to get us to take action.

Consider the various claims made in the halls of our legislatures, neglecting to include *qualifiers* or *reservations* and thus becoming albatrosses around our necks. For example, the Gulf of Tonkin resolution lacked these two elements, thereby allowing the President to wage war without congressional sanction. The resolution authorized the President to take *all* necessary steps, including the use of armed force, to help any SEATO nation defend its freedom. The absence of *some* kind of limit on the power of the chief executive led to a decade of congressional debate, numerous counterstatements and resolutions, culminating in the overwhelming repulsion that accompanied Lyndon B. Johnson as he left office in 1969.

The same kind of example could be cited from other periods of history and other issues. For instance, from 1836 to 1844 the U. S. House of Representatives operated under various forms of a "Gag Rule," which stated in essence: All petitions, memorials, resolutions, propositions, or papers relating in any way, or to any extent whatsoever, to the subject of slavery or the abolition of slavery, shall, without either being printed or referred, be laid on the table, and that no further action whatever shall be had thereon. It was an *unreserved* and *unqualified* rule, which led to numerous problems as territories sought to incorporate slavery or not to incorporate it. The definition of "executive privilege," or the right of a President to disallow the testimony of aides, former aides, documents, or tapes nearly caused a crisis during the Watergate hearings. The point is that most issues are not clearcut *yes* or *no* situations. Instead, there are complex and interacting factors that need to be taken into account—and can be by means of the qualifier and the reservation. At the same time, unfortunately, they may also provide the possibility for "loopholes" (e.g., the phrase "with all deliberate speed," which the Supreme Court inserted into its 1954 *Brown* v. *Board of Education* decision to desegregate schools). The persuadee needs not only to request reservations and qualifiers but also to demand that they be clearly and operationally defined.

The final element in Toulmin's system for showing the tactics of argument is called the *support*, or sometimes the *backing*, for the warrant. Toulmin observed that many issues hang on this element—that it justifies acceptance of the warrant. Suppose the persuadee does not consider the warrant to be true or that he doubts some part of it. The persuader must then provide some kind of proof that would *support* or *back up* the reasoning expressed in his warrant. In a sense, there is a whole separate argument with a separate claim, data, and warrant going on when support is offered for a warrant. Essentially the persuader is claiming that his warrant is acceptable because of the support or backing he offers. The backing is really data for this second claim. This same process of claim-data-warrant within claim-data-warrant can go further and often does—and creates the complexity surrounding most controversial and philosophical issues. (Figure 5–2 depicts a persuasive argument in these terms: (1) *claim* made by the persuader, (2) *data* provided by the source, and (3) emergence of the *warrant*.)

We can now see that the tactics of persuasion are not usually encapsulated into simple syllogisms. Instead of making statements like "If A then B; A is true; therefore B is also true" or "Either A is true or B is true; B is false; therefore A must be true," most persuaders make claims that persuadees may (1) buy outright with no questions asked, (2) reject outright, or (3) ask for proof. Persuaders then can provide data, which again can be accepted, rejected, or questioned. If the persuadee continues to request more of the persuader, he (the persuader) ultimately provides his warrant or reason for linking his proof to his request. Given enough time, three other elements may enter into the persuasive appeal:

1. The qualifier (which limits the force or universality of the claim or request)

Step 1
Claim Made by Persuader
"We don't need an in-class
exam since take-home exams
are the same."

(Option 1 — O.K.)

(Option 2 — Nope)

Option 3 — Request for proof or evidence

Step 2
Data Provided by Source
"Experiments at Slippery
Rock and elsewhere show
parallel nature of the
two types of tests."

(Option 1 — "O.K., I
believe")

(Option 2 — "It doesn't
make any difference")

Option 3 — Persuadee wants to know what is the relationship
between evidence or data and claim

Step 3
Warrant Emerges (Assumptions and philosophical position)
"Learning time together
is the most valuable asset
teacher and student have.
Tests take away from this
time; therefore take-home
tests are preferred if
they are equivalent."

(Option 1 — "O.K., we won't
have an in-class
test")

(Option 2 — "It still doesn't
make any difference
to me. We will have
the test.")

Option 3 — There are several possibilities (Step 4):

1. persuadee may ask for qualifier (*probably*).
2. persuadee may ask for reservation (*unless*).
3. persuadee may ask for backing (*as shown by . . .*).

Figure 5–2

2. The reservation (which states the conditions under which the warrant operates)
3. The backing (which supports or provides evidence to substantiate the validity of the warrant)

Some of you will be asking now how the persuadee gets his input noticed and considered. After all, there are thirty or more people in most classes, and not everyone will get a chance to participate; and the problem is compounded as time goes on and as the audience gets larger, as in political campaigns. Although that is true, you must also remember that in another sense the persuadee *always* gets his input; he always is "heard" in a way. The persuader who knows anything about his audience will anticipate the kind of questions the persuadee *might* ask if he had the opportunity. Furthermore, if not satisfied with the completeness of the argument offered by the persuader, the persuadee may decide not to follow the course of action suggested by the persuader and thus signal that he wants more proof, reasoning, qualification, backing, or reservation. Finally, the function of the persuadee is to dissect the persuasion he hears so that he will know *when* and *if* he wants to be persuaded; it doesn't matter whether the persuader is exposed to all of this analysis (though he ought to catch on if fewer and fewer persons buy his product or vote for him or give him rewards). What does matter is that the persuadee is aware, critical, and fairly sophisticated and systematic as he is exposed to persuasion. Toulmin's system for analyzing the tactics of persuasion provides us with a simple but discriminating tool, which operates well with the kind of persuasion to which we are exposed every day.

For the persuader, there are a few simple pieces of advice, if he intends to structure his persuasion with Toulmin's system in mind. First, he must anticipate his audience's probable response. Second, he needs to provide data if a claim is likely to be questioned. Many persuaders merely restate a claim if it is not accepted—a more appropriate course of action would be to provide the persuadee with good reasons (data) for following the advice of the claim. If he wishes to bolster his persuasion, he needs to demonstrate his reasoning, or the warrant of his case. Finally, the probability of getting audience acceptance for his case will increase to the degree that it is less dogmatic and is well documented; therefore, it is wise to qualify claims, taking any reservations in the warrant into account, and to provide substantial backing for the data.

Now that we have looked at how persuasion operates on this rule-governed or procedural or *content* level in strategic and tactical ways, let us consider what we do know about logical thought processes and the human responses to various kinds and amounts of evidence or proof.

Experimental Evidence on Evidence

Since its inception, the field of speech communication has been interested in the nature of evidence—what it is, what types may occur, how much of it is necessary, who is most likely to be persuaded by certain types of evidence, and other similar issues. Aristotle, in his study of persuasion, observed persuasion and categorized the types of reasoning and evidence into what he called *topoi,* or topics or places where arguments of a rational nature could be found. The philosophers of the New Science during the Renaissance tried to establish scientific methods of proving things to be true or false.

Basically, *evidence can be thought of as an example in some form, which is in support of or which gives credence to an argument or conclusion.* If the evidence is statistical, then the support is the result of compiling numerous examples; if it is expert testimony, then the testimony is an example of the point being made; if the evidence is analogical (literal or figurative), it is also a kind of example. It is a "narrative," expressed numerically or dramatically, that supports a premise or leads to a conclusion.

Behavioral scientists have recently tried various "scientific" means to test the impact of such things as evidence types, organization, and concreteness. A number of presumably typical persuadees (e.g., several hundred freshmen in college speech or psychology classes or a number of high school students or possibly a group of debaters) are given varying degrees or levels of certain types of persuasion and evidence (e.g., opinionated versus nonopinionated statements, emotional versus logical evidence, "good" evidence versus "bad" evidence, "good" delivery of evidence versus "poor" delivery of the same evidence, or some other similar variation on the general theme of evidence). Following this treatment, the subjects' attitudes are measured, using an attitude measure. Then the results are compared with pretreatment scores on identical or similar measures, and the difference between scores is compared, by statistical methods, to determine the effects of the varying degrees or types of evidence characteristics.

Unfortunately, the overall results of the numerous studies have not shed much light on the questions that were bothering the ancients (e.g., What kinds of evidence persuade best? What amount of evidence is enough? When should you use what kind of evidence?). Rather, the results are often contradictory or inconclusive. Richard Gregg observed that the overall results of these studies were disheartening when he noted that ". . . the audience reaction to an argument may have little or nothing to do with whether the argument includes fully documented evidence, relevant or irrelevant evidence, weak or strong evidence or any evidence at all."[16] Yet we do know that people ask for evidence when in doubt. In spite of the pessimism suggested by Gregg, we do know *some* things about evidence, as a result of 15 to 20 years of behavioral study:

1. Evidence increases persuasive effects if the persuader is unknown or has low to moderate credibility.[17]

2. There seems to be little difference in the persuasive effects generated from emotional as opposed to logical evidence.[18]

3. Usually some evidence is better than no evidence.[19]

4. "Reluctant" evidence (that given by someone against himself or his own interests) is no more effective than biased or unbiased objective evidence.[20]

5. Good delivery can enhance the potency of evidence (but perhaps only when the source is unknown or has low credibility, so that the delivery makes him and his evidence more believable and therefore more persuasive).[21]

6. Evidence can make persuasive changes more permanent.[22]

7. Evidence is most effective when the persuadee has not heard it before.[23]

8. The method of transmitting the evidence (live, on tape, etc.) seems to have no effect on evidence potency.[24]

9. People are likely to believe evidence that agrees with their own position more than evidence that does not.[25]

---

[16] Richard E. Gregg, "Some Hypotheses for the Study of Psychology of Evidence," as quoted in James C. McCroskey, "A Summary of Experimental Research on the Effects of Evidence in Persuasive Communication," *Quarterly Journal of Speech*, 55 (April 1969), 167.

[17] See the discussion on evidence by James C. McCroskey, cited in fn. 16; and Gerald R. Miller and John Baseheart, "Source Trustworthiness, Opinionated Statements, and Response to Persuasive Communication," *Speech Monographs*, 36 (March 1969), 1–7.

[18] See McCroskey, cited in fn. 16; Cronkhite, *Persuasion: Speech and Behavioral Change*, cited above (fn. 10); and Cronkhite, "The Relation of Scholastic Aptitude to Logical Argument and Emotional Appeal," cited above (fn. 10).

[19] See the McCroskey summary cited above (fn. 16); and Robert S. Cathcart, "An Experimental Study of the Relative Effectiveness of Selected Means of Handling Evidence in Speeches of Advocacy," Doctoral dissertation, Northwestern University, 1953.

[20] William E. Arnold and James C. McCroskey, "The Credibility of Reluctant Testimony," *Central States Speech Journal*, 18 (May 1967), 97–103.

[21] James C. McCroskey and R. Samuel Mehrley, "The Effects of Disorganization and Nonfluency on Attitude Change and Source Credibility," *Speech Monographs*, 36 (March 1969), 13–21.

[22] See the McCroskey summary cited above (fn. 16).

[23] See the McCroskey summary cited above; and Karl Anatol and Jerry Mandel, "Strategies of Resistance to Persuasion: New Subject Matter for the Teacher of Speech Communication," *Central States Speech Journal*, 23 (Spring 1972), 11–17.

[24] James C. McCroskey, *Studies of the Effects of Evidence in Persuasive Communication*, Report SCRL, 4–67, Speech Communication Research Laboratory, Michigan State University, 1967.

[25] Victor D. Wall, Jr., "Evidential Attitude and Attitude Change," *Western Speech*, 36 (Spring 1972), 115–123.

10. Highly dogmatic persons differ from persons who are not so dogmatic, in that the dogmatic are more affected by evidence.[26]

For the most part, these findings are not surprising or unpredictable. Many of them seem to be common-sense conclusions, and that fact has prompted many researchers to attempt to investigate the effects of evidence from a different perspective—that is, by observing persuasion as it operates in the "real world." After observing a number of both successful and unsuccessful persuasive efforts, the researcher tries to draw some conclusions based on the general patterns he has observed. By now, you will have concluded that this is the admonition repeated in almost every chapter of this book—observe, search for a pattern, try to draw some conclusions about the persuader and the persuasion on the basis of these patterns, and then and only then respond to the persuasion confronting you.

Several patterns seem to emerge from the discussion in this chapter and from the assumptions underlying Chapters 2 and 3. First, evidence is probably most effective when it encourages audience participation. Earlier we noted that, in using emotionally oriented evidence, the persuader is most effective if he can present his audience with a dramatic scene or setting and can then ask the audience to empathize with the character acting within that setting. By participating vis-à-vis their imaginations, members of the audience co-create the proof, and in this way incorporate the proof into their own frames of reference—the persuasion thus achieved is more permanent and potent. In using intellectually oriented evidence, the effective persuader presents claims and perhaps data to support them. He hopes that warrants will be provided by the audience he is persuading; but even if they do not supply the linkage that is needed and instead question the persuader's conclusions, they are still participating in their own persuasion when they begin to play the game (i.e., co-create a proof with the persuader).

Consider the following piece of persuasion from an admittedly white racist publication:

> Leftist forces have long waged a relentless battle to have the death penalty abolished. Jack Greenberg . . . is representing negro Lucius Jackson Jr. . . . He was sentenced for raping a White doctor's wife . . . What the Jew lawyers . . . have failed to tell the court . . . is the fact that blacks commit over 80 percent of all forcible rapes in this country. Remember that negroes are only 13 percent of the population, therefore their crime rate is far out of proportion to their numerical percentage in this country . . . the negro constitutes by far the most dangerous criminal element in America. Over half of all black males are expected to be involved in some crime during their lifetime.

---

[26] Gary Cronkhite and Emily Goetz, "Dogmatism, Persuasibility, and Attitude," *Journal of Communication*, 21 (December 1971), 342–352.

> There is no way to rehabilitate this entire race of people . . . We want to save White people from further murder, rape and plunder . . . Let's bring back peace, prosperity, safety, low taxes and all the improvements resulting from the elimination of slum ghettos and violent crime will be reduced by an astounding 85%.[27]

The publication then repeatedly appealed for help in promoting a "Back to Africa" movement to deport all blacks as soon as possible. For a moment, try to overlook your immediate *emotional* response to the quotation and instead look at it as a piece of persuasion, which attempts to use both kinds of evidence discussed in this chapter. There is a clearcut attempt to appeal to the emotions and biases inherent in the audience; at the same time, there is an attempt to appeal to the audience in intellectual ways (e.g., the citing of statistics and giving examples). In all likelihood, most nonsubscribers reading this newspaper article would not be persuaded by it—they would probably observe that it was more garbage from another right-wing organization. Yet it demonstrates some of the things which we have been talking about. The article creates a dramatic scene with great potential for action. It includes data in support of claims and even draws the conclusion in some cases (e.g., ". . . therefore their crime rate is far out of proportion to their numerical percentage in this country"). Why does it fail as persuasion? Examine it more closely. The situation drawn by the persuasion is dramatic, but it does not allow participation or empathy (except perhaps on behalf of the Negro defendant in the death penalty case). The audience is not invited into the drama—it isn't asked to use its imagination. The same thing occurs with the intellectually oriented parts of the message. This passage is a good instance of not allowing the auditor to participate in his own persuasion. The conclusion that black crime rates are higher than black population ratios is one that is easily drawn from the 80–13 percent figures, but the author *insists* on drawing the conclusion for you. The probable response to this kind of paternalistic persuasion is to question the conclusion that *is* drawn. The unparticipating persuadee wants to get in on the action; and since there are no openings here for him, he finds one on the opposite side of the case. He starts to convince himself that the persuasion he is hearing or reading is not accurate or true. He starts asking questions about the data given (e.g., Isn't crime caused by environmental factors like poor home life?). He starts looking for faulty relationships or linkages. He wonders how lower taxes fit in with deporting people—it seems like an expensive plan at best. And sooner or later he rejects the whole argument. This isn't meant to say that the citation could be doctored up

---

[27] From an article entitled "Black Rape of White Women Grows," *The Thunderbolt*, February 1972, p. 2. The publication is published irregularly by the National States Rights Party, Marietta, Georgia.

to be persuasive in any meaningful sense; probably it is so extreme that it rules that possibility out. However, if the persuader had not tried so hard to lead the persuadee through the message, drawing conclusions for him and so forth, his chances for success would have been better. We are never invited to join the drama the persuader is presenting—he makes the picture too complete.

A second characteristic that seems to help, in using evidence for "logical" or content-oriented persuasion, is to highlight the evidence in one of two ways—either as part of a narrative or by use of some form of analogy. People are fascinated by stories; our entire history reflects this tendency. The preponderance of television shows presented in any single evening or afternoon, or on any single network or channel, is dramatic in tone and substance—even the news programs attempt to cast their facts into dramatic structures. Seemingly, evidence is more effective and memorable if it is presented in the framework of the narrative or dramatic.[28] Closely related to this narrative mode of presenting evidence is the analogy. The narrative provides a kind of perspective (i.e., we see the evidence *in terms* of the story) and a participatory *machina* for evidence (i.e., we can imagine ourselves in the narrative). The analogy has elements of both of these two characteristics. When we hear about the death rate on highways compared with that caused by lung cancer, heart attack, and stroke combined, we are *hearing* an analogical presentation of evidence, but we are also *seeing* highway deaths *in terms* of something else. We can also *participate* by imagining or picturing the details of the evidence presented. Both methods of presenting evidence rely on our ability to learn vicariously (see footnote 3) and on the audience's own artistic abilities (i.e., their ability to dramatize and imagine what the proof was like or how they themselves are similar to the characters in the mini-drama being presented in the narrative).[29]

Finally, it seems clear that evidence presented in a structured form is more effective than evidence that is not. Structure does not necessarily mean the kind of thing you learned when you were told that the good outline always has a roman numeral II for each numeral I and a "B" for each "A." Instead, evidence needs to be presented in some form that makes it possible for the audience to see relationships and to remember it. The narrative is one such method, and so is the analogy. Here are others:

Comparison and contrast is another form of the analogical method of presenting evidence. We say, for example, that the Nixon administration had as much deficit spending and increased the national debt

---

[28] See Bormann, cited above (fn. 6).
[29] See Hume, cited in fn. 12.

as much as the combined total of all previous administrations. By doing this, we are contrasting and comparing. We are also providing a frame of reference or perspective for the facts.

The *example* is similar to the narrative, in that it is meant to provide a dramatic sample occurrence of whatever we are talking about. Hopefully, the persuadee will vicariously imagine and interact with the example. For instance, we might try to prove the value of cable-television franchises by saying that one benefit is that people do their grocery shopping by tuning in the market and ordering their purchases electronically. The audience sees itself as acting through or in the example.

Sign argument observes certain symptoms, which usually indicate other things. For example, you might tell your parents that they are too conservative as shown by their unwillingness to get a faster car or by their doubts about college morals. You argue from symptoms here—the symptoms you cite are signs of conservativism. In a sense, this argument is a kind of analogical presentation, since it provides perspective or a frame of reference for the audience—it correlates two perspectives.

Statistics are usually just large examples or generalizations generated from many examples. It is important to make them meaningful and clear for the audience. For instance, it would be better to observe that there are twice as many chances of being born seriously sick if one is the child of a poverty-stricken family than to point out that there are 1,567,900 children born with serious defects to poverty-stricken families and only 780,700 to average-income families. Again the principle of the analogy and the narrative are operative. If we see evidence *in perspective*—in terms of something else—we are more likely to accept it and be persuaded by it.

A Review and Conclusion

Content premises do not necessarily rely as much on the internal states of each individual persuader as do process premises. Instead, they rely more on universally agreed upon *norms or rules*, in contrast to individualized *processing* of bits of information.

In a sense, evidence is either dramatistically oriented or it is intellectually oriented. Users of dramatistically oriented evidence may lead persuadees to a "logical" conclusion, to be drawn from a content premise, by creating a dramatic scene for the audience and then by inviting the audience to join into the drama and "prove" the validity of the premise to themselves. Users of intellectually oriented evidence, on the other hand, may lead their persuadees to "logical conclusions" by presenting them with a set of *data* in support of a certain *claim* or content premise.

The persuadees provide the connective between this data and claim in the form of a *warrant*.

Both types of evidence rely upon a kind of *self-persuasion* on the part of the persuadee. The persuadee ought to participate in some way in his own persuasion, whether the evidence is intellectual or dramatistic—that is the basic principle. Some of the most fascinating research done in persuasion has focused on self-persuasion. Much of this research is based on Festinger's theory of dissonance, and studies usually ask persuadees to state arguments that are contrary to their own beliefs or that are counterattitudinal (e.g., why a dull experiment was interesting, why strange foods taste good, or why they might accept some group or idea that is counter to their beliefs). Having engaged in this kind of participation, the respondees tend to change their beliefs in accord with the false or counterattitudinal message they advocated. Though this issue has been plagued with problems in research measurement and design, the findings have been fairly consistent—when we engage in self-persuasion, even if it runs counter to our own beliefs, the effect of the participation is powerful.

From a strategic point of view, the traditional syllogism usually forms the skeletal structure of an overall argument or content premise. Within this overall structure, the tactics or particular arguments or premises are represented by claims supported by data and hopefully linked by audiences through warrants.

Finally, of the types of evidence available to the persuader, several seem more important than others. First, probably, are those that support the three major linkages: *cause-effect, symptoms*, or *congruency*. Also, evidence that provides perspective for the audience is probably more effective than evidence that does not. We have focused on two particularly effective methods of providing this perspective—the use of the analogy, which provides a comparative perspective, and the use of the narrative, which has the same ability to provide a perspective within a dramatic frame of reference. Both are also "artistic," in the sense that neither merely presents information; both depict evidence in dramatic or pictorial formats.

Perhaps the capture and murder of the members of the Israeli Olympic team at the 1972 Olympic games demonstrates our conclusion about the potency of evidence better than lengthy explanations. Imagine yourself listening to a pro-Arab spokesman citing statistics about the numbers of displaced Palestinian refugees, the number of acres of land lost to Israel during the Six-Day War, the cost of housing and feeding refugees, and so forth—he cannot persuade you to even listen to him. Try to imagine your response to this hypothetical case. Now compare that with your response and attention to the single and dramatic event at the Olympic village in 1972. Your attention was probably fixed on the problem of Arab-Israeli relations as it never could have been by the long-winded spokesman. The use of "dramatic" and, in this case, sadly tragic evidence has a potency difficult to estimate—it suddenly forces us to re-think and to participate, emotionally and empathically, with the premises presented to us. We are persuaded by our own participation.

Questions for Further Thought

1. What are the three types of linkages? Give examples of each from news advertisements, political speeches, or some other source of persuasion.

2. Define proof. What constitutes adequate proof for you? Does it change from issue to issue? If so, in what ways?

3. Review some of the magazine commentary concerning a particular issue and attempt to identify the pieces of data which are offered. What kinds of evidence are they? Are they dramatic? If so, in what ways? If not, are they persuasive and why or why not? What is the underlying syllogistic structure inherent in the discussions of the issue?

4. Read a contemporary discussion of some ideological issue (e.g., Germaine Greer's *The Female Eunuch*, Robert Townsend's *Up the Organization*, or Charles Reich's *The Greening of America*). Try to identify the claims put forth. What kind of evidence is used to support them? Do the warrants for linking data and claim appear in the book? Are there qualifiers or reservations? Where is the argument most persuasive and why?

5. Identify several forms of proof in the source used for question 4.

6. Identify various forms of proof (e.g., intellectually oriented or emotionally oriented; analogical, dramatic, etc.) in an issue being debated on the editorial pages of your daily newspaper.

7. What is the difference between intellectually oriented evidence and emotionally oriented evidence? Give examples and explain how they differ.

8. Give examples of the following: (a) comparison and contrast, (b) example, (c) sign argument, (d) statistics.

Experiences in Persuasion

1. Read the "Letters to the Editor" section of a popular magazine (e.g., *Playboy, Jet, Time*, etc.). A group of letters will usually refer to an article included in the magazine's earlier issues. Go back to this earlier article and see what prompted the letter to the editor. What kind of persuasion and evidence seems to have prompted the letter writer to go to the work of writing to the editor? Was he emotionally or intellectually stimulated? Was his response based on intellectually or emotionally oriented evidence? If you were to answer the letter, how would you go about doing it? Try to

compose an answer utilizing the same kind of persuasion or evidence used by the author of the letter, by the author of the article, and by the author of a competing letter if there is one.

2. Tape record a discussion on a television-talk program involving persons who are not entertainment personalities but who are associated with an issue. Trace the argument over the issue utilizing the Toulmin system of analysis. Retrace it using syllogistic analysis. What happened? How could it have changed? What kind of position and line of reasoning do you suppose would be used by the participants on other issues—such as using quotas for hiring minorities or busing school children to achieve racial balance or if the President knew about Watergate?

3. Involve yourself in a discussion with your parents, friends, or students in your dormitory over some emotional issue (e.g., giving birth control pills at the health clinic on campus, trial marriages, etc.). As you discuss the issue, try to identify the path of the discussion. Does it go from claim to data to warrant? If not try to make it do so by asking for clear articulation of claims; ask for evidence or data; question the philosophical basis on which these two are related; and see if the resulting discussion leads to the addition of qualifiers or reservations to the discussion.

4. Rewrite a piece of intellectually oriented persuasion so that it makes the same requests but is emotionally oriented. Now do the same thing with an emotionally oriented piece of persuasion. (*Note:* You will probably be able to find instances of both; but if this is difficult, read the speeches of a flamboyant persuader such as George Wallace or Huey P. Newton for emotionally oriented persuasion. Read an article from a magazine such as *Harper's, Saturday Review,* or *Intellectual Digest* for examples of intellectually oriented persuasion.) Identify the rational or reasonable elements in both pieces of persuasion. After rewriting the two, be prepared to argue for the relative effectiveness of one version over another.

Readings for New Dimensions

Anderson, Jerry M., and Paul J. Dovre, *Readings in Argumentation* (Boston: Allyn and Bacon, 1968). This collection of sources on reasoning and argument is particularly interesting because of the diversity of material. In particular, the selections by Scott, Mills, Smith, Thonssen and Baird, and all of parts IV and V on reasoning and evidence are of value. The discussion by Gary Cronkhite mentioned in footnote 10 is also in this book ("Logic, Emotion and the Paradigm of Persuasion").

Becker, Samuel L., "Research on Emotional and Logical Proofs," *Southern Speech Journal, 28* (Spring 1963), 198–207. Becker examines the kinds of research undertaken on the relationship between emotional and logical persuasive techniques. He concludes that most of the research has been in little of value and attributes the problem to the emotion-logic distinction, which so many researchers and textbook writers in persuasion have made. The article is of particular value for the review of research concerning this question.

Beisecker, Thomas D., and Donn W. Parson, *The Process of Social Influence* (Englewood Cliffs, N. J.: Prentice-Hall, 1972). This collection of articles from various fields (speech, psychology, sociology, etc.) focuses on various aspects of persuasion. In particular, the selections by McCroskey, Koehler, and Jones are of value for the study with Chapter 5. The whole book is a valuable addition to anyone's persuasion library, as it collects a number of articles from various sources and groups them around four major issues: *the psychological content* of persuasive messages; the properties of *the source* of persuasive messages; the properties of *the message* itself; and finally *the effects of persuasion.*

Brockriede, Wayne, and Douglas Ehninger, "Toulmin on Argument: An Interpretation and Application," *Quarterly Journal of Speech, 46* (February 1960), 44–53. This article provides a concise explanation of the Toulmin system of diagraming arguments, as well as numerous examples of how the system can structure a variety of persuasive methods, such as argument from sign, analogy, and so forth. The authors clearly and concisely discuss the advantages of the system over more traditional approaches.

Cronkhite, Gary, "Logic, Emotion, and the Paradigm of Persuasion," *Quarterly Journal of Speech, 50* (February 1964), 13–18. Numerous references have been made to this selection in Chapter 5. In it, Cronkhite argues that viewing persuasion as "emotional" or "logical" may be an outdated perspective. Instead, he suggests that the terms "activation" and "cognition" are better substitutes. He also describes what happens, theoretically, when persuasion occurs—cognitions about object concepts are linked to motivational or activational concepts by the author. That is similar to the argument put forth in this chapter (that it is in *participation* in the argument that the receiver is really persuaded).

Cronkhite, Gary, *Persuasion: Speech and Behavioral Change* (New York: Bobbs-Merrill Co., 1969). The first 70 pages of this book provide a most comprehensive and concise review of the study of persuasion from Aristotle to the present. Of particular interest to the student and to the study of Chapter 5 are Cronkhite's discussions of conviction-persuasion duality, message organization, reasoning and evidence, and the Toulmin approach. His own paradigm for persuasion is similar to the "participative" approach suggested here. Also of interest is that Cronkhite's own early research was in attempts to distinguish between emotional and logical persuasion. He was unable to discover any measurable differences.

McBurney, James H., and Glen E. Mills, *Argumentation and Debate: Techniques of a Free Society* (New York: The Macmillan Co., 1964). This book, particularly pp. 119–134 and 145–153, provides what most would call the "traditional" discussion of syllogistic argument, inductive and deductive methods, and types of proof.

McCroskey, James C., "A Summary of Experimental Research on the Effects of Evidence in Persuasive Communication," *Quarterly Journal of Speech, 50* (April 1969), 169–176. This article provides a good review of behavioral research to 1968 concerning evidence effects, with results grouped around certain issues. The only problem with the selection is that it refers to a series of studies, not generally available at most libraries, conducted through the Speech Communication Research Laboratory at Michigan State University. The author generously offers to provide these studies on request, however. The article would be of particular value to students needing a quick review of research findings and suggestions on what might be studied further.

Rosnow, Ralph L., and Edward J. Robinson, *Experiments in Persuasion* (New York: Academic Press, 1967). This book collects a number of articles, most of which are found in "non-speech" journals. Several of them directly address the emotion versus logic issue. See especially "A Field Experiment on the Comparative Effectiveness of 'Emotional' and 'Rational' Political Leaflets in Determining Election Results," by George W. Hartman. The book would be a valuable addition to one's persuasion library, since it collects a variety of research items from psychology and social-psychology perspectives.

Toulmin, Stephen, *The Uses of Argument* (Cambridge: Cambridge University Press, 1969). Toulmin's discussion of the nature of argument is quite philosophical and involved. Students may wish to look in particular at two chapters —Chapter 3, "The Layout of Argument," and Chapter 1, "Fields of Argument and Models," since the two provide the basic elements of the Toulmin theory of persuasive discourse.

6

Societal and Cultural Predispositions to Persuasion

Each culture seeks to train its members in the ways of that culture—its beliefs, its modes of behaviors, its folkways, and its norms. This training builds a set of predispositions for persuasion in each member of that society and culture. These predispositions are very much like the premises discussed in Chapters 4 and 5. They are understood by the audience, appealed to by persuaders, and reacted to by individual audience members. The only difference between cultural and societal predispositions to persuasion and the process and content premises mentioned earlier is that cultural and societal training has been so pervasive and so consistent throughout most of our lives that we are only faintly aware of the results of that training. In other words, cultural and societal predispositions for persuasion occur at such a low level of awareness that we must look carefully at our behavior patterns to discern these predispositions. Consider the following instance of cultural patterning:

Suppose that you are a member of an Eskimo-Indian tribe called "People of the Deer," whose sole means of sustenance derives from a spring and an autumn slaughter of caribou as the animals migrate following food supplies. You kill enough animals in the spring to last the tribe until the fall, when again the animals migrate south following the food supply. The tribal custom is to kill and preserve these deer in a period of a week or two. The tribes are perhaps 100 persons strong. Suppose that we have just finished our fall hunt, and we discover that we face a severe winter without having killed enough caribou to feed the tribe until the spring migration. Death, though not imminent, is certain without sufficient supplies of meat and fat.

Imagine that you are part of a tribal meeting called to consider the matter. What would you do in this situation?

In several persuasion classes, students brainstormed for solutions to this problem and came up with these suggestions in this approximate order:

1. "Let's follow the deer and kill enough."
2. "Let's seek an alternate food supply—we can eat berries or fish or birds."
3. "Let's send a band of the tribe to get help."
4. "Let's ration food to make it last longer."
5. "Let's use all the parts of the deer—skin, horns, everything—in order to increase the supply."
6. "Let's send some of the people away to another place where food is more plentiful and thus decrease demand."
7. "Let's kill some of our tribe in order to decrease demand."
8. "Let's kill the most useless—the old first, and the very young next."
9. "Let's resort to cannibalism along with the killing."

In an attempt to get out of the predicament, the most practical, situation-oriented solutions emerge first and then are escalated to more serious and stringent solutions until cannibalism is suggested. The actual People of the Deer literally *do nothing*—they eat the food at their regular rates, knowing full well that they will not live through the winter, and then they sit and wait for death. The whole tribe does not enter into the problem-solving frame of mind typical of Western culture. Instead everyone accepts the fates. This possibility just doesn't enter into our action-oriented, problem-solving culture, just as sending someone off to hunt other sources of food doesn't enter into the frame of reference of the People of the Deer. They have a cultural predisposition to accept a problem and do nothing, while we have a cultural predisposition to try immediately to find solutions for any problem we encounter, even though the problem may be insoluble. We literally cannot *not* do something. In our culture, persuaders will be successful if they depict a problem and then start suggesting solutions or alternatives to the status quo. In other cultures, the same persuaders would not meet with success.

A classic example is the hero of the musical *The Music Man*, Professor Harold Hill. He comes into River City, Iowa, intent on selling band instruments, but he must create a *need* for these instruments. He calls the citizens of River City together and begins to create a problem for them—trouble. He says, "There's trouble, my friends, in River City; I said trouble, trouble, trouble . . ." and then proceeds to point out the particulars of the trouble—some boys buckle their knickerbockers below the knees after leaving the house, others have nicotine stains between their fingers, still others are using slang words (like "swell" and "so's your old man"), and downtown you can see "scarlet women" and "libertine men." By the time Professor Hill is through, he has created such a real problem that the people of River City aren't about to sit still as the People of the Deer might. They want action and a solution now. Professor Hill gives them one—he says that since "trouble" starts with the letter "t," which rhymes with the letter "p," which might stand for "poolhall," the parents should buy band instruments to keep their children busy after school instead of off playing billiards. Thus, the need for action is met—a cultural premise forms the basis for Hill's appeal.

There are several ways to deal with cultural patterns and societal norms and how these relate to persuasion. For our purposes, we consider three sources of patterns, all seemingly related to cultural training: (1) the development of cultural images or myths, (2) the presence of an American or Western value system, and (3) the use of nonverbal messages and cues. As these are discussed, bear in mind the nature of a *value*—here defined as a conception of the "good" or the desirable that functions as a standard for assessing means or as a goal in motivating human behavior. Examples of values are concepts such as honesty, justice, beauty, efficiency, safety, and progress. Because the value system held by an audience is a major source of a persuader's leverage, you may want to assess the ways in which a persuader attempts to link his proposal and arguments to specific values held by that audience.

Cultural and Societal Pressure

I am sure that everyone has heard stories about the children of various Indian tribes in the 1800s. Supposedly, the children never cried because it was culturally essential not to frighten off game. Anyone who has been around a newborn infant probably doubts that these stories have a whit of truth to them. Children cry when they are uncomfortable, when they are lonely, when they are hungry, or even for exercise. As long as the child has no language besides his cry, it would be doubtful that an Indian mother could get across the message "Hush, there are some elk near and we need to kill them for our meat." How, then, did Indians train their children not to cry out?

Researchers into the Sioux culture found that during the first hour of life, whenever an Indian baby cried, its mother or some other adult clapped her hands over the child's mouth and nose, thus suffocating it.

The hand was removed only if the child stopped crying or if it seriously began to smother. If done within the first hour of life, this extreme utilization of the "Stimulus plus Negative Response equals Extinction of Stimulus" pattern worked remarkably. Of course, as the child grew the pattern was seen by him over and over again; his parents and the tribal elders spoke of the power of silence; they valued quiet and stealth in stalking game; and the Indian brave was tested and proved his courage by experiencing pain and not crying. Thus the pattern introduced in an almost brutal way at birth was continually reinforced throughout life by the values placed on the pattern and the respect given to it by Indian culture and society as a whole. Each of us goes through essentially the same learning process, no matter what culture we are born into. Cultural values, images, myths, and manners of behavior are introduced, demonstrated, and valued by those around us, and as a result we adopt the values.[1] They become rules for governing ourselves as we interact. Eventually (some psychologists estimate by age five) most of these patterns are so ingrained that we do not even notice that they are there; instead, we respond almost instinctively to them. Only when we deliberately examine them or when we are thrust into another new culture do we ever realize how many of our ways of believing and behaving are culturally determined.

This pattern of cultural training and patterning underlies each of the three kinds of predispositions we are going to investigate. In each case, these ways of believing and behaving lurk beneath our surface thoughts and acts. Sophisticated persuaders perceive the patterns and can appeal to them directly and cleverly. Even if persuaders do not do "in-depth cultural analyses," they nonetheless can appeal to cultural and societal pressures, if only because the appeal fits their own cultural and social pattern. They can appeal to cultural and societal premises because they believe in them themselves and hope that their audiences do also.

Cultural Images and Myths

Every culture has its own myths and sets of heroes who do things valued by that culture, although they may not be valued by other cultures. This phenomenon even occurs within countries with the

[1] For a good discussion of the trials by pain used by Indians, read *Black Elk Speaks* by John Niehardt (Lincoln: University of Nebraska Press, 1961). The Sioux's use of smothering to prevent crying is included in *These Were the Sioux* by Maria Santos (New York: Dell Publishing Co., 1961), p. 19.

same general cultural heritage. For example, early Greek society developed a series of myths surrounding the sin of hubris—the sin of pride. Eventually the myths became institutionalized in many of the Greek dramas (the Oedipus trilogy, the Agamemnon dramas, and others). Parts of the myths related to physical acts like walking on a purple carpet, thereby insulting the gods. Other parts of the myths, like trying to control one's own destiny, were repeatedly discouraged. Eventually Greek citizenry believed in and responded to this legend—they placed a high value on avoiding prideful action; they elected leaders who were humble, and they valued humility. Americans have similar beliefs. As a student, you probably know that the overproud student is less likely to be elected to office or chosen as team captain than the more humble person. We seem to value humility as much as the Greeks did—parents warn us against setting ourselves up for the big letdown, and we are often called upon to observe the antics of a pompous person. We ridicule needless pride. At the same time, our culture differs from the Greeks in other ways—particularly in the myths we hold in esteem.

What are some of the cultural myths or legends or images underlying American culture and society and how do persuaders use them? Are these images capable of being changed? If so, how? Are they being changed at present and if so, how? These are questions the perceptive persuaders and persuadees need to ask as they prepare to send and receive messages in an age that offers each person more information and many more choices than he can ever assimilate or take. Let us consider a few of these cultural myths or images.

Wisdom of the Rustic

One of the most pervasive images or legends in American literature, and one with great persuasive impact, is the belief in the common sense of the plain and uneducated but sincere and clever rustic, who because of his simplicity will win out in the end. No matter how devious or sophisticated the opposition, let the simple wisdom of the backwoods emerge, and truth will become clear. Numerous folk tales rely on this image—all of the Daniel Boone tales, the stories about the inventiveness of Paul Bunyan, and the incredible number of sage Lincoln stories. Even today, we have faith in the humble beginnings of persons when we look for leaders. Often the small-town boy is chosen team captain, more and more persons from the lower middle class are sending their children to school, and so forth. As Americans we have a belief that humble beginnings and the world of obstacles and difficulty can teach even the most uneducated of us to be wise in a worldly way.

Persuaders have repeatedly used the image, portraying themselves as rustics who have wisdom. There are obvious examples—Lincoln, George Wallace, the advertisements focusing on the cleverness of rustics (e.g.,

Mrs. Olson, the Folger's lady; or Josephine, the lady plumber). Inculcated in these images are several cultural values and predispositions: a faith in common sense; a belief in the spontaneous and instinctive act (think of maxims like "trust your initial judgment"); and a reliance on physical and mental prowess.

At the same time that we seem to value the simple, impulsive common-sense attributes of the rustic, we have a corresponding set of norms that devalue or hold in low esteem the intellectual and the deliberate attributes people associate with the educated. DeToqueville, in his book *Democracy in America* written in the 1830s, observed the same distrust:

> The nearer the people are drawn to the common level of an equal and similar condition, the less prone does each man become to place implicit faith in a certain man or a certain class of men [intellectuals]. But his readiness to believe the multitude increases, and opinion is more than ever mistress of the world. Not only is common opinion the only guide which private judgment retains . . . it possesses a power infinitely beyond what it has elsewhere.[2]

Hofstadter has also written about this anti-intellectualism in several places,[3] and persuaders often use the reverse side of our value system in the wisdom of the rustic. George Wallace aimed his rhetorical barbs at "pointy-headed professors," while Spiro Agnew condemned with great effect a group he called "an effete corps of intellectual snobs." The list could go on, and you can undoubtedly observe this feeling simply because you are at college. Perhaps persons in your family or neighborhood who have never been to college distrust the kind of education you are receiving. Phrases like "the godless universities" were in vogue in the 1960s, and with the student-power demonstrations of the 1970s, colleges, their faculties, and their students have become increasingly distrusted by most persons. The phenomenon is not a new one—it has roots in the fundamental values placed on the spontaneous, common-sense wisdom of the rugged individual. He wore a coonskin cap on the Kentucky frontier, or a rough rider's hat in the 1890s, or a straw hat on the Midwestern farm; in the 1970s he probably wears a steelworker's hat.

Possibility of Success

You often hear reference to the Horatio Alger myth, which was based on a number of novels written by Alger in the nine-

---

[2] Alexis DeToqueville, *Democracy in America* (New York: Mentor Books, 1965), p. 148.
[3] Richard Hofstadter, *Anti-intellectualism in American Life* (New York: Alfred A. Knopf, 1963).

teenth century. They always told of a young man who through hard work, sincerity, honesty, and a faith in the future was able to make good—even to rise to the top and to own his own company, to have a beautiful wife, to have a fine life, and to be able to do good for others. The myth was an appealing one and was warmly embraced by immigrants, the poor, and middle-class Americans. They passed it on, either by reference to themselves or to others, to their children, admonishing them to work hard and to "make it." In 1962, one of the slogans on college campuses was "Get a degree, get a job, and get ahead." That slogan probably was a remnant of the Alger myth, which parents have repeated over and over again like the Indian value of silence.

In a sense, this myth—the Possibility of Success—links up with the Wisdom of the Rustic myth. "If you follow the advice of the common man and use common sense, with sincerity and hard work, you will be a success" would be the articulation of this myth. It has the values of hard work, sincerity, honesty, and law and order embodied in it. Some persons have claimed that the myth was established to enslave the common man and to keep him on a treadmill—that it is a propaganda device designed to keep "the establishment" in power. If you think that you have a chance to achieve success, you won't risk questioning authority figures or established value systems; instead, you will submit to them and try to gain power for yourself. Again, this myth was observed by DeToqueville:

> No Americans are devoid of a yearning desire to rise; . . . All are constantly seeking to acquire property, power, and reputation . . . What chiefly diverts the men of democracies from lofty ambition is not the scantiness of their fortunes, but the vehemence of the exertions they daily make to improve them. . . . The same observation is applicable to the sons of such men: they are born . . . their parents were humble; they have grown up amidst feelings and notions which they cannot afterwards easily get rid of; and it may be presumed that they will inherit the propensities of their father, as well as his wealth.[4]

You probably can see your parents and your relatives in this description; and if DeToqueville is right, you may well see yourself also. You may be predisposed to persuasion that articulates the possibility of success if you follow the values prescribed by the myth—work hard and honestly for your grades or job or pay and, if you have the faith and stamina, you will succeed. This myth was used by Richard Nixon in his 1972 campaign, and it will probably be used by one candidate or the other in many elections to come. It usually tries to cast intellectual, lofty, and

---

[4] DeToqueville, pp. 156–158.

idealistic aims in opposition to itself. As a persuadee, you should expect to hear appeals for one myth and against the other. Persuaders will offer success as just around the corner, if only you will follow them and not the false prophets. They will offer the "big break" and the chance to have a better life for you and your children.

Coming of the Messiah

Perhaps because Americans are so deeply steeped in the Judaeo-Christian value system, they expect to be saved from dire circumstances by a great prophet or savior. We sketchily mentioned this myth in Chapter 3 as one of the metaphors often used by persuaders. It is also one of the dramatic plots used in campaigns to be discussed later. Let us investigate the values this image inculcates in more depth.

First, what does the myth claim? Well, there are times when a situation becomes so difficult, so confusing and chaotic, or so unbearable that escape from it seems impossible. For the unemployed during the Depression, it was the total lack of job opportunities and the prospect of more of the same (no food for families, property foreclosures, etc.); for the citizenry of the 1950s it was the increasing encroachment of Russian Communist domination (in four years, Communist governments were established in China, North Korea, Poland, Czechoslovakia, Hungary, Yugoslavia, Latvia, Estonia, Lithuania, Romania, Finland, and others); for America in the late 1960s, there were two problems: (1) a serious breakdown of traditional values and lifestyles, expressed in such trends as civil riots in major cities, the use of hallucinogens and other drugs, common-law marriages, and the development of communes and (2) the seeming inability of public opinion to deter the war policy of the Johnson or Nixon administrations.

The first element of the messianic myth, then, is an insoluble problem. The second element in this myth is a man of great character and insight. In the 1930s he was a patrician with a common touch who combined great vision tempered by adversity—Franklin D. Roosevelt. There were others proclaiming that they had the same messianic qualities—Huey P. Long of Louisiana, Floyd B. Olson of Minnesota, "Father" Divine (who actually declared himself god), and Father Coughlin, for example. In the 1950s there were also several would-be prophet-messiahs: Senator Joseph McCarthy, who charged repeatedly that Communist agents had infiltrated government and that the State Department was riddled with traitors, Douglas MacArthur who held similar views, and others. All of them claimed to have the insight and wisdom to be the savior of the country. Unlike the 1930s, the 1950s must not have demanded as much, for the electorate chose a reluctant war hero—Dwight Eisenhower—and a witty intellectual—Adlai Stevenson—as major candidates and rejected the would-be messiahs. In the 1960s, other messiahs emerged to solve the insoluble—George Wallace, Eugene McCarthy, Robert Kennedy, and George McGovern. Again the situation evidently was not dire enough to demand the ultimate success of the messiah. At the same time that Americans are fascinated by the messiah or the savior, they are reluctant to follow him too zealously; and they often choose a technician to solve the problem (Eisenhower in the 1950s and Nixon in the 1960s).

What values does this myth encompass? First, a belief that there is no problem too great if the right man is given the proper insight and opportunity. This intense optimism, which many persons from other countries have difficulty believing as genuine, is at the core. Another value emerging from this myth is that there are superhumans or godlike figures who come to the fore in difficult times. We talked, in another place, about the TV saviors—Mrs. Olson and her coffee, Mr. Clean, and the Man from Glad. In a way, this expectancy of a messiah encourages docility and long suffering as values, not to the degree that we lose sight of the problem or of potential solutions but sufficiently to discourage revolt. Finally, the myth sets idealism and technology in opposition to one another. Though the myth does not directly place a higher value on technology, the fact that the technocrat has so often been chosen in times calling for a messiah suggests that one of our values—one of our God terms, going back to Chapter 3—is technology.

Presence of Conspiracy

Associated with the messianic myth is another societal belief or presupposition. Richard Hofstadter has called it the "paranoid style," or the belief that when problems appear great, the only reasonable explanation for them is that a powerful and insidious group has conspired to cause these problems.[5] This argument—the conspiracy argument—has recurred throughout American history, according to Hofstadter. At one time or another persuaders claimed that there were Papist conspiracies, Masonic conspiracies, and Populist conspiracies. We have heard the conspiracy argument several times in the last thirty years—Franklin D. Roosevelt used the argument to explain the Great Depression (money interests and the great banking houses had caused the depression and should be "thrown out of the temple"); Joseph McCarthy and right-wing groups claimed that Communists were conspiring to take over the world (some even claimed that Dwight D. Eisenhower and his brother Milton were working hand in hand with John Foster Dulles and his brother Allen Dulles, head of the CIA, and

---

[5] For a more complete discussion of the conspiracy argument, see *The Paranoid Style in American Politics and Other Essays* by Richard Hofstadter (New York: Vintage Books, 1967).

that all four were paid agents for the USSR); several groups explained the John Kennedy assassination by claiming conspiracy; McGovern claimed a presidential conspiracy when the Democratic headquarters were "bugged"; and several groups have claimed that the Vietnam war was caused by a conspiracy of industrial concerns, the defense establishment, and groups of higher education administrators who wanted to increase college enrollments by encouraging college deferments from the draft and also to get research contracts. These last "conspiracies" invited further elaboration, and several groups saw the war as a systematic way to exploit blacks and the poor; as a tool to ruin freedom of the press and freedom of speech; and as a device to get the electorate so disturbed that they would turn to a leftist-inspired rebellion.

Though this myth does not really inculcate *values* of our culture, it does demonstrate a cultural pattern of response. If you hear a conspiracy argument being articulated (whether there actually is a conspiracy or not), chances are the persons using the conspiracy notion to persuade hold these views:

1. That they have something of value to lose (they are in possession of some kind of power or property)
2. That they see themselves as either in danger of losing some or all of this power or property or as already having lost some of it
3. That they see themselves as relatively helpless as individuals to prevent their loss

It is easy to see how these kinds of perception link up with the messiah —he and perhaps his movement can help the hamstrung individual prevent the loss he perceives. The messiah can defeat the insidious conspirators and thus "save" the endangered culture or society. Herein lies one of the dangers and excitements of the conspiracy argument—it invites the mass movement and the charismatic leader.[6] Thus, in times of trouble and confusion, we may see the rise of mass movements led by charismatic charlatan leaders—and charismatic heroes or saviors. Perhaps this tendency explains why we are so reluctant to elect "messiahs" and instead often choose technocrats.

Value of Challenge

Associated with the messiah or savior myth is a final myth or image (though there are undoubtedly more which you can explore)—belief in the value of challenge. The myth is fairly simple and

---

[6] For a good discussion of the degree to which persons will follow charismatic leaders, see Eric Hoffer, *The True Believer* (New York: Harper & Row, 1951).

may be related to tests of strength and character that appear in most tribal cultures. The myth suggests there is a kind of wisdom that can be gained only through great challenge and testing. There is a "rite of passage" or initiation, which, having been experienced, imbues the initiate with power, character, and knowledge.

You are probably now going through an experience that demonstrates this myth very well. For many years our culture has assumed that going to college was a test of endurance more than a training ground for a specific job (except for the professions). College graduation signaled that you could meet a challenge and handle it; that you had matured; that you had learned how to learn. Employers thus hired college graduates and then trained them for a job *after* college. Boot camp offers another example of belief in the value of overcoming difficulty and in meeting challenges.

The more dramatic the challenge, of course, the more persuasive is the myth, and the appeals to it become more potent. Good examples from the past of persuasive uses of this myth were Hitler's references to his imprisonment as a test, the reminders of Roosevelt's physical and emotional testing when he was crippled with polio, and Robert Kennedy's references to his testing during and after his brother's assassination (it will be interesting to see if Edward Kennedy will appeal to a similar kind of example in 1976). Recall, too, that John F. Kennedy challenged Americans to explore "The New Frontier" and he sounded the call "Ask not what your country can do for you—ask what you can do for your country."

The rite of passage or the meeting of a challenge underscores several values that persuaders can use as appeals in our culture. First, it suggests that there is something inherently "good" about suffering—you learn from it and grow emotionally as a result of it. Persuaders often refer to this value when they suggest that, though the going might be difficult, the lessons learned along the way are worthwhile. (Remember your parents telling you how "good" it was for you to suffer through trigonometry or Latin?) Secondly, the myth suggests that there are certain signs of maturity, one of which is the ability to behave admirably and with character when under duress. Finally, the myth suggests that greatness needs to be tempered in adversity—Roosevelt would never have been a good President if he had not been crippled, Nixon would not have been a success if he hadn't failed so many times, and so forth. Our gods had better have a few scars if they don't have clay feet.

Presence of an American Value System

What we have just been talking about is a kind of dramatic or literary representation of cultural and societal values. There are more systematic investigations of values that have been and can be conducted. One does not need to identify and interpret the fantasy worlds and myths that seem to have power in society in order to determine values. He can ask people about values, or he can search for the values articulated in various credos or used by various groups and persuaders. The platforms of political parties may provide a reflection of shifting values. The Boy Scout laws may even give the researcher a glimpse into prevailing values. (Certainly the notions of being prepared, and of being friendly and helpful and reverent, are all related to values deeply ingrained in American culture and reflected in the actions and beliefs of the populace.) One might look at the movie offerings in major cities and determine what public taste might suggest about values. In short, there are many fairly systematic reflections of value systems in our culture.

One of the early speech-communication studies that explored values was conducted by Edward Steele and W. Charles Redding.[7] They looked at the communication of several political campaigns and tried to extract core and secondary values to be reflected in the campaign discourse by all candidates. These were the core values observed by Steele and Redding:

Puritan and pioneer morality, or the willingness to cast the world into categories of foul and fair, good and evil, and so forth. Though we tend to think of this value as "outdated," it is interesting to see how persons who claim to reject such values actually reflect them under different guises. For example, though rejecting Puritanism, most New Lefters would readily talk in "good/bad" or "just/unjust" terms when talking about the 1972 election and its candidates or about the Vietnam war.

Value of the individual, or the ranking of the rights and welfare of the individual as above that of the government and as important in other ways. Again, this value seems to persist. Both the political left and right claim they hold this principle in esteem. Barry Goldwater's renunciation of bureaucracy and big government in 1964 is not very different from the "Power to the People" philosophy of the 1970s.

---

[7] Edward Steele and W. Charles Redding, "The American Value System: Premises for Persuasion," *Western Speech,* 26 (Spring 1962), 83–91.

Achievement and success, or the accumulation of power, status, and property. This value seems to have been somewhat rejected by the counterculture lifestyle; but while disclaiming interest in these things, most followers of counterculture values also work to achieve political power, recognition, and in many cases property. Though Abbie Hoffman entitled his book *Steal This Book,* he made a good deal of money from royalties. The prime philosopher of the counterculture, Herbert Marcuse, recently observed that it may take another century before these values begin to fade (see his *Counter-revolution and Revolt*). He even advises those favoring the counterculture to follow traditional achievement goals. Encyclopedia salesmen often appeal to this value.

Change and progress, or the belief that society develops in positive ways measured by progress. Though this value is probably the one most often questioned today (Westinghouse doesn't claim that "Progress Is Our Most Important Product" any more, and environmentalists want to know the cost of progress), it still has a good deal of persuasive potency. Recall the frequency of maxims suggesting "You can never stand still; if you do, you fall behind." Again, even the most vehement opponents of industrial and technological progress (e.g., antispace exploration groups or ecologists) still want change and merely define progress as the movement away from technological change and toward change and progress in lifestyle. Most auto advertisements suggest the value of change and progress.

Ethical equality, or the view that all persons are equal in a spiritual sense and ought to be in realm of opportunity. Though the "equal in the eyes of God" aspect of this value has changed since the 1950s, the opportunity element remains potent. HEW's Affirmative Action proposal and the Equal Rights amendment to the Constitution witness the power of this value. Most revival movements appeal to this value.

Effort and optimism, or the belief that hard work and striving will ultimately lead to success. This value is clearly inculcated in several of the myths discussed above—the value of challenge and the possibility of success, for example. Retirement programs are ballyhooed with this value.

Efficiency, practicality, and pragmatism, or the value placed on solution-oriented as opposed to ideologically oriented thinking. (See our earlier discussion in this chapter of the often held disregard for intellectuals and of the pragmatic style in Chapter 3.)

Even though these values were cataloged over twenty years ago, they still have a great deal of relevance. This, if nothing else, suggests their basic quality. The fact that political position has less to do with the strength of these values than the method of enacting them seems to underscore the probability that these are core values for Americans. Our culture has been effective in instilling a set of values in all, or very nearly all, of its members—radicals, moderates, and reactionaries all believe in the same things, but just operationalize them differently. The power of a social system or culture to train its members is immense, even though the members do not often realize this as they react to the dictates deeply ingrained in them.

Does this mean that values remain essentially static and cannot be changed? Not necessarily. It only means that values are so deeply ingrained in a culture that its members often forget how strong their pressures are. The model of reinforcement suggested by B. F. Skinner is probably the one which acculturates most often, and extinction of any set of responses, once learned, is difficult. Only by changing behavior patterns consistently will attitudes and values follow suit. In its early stages, the basic idea behind the philosophy of the counterculture was precisely that—change behavior patterns (i.e., lifestyles) and changes in attitudes and values will ultimately follow.[8] That is why there was a great increase in the number of communes, group marriages, use of drugs, and so forth in the late 1960s and early 1970s. The idea was that if you lived out the new value system you would believe it and soon others (eventually the entire culture) would also begin to embrace those values. Interestingly, most of these experiments failed because they rejected the old culturally and socially inculcated values.[9] The rest of the 1970s and perhaps the 1980s will probably witness a further challenging of these traditional core values, but again we will probably see the tremendous power of the old values to draw members of the American culture and society away from experimental value sets.

Use of Nonverbal Messages and Cues

A final kind of cultural or societal predisposition for persuasion relates to symbolic behavior that is not spoken or articulated. The whole field of nonverbal communication is relatively new and the

---

[8] See Theodore Roszak, *The Making of a Counter Culture* (Garden City: Doubleday & Co., 1969); Charles Reich, *The Greening of America* (New York: Random House, 1970); and Herbert Marcuse, *Eros and Civilization* (Boston: Beacon Press, 1955), *One Dimensional Man* (Boston: Beacon Press, 1964), *An Essay on Liberation* (Boston: Beacon Press, 1969), and *Counter-revolution and Revolt* (Boston: Beacon Press, 1972).

[9] The report on the Twin Oaks commune near Richmond, Virginia, provides a good discussion of the problems of adapting communal values in our culture. A brief discussion of this experiment can be found in "A Walden Two Experiment" by Kathleen Kinkade, *Psychology Today*, January 1973, pp. 35–40.

research is extremely broad—far too broad to be adequately covered in part of one chapter. To limit our consideration here, we will not consider those nonverbal signal systems that seem to be biologically oriented (e.g., the fact that humans are right- and left-nostriled as they are right- and left-handed and that you use your dominant nostril to "sniff out" a new acquaintance for the olefactory cues he gives off—fear, hate, love, lust, or joy odors). Instead, we will just look briefly at the kinds of nonverbal signals that seem to be culturally related—that differ from culture to culture and that can increase or destroy persuasive potential. We will look at the use of artifacts or objects, the use of space, and the use of touch.

Use of Artifacts

We are probably not so very far removed from animals, but there are some differences. Though birds feather their nests with bits of string, straw, hair, and wood, they do it for purely functional reasons—to keep their nests intact and cozy. We humans feather our nests not only for those reasons but also for highly symbolic reasons. The best way of discovering how this happens is to look at your work area in your dorm room or at the work area of your roommate or spouse. It is not only arranged so that work can get done, but the person has feathered the nest with objects—artifacts—that symbolize him. His arrangement is also symbolic (certain types of persons have messy desks, while others have extremely neat desks, with each pencil sharpened and papers stacked in neat piles). Our culture has taught us to react in certain ways to the artifacts of others and how they are used. These patterns of responses form premises for persuasion.

A common type of artifactual cosmetology is revealed in the objects surrounding a persuader in a message situation (e.g., in a public speech situation the banners, the bunting, the use of flags, the insignias)—all lending to the ultimate success of the persuasive attempt. Another type of artifact is clothing. What one wears sends signals about what he is like (think of the differences between casual sports clothes and a tuxedo), what he believes (e.g., a priest's collar or an army officer's uniform), or with whom he is likely to associate (e.g., the "uniform" of the hippie indicates that he will probably not meet and associate with too many go-getting young IBM salesmen). Thus, the persuader symbolizes himself and his purpose through his plumage.

Another type of artifact is exemplified in the personal objects surrounding a persuader. Consider how you feel when you go into a doctor's office with diplomas on the wall—no art, no colorful posters, or any other kind of decoration—just diplomas. What cultural signal do you receive about the type of person the doctor is likely to be? Compare that with the feeling you have as you enter a college professor's office with posters or abstract art on the walls. The artifacts symbolize the kind of persuasion you will be likely to hear—in one case, professional, concrete, and probably prescriptive and, in the other, abstract.

Large objects, like furniture, can also give off signals. We can expect a certain kind of communication to occur when we are told to sit down at a table and the persuader sits on the opposite side of the table. If the persuader puts a lectern between himself and his audience, he will probably engage in a certain kind of communication—probably very formal—whereas if he steps out from behind the lectern or walks around while talking, he may well be more informal. Types of furniture can also symbolize certain characteristics. What kinds of persuasion and what kinds of persons would you associate with French Provincial furniture? What kind of persuasion is likely to occur in a room with industrial metal furniture? What kind in a Danish Modern room? Or Early American?

Use of Space

The way a person structures the space around him is also a factor in communication that seems particularly related to cultural training. He can, if he wishes, signal to his fellow communicators that he feels superior and that formal communication is called for; he can suggest that informal communication is called for; or he can suggest that intimate and extremely frank communication is called for. Edward T. Hall notes four general distances used by persuaders in American culture:[10]

Public distance, or distances we often find in public speaking situations where speakers are 15 to 25 or more feet from their audiences. Informal persuasion probably will not work in these circumstances. Persuaders who try to be informal in a formal situation will probably meet with little success.

Social or *formal* distance, or the distances used in formal but non-public situations like interviews or committee reports. The persuader in these situations, though formal in style, need not be oratorical. Formal distance runs about 7 to 12 feet between persuader and persuadee. You would never become chummy in this kind of situation (regardless

---

[10] Edward T. Hall, *The Silent Language* (Garden City: Doubleday & Co., 1959), *The Hidden Dimension* (Garden City: Doubleday & Co., 1966), and "Proxemics—A Study of Man's Spatial Relationships" in *Man's Image in Medicine and Anthropology* (International Universities Press, 1963) all provide further insights to the use of space.

of whether you were persuader or persuadee), yet you wouldn't deliver a "speech" either.

Personal or *informal* distance, or the distance used when two colleagues or friends are discussing a matter of mutual concern. A good example might be when you and your roommate are discussing this class or problem you both share. In these situations, communication is less structured than in the formal situation; persuadee and persuader are both more relaxed and interact often with one another, bringing up and questioning evidence or asking for clarification. Informal distance, in our culture, is about 3½ to 4 feet—the eye to eye distance, if you sit at the corner of a teacher's desk while he sits in his chair, as opposed to the formal distance created when you are asked to sit across the desk from him.

Intimate distance, or the distance one uses when he mutters or lovingly whispers a message he doesn't want others to overhear. Persuasion may or may not occur in these instances; usually the message is one that will not be questioned by the receiver—he or she will nod in agreement, follow the suggestion given, or respond to the question asked. When two communicators are in this kind of close relation to one another, their aims are similar, in all probability. The distance ranges from 6 to 18 inches.

When distances are used to encourage or discourage a certain kind of persuasion or when a persuader oversteps the boundaries "agreed upon" by the persuadee, results can often be startling. For example, during the 1972 presidential campaign, George McGovern, after being heckled during a speech, walked up to one of his hecklers and when he was in intimate distance said to him "kiss my ass" and walked away. The message—an intimate and certainly not a persuasive one—was overheard by some members of the press and then written up in the evening newspapers and related over the television news—a public kind of exposure. The response did not help the candidate's image.

In studies of communication flow and its relation to ease of conversation, leadership emergence, and a number of other variables, researchers discovered that the most used communication channels at a conference table (see Figure 6-1) were those across the corners of the table (or informal distance), the next most often used channel was directly across the table (or about the distance we have called formal distance), the third was down the length of the conference table (or about what we have called public distance), and the least used was between persons sitting next to one another (or about what we have called intimate distance). In conferences, we feel fairly comfortable to converse, to discuss, to persuade in informal ways; we don't often engage in intimate conversation and thus avoid speaking with those next to us. (Most persons form few intimate relationships and probably feel uneasy responding *as if* in intimate relation with another person. Think of what you do in the front seat of an auto when there are three persons or at a banquet table when you have to talk to the person next to you —see footnote 11. You probably move away from that person's face or you speak to a spot in midair—perhaps the windshield of the car or a centerpiece on the banquet table. You rarely allow yourself to communicate in intimate distance unless you are on an intimate basis with a person.)

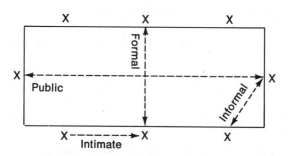

Figure 6–1

If you want to encourage communication flow, try to arrange informal spaces for persons to use; if you want to discourage communication, arrange intimate spaces for persons to use. Be alert to the persuader who is adept at using space this way and to the persuader who seems to have misjudged his relationship with a listener. In either case, the use of space indicates something about the persuader.

In *The Making of the President: 1960*, Theodore H. White tells an interesting anecdote about the use of space in describing the 1960 election-eve activities at the Kennedy compound in Hyannisport. Throughout the early evening hours, the "Irish Mafia" and aides who had helped John F. Kennedy in the campaign sat watching television election returns while they ate popcorn and drank beer and wine. Later in the evening it became apparent that the final results would be close and not decisive until at least the next morning. J. F. K. went to bed. He awoke the next morning in his private cottage to the radio and television news that Illinois had gone Democratic, thereby assuring him the adequate electoral majority—he was the President-elect. He dressed and went out to the front steps of the cottage where his friends and aides waited. None of them seemed willing to enter a 10- or 15-foot circle of space around the President-elect until he gestured for them to come forward. They seemed to feel as if their former informal or even intimate relationship was not now called for, and they would have to be invited by President-elect Kennedy. Many persuadees and persuaders are not as perceptive as the Kennedy aides—they assume intimacy or informality when other patterns are called for.[11]

Use of Touch

One of the strange inconsistencies in American culture is the way we regard physical touch between human beings. One often sees the heads of state in various European countries hugging and kissing one another when they meet after trips. Can you imagine what the press would do with a televised and photographed incident in which our President and Vice-President hugged and kissed after the President had returned from a trip abroad? In spite of new freedoms granted to homosexuals, public opinion would probably not be in favor of physical suggestions of homosexuality between public officials, even if there were no doubt in anyone's mind about the relationship. At the same time we have no strange feelings when the wives of the President and Vice-President hug and kiss. Touch is perfectly acceptable between two men on a football field or between two grade-school chums or between a man and a woman. Certainly touch is one of the most important systems of communication with infants—the sureness of a mother's or father's touch can calm and soothe an infant in distress.

Generally, in Western culture touch between men is limited to shaking hands or backslapping. Persuaders who are too "touchy" with persons around them (e.g., with fellow candidates for office, with other persons on interview shows, or with other members of the board of directors) are likely to offend not only the person touched but also the persons observing the touch. Credibility can be drastically undermined if persuaders misread a relationship and respond inappropriately with touch. A good example occurred at a recent Speech Communication convention. Conventions are traditionally more "touchy" than other occasions—friends see one another after a long time, there are receptions and cocktail hours, and informal job interviewing goes on. A young attractive graduate student was visiting with other students and faculty members. As she turned to leave the room, one faculty member used his arm and hand to direct her movement (although people usually know where they are going, such "guidance" is acceptable and often used). The problem was that his arm and hand made physical contact with parts of the girl's body. If the contact had been just across the back or shoulders the touch might still have been acceptable—it wasn't and, combined with the actual physical touch, had a negative effect on the

[11] See Erving Goffman's *Behavior in Public Places* (New York: The Macmillan Co., 1963); A. Paul Hare and Robert F. Bales, "Seating Position and Small Group Interaction," *Sociometry, 26* (December 1963), 480–486; and Robert Sommer, "Leadership and Group Geography," *Sociometry, 24* (March 1961), 99–110.

professor's credibility, not only in the view of the girl touched but in the minds of the other graduate students who watched. They concluded that the faculty member was a "lech" or a "dirty old man" or that he was "horny" and looking for action. None of these messages may have been intended; but whatever the professor's motivations, his use of touch elicited a culturally learned response—he was on the make in the carefree atmosphere of the convention.

Persuaders and persuadees should be alert to the uses of touch around them. The kinds of touches and the ways in which touches are made signal not only what kind of a relationship may exist between two persons but also the intentions of persons. Again, the accurate as well as the inaccurate "readings" by persuaders need to be noted, for they may signal the persuader's sensitivity to the feelings of others, his motives, and his ability to respond to situational and interpersonal cues.[12]

Using Nonverbal Behavior

Again, we need to emphasize that nonverbal behavior—like the other cultural predispositions for persuasion—occurs at a very low level of awareness, almost instinctively or automatically without our being aware of it. Nonetheless, we respond to nonverbal uses of objects, space, touch, and other symbolic cues like facial expression; we feel at ease with what has happened or with what we observe if the observed actions are consistent with what our culture has taught us and if they seem sincere. We began this discussion of nonverbal cues in persuasion by saying that though man may not be far from the animals, he engages in the symbolic use of artifacts, touches, and space when he attempts to persuade. The same notion applies as we receive messages—we trust our nonverbal reactions because of what we believe these unspoken messages symbolize about the persuader. We don't look at the use of touch or plumage as happenstance; we see it as intentional, even if only at a low level of awareness. There is "leakage" in nonverbal cues—though we may try to pretend or to fake nonverbal signals, we are unable to prevent our true motives from seeping through. The perceptive and sensitive persuadee will be on the alert for these cues.

Obviously, the use of artifacts, space, and touch are not the only nonverbal dimensions with persuasive impact. In evaluating persuasion, you should also consider the roles and meanings of such nonverbal cues

---

[12] For further discussion of the communicative function of touch, you might look at Hall's discussions of "Tactics" in the books cited above (fn. 10); Donna C. Aquilera, "The Relationship between Physical Contact and Verbal Interaction between Nurses and Patients," *Journal of Psychiatric Nursing and Mental Health, 5* (May–June 1967), 5–9; and Chapter 6 of Julius Fast's *Body Language* (New York: M. Evans and Co., 1970).

as tone of voice, directness of eye contact, facial expressions, and gestures. And in a persuasive situation, what meanings may be attached to silence on the persuader's part?

A Review and Conclusion

As you have probably felt by this time, the world of the persuadee in an information age is not an easy one. There are so many things to be aware of—the persuader's self-revelation using language, his stylistic choices, the internal or process premises operating within each of us, the interactive rules for content premises, as we have called them, and now we have glimpsed at societal and cultural predispositions for persuasion—which may also act as premises in persuasive arguments. Persuaders, either because they have studied and analyzed our cultural predispositions or because they instinctively appeal to these trends, rely on the societal training and shaping of belief and action in the persons they are trying to reach. On at least three separate levels, this training has an effect on each of us—in the cultural myths or images we respond to, in the sets of values we consciously articulate, and in the nonverbal cues we respond to (uses of artifacts, space, and touch, to mention a few).

Questions for Further Thought

1. What are the three types of culturally or socially inculcated predispositions for persuasion? Give examples of each from your own experience.

2. How does culture or society train its members? Give examples from your own experience.

3. You are in school for a reason: What is it? How did you become motivated to come to college? Why? Is this related to any particular myth or image repeated to you? What were the elements in it? (For example, as the child of immigrant parents, I was repeatedly told that though "they" could take away your house and job, "they" could never take away an education—it spelled success in America.)

4. How do you rank the core values mentioned in Chapter 6? How do you operationalize them (i.e., put them into practice)? Are there other values in your own value system not mentioned by Steele and Redding? What are they? Are they restatements of the core values? If so, how? If not, how do they differ?

5. How do you use space in the classroom? How far does the teacher in your favorite class stand from the members of the class? In your worst class? In classes in which you were most successful when it comes to grades, what kind of distance was used most often (social, intimate, etc.)? Which are you most familiar with or most at ease with? How do you use space when you interact with persons where you live (observe your behavior at mealtime, in conversations, etc.)?

6. How much do you touch others? Try to increase the number of touches you use and observe the responses of others. Does the increase cause a different effect? If so, how?

7. What are the artifacts you surround yourself with? What do they mean to you? (Some students have reported that the first thing they do after unpacking for dormitory living is to purchase "conversation pieces" or artifacts that symbolize themselves.) What about your roommate? What artifacts does he use? Do they symbolize him? What about your family members?

Experiences in Persuasion

1. In a group of four or five, observe a television talk show without the sound being turned on. Concentrate on one participant and his nonverbal gestures and movements. Report on the nonverbal interaction between guests and host and between other guests. (This exercise is particularly revealing if the show is a controversial one in which emotional behavior is exhibited.)

2. Observe the entertainment page of a newspaper from a town or city other than your own. What kinds of values might you predict for the inhabitants of that city based on your observations. Justify your conclusions.

3. Go to an adolescent fiction section of a public library. What do the plots of the novels suggest about cultural myths? (Examine several novels using the flyleaf of the book for plot synopses—15 or 20 can be checked relatively quickly this way.) Now observe the television advertisements during a 3-hour period of prime time (6 or 7 o'clock until 10). Compare the plots of the novels with the "plots" of the advertisements and discuss similarities in character, image, or action. Discuss differences.

4. Rearrange the personal artifacts and space of your roommate or a family member. Observe and record his reactions. Interview him after your experiment and see which objects mean most to him. Find out why. Report on your findings.

5. Interview foreign students on campus or persons of foreign background with whom you are acquainted. Try to find out what their culture inculcates through the use of myths or images. Through values. How does their nonverbal system differ from ours. You might also want to talk to persons who have recently returned from a trip to another country to see what kinds of cultural differences they observed. (For example, in Sweden the Horatio Alger success image has little potency as a persuasive premise—income and opportunity is relatively equalized and restricted there, so the myth has no believability).

6. If there is a film society or cine-club on your campus, attend several of the films throughout the term. Try to sample both domestic and foreign films and from a variety of time periods. As you watch the films, try to identify the myths or images being portrayed by the film maker and the kinds of values he seems to emphasize. (For instance, a Bergman film may emphasize the value of experiential images, whereas a film by DeMille may emphasize individualism through strong central characters). Report on the differences you observe throughout the term and of the recurring similarities.

7. If you are divided into study groups, select a source relating to nonverbal communication (see the readings list at the end of this chapter and footnotes for a starting point) or select several sources and have each group member choose one. Read the source, or sources, and present a report to the class that elaborates on the material presented in this chapter.

8. Interview psychiatrists or psychiatric counselors in your community (try the health service on your campus). Try to find out the kinds of values and cultural demands that individuals tend to have difficulty handling in American society. (Supposedly, one out of every three persons sees a psychiatric counselor in his lifetime and probably even more would if given the opportunity.) Speculate on the kinds of values that might cause problems for you in the future. How might persuasion be directed to appeal to these values (the ones repeatedly causing difficulty for others or yourself)? Identify television or print media appeals which do aim at these values.

9. Go to a local television station. Ask for old television commercials (they are usually thrown away). Select one or more of the core values cited by Steele and Redding or one of the myths or images suggested here. Try to demonstrate values or images in action in advertising. (*Note:* You might have to splice several commercials together, but this is relatively easy. Ask the radio-television faculty for advice.)

Readings for New Dimensions

Ardrey, Robert, *The Territorial Imperative: A Personal Inquiry into the Animal Origins of Property and Nations* (New York: Atheneum Publishers, 1966). This discussion of the human use of space and territory is interesting, particularly in comparison with Hall's consideration of the same topics. The examples are pointed, and Ardrey's style is easy. He is outspoken and overstates his case for the biological drive for territorial boundary lines, but the discussion is captivating. You can often see Ardrey on television interview shows promoting his latest book. Having read him makes the interview sessions meaningful. He is controversial but stimulating.

DeToqueville, Alexis, *Democracy in America* (New York: Mentor Books, 1956). DeToqueville came to America in 1831 to observe how democracy worked, in view of democracy's miserable failure in France in 1789. He traveled around the country for about a year and then returned to France, where he wrote this book. Even though it is over 100 years old, it is remarkable for its insights and prophesies about America and the experiment in democracy. The first part is especially important, with its discussion of "The Tyranny of the Majority"—clearly a problem in the twentieth century. The last part investigates American values in depth. The book is divided into short sections and can be read off and on as you wish. You will be delighted with the contemporary nature of the insights.

Fast, Julius, *Body Language* (New York: M. Evans and Co., 1970). Fast's book was on the bestseller lists for some time. It is a slick explanation of some hard research in the area of nonverbal communication. The book claims to be able to train you to manipulate the world around you, from winning conferences to succeeding sexually. Although the claims are inflated, it is a quick and enjoyable introduction to some of the areas of nonverbal research —you can finish it in an evening. The examples included in it are valuable, and you will find yourself referring to them often and becoming more observant of nonverbal cues; for this reason alone it is worth reading. It can provide you with enough background to prepare an interesting speech or paper; it also has a good bibliography.

Hall, Edward T., *The Hidden Dimension* (New York: Doubleday & Co., 1966); *The Silent Language* (New York: Doubleday & Co., 1959). Both of these books are inexpensive and easy to read. They provide a wealth of examples from nonverbal communication that show differences in cultural communication. You will enjoy Hall's style, and the two books should provide a more than sufficient introduction to nonverbal and cross-cultural communication. Most of Hall's conclusions are based on observation, so it may be wise to take some of them with a grain of salt and to check them out in other sources or with your own experience.

Hoffer, Eric, *The True Believer* (New York: Harper & Row, 1951). Hoffer's book is an analysis of mass movements and the kinds of persons who are likely to join them. It would be a good source for Chapter 7, but is also important here because it reveals many of the things our society values highly—change, individuality, men of words, and others. The book reads easily and is also divided into short sections that can be read off and on. Hoffer is also available on film discussing his ideas.

Hofstadter, Richard, *The Paranoid Style in American Politics and Other Essays* (New York: Vintage Books, 1967). This book presents the conspiracy argument, briefly discussed in this chapter. It is clearly and concisely written, with numerous examples. This image of the conspiracy is a pervasive one, and no student of persuasion should overlook reading about the development of its style and recurring character. Interestingly, this criticism of style comes from a scholar in the field of history, not speech communication. There are also several other good essays, particularly those dealing with conservative thought.

Mehrabian, Albert, *Silent Messages* (Belmont, Calif.: Wadsworth Publishing Co., 1971). Mehrabian's book is a brief, highly readable, and enjoyable discussion of various aspects of nonverbal communication. His book takes much research conducted since Hall's early writings into account and is thus an up-to-date and informative source. Students interested in the persuasive effects of nonverbal cues should make Mehrabian's book must reading.

Morris, Desmond, *The Naked Ape: A Zoologist's Study of the Human Animal* (New York: McGraw-Hill Book Co., 1967). This book became popular along with the explosion of interest in nonverbal communication in the late 1960s. It is sometimes technical, but provides excellent insights into some nonverbal characteristics of human behavior. The book may give you a look into the symbolic impulse discussed in Chapter 2 (e.g., though chimps enjoy scribbling, as children do, they never move beyond the drawing back and forth stage to draw symbols such as faces). The discussion of physical responses to various emotions relates to our discussion of nonverbal communication.

Wills, Garry, *Nixon Agonistes: The Crisis of the Self-Made Man* (Boston: Houghton Mifflin Co., 1970). This book, critical of Nixon, is an excellent source for instances of the belief in cultural myths (see, for example, Wills's chapters on "The Common Man" or "The Hero," or "The Succeeder," or "Making It") and the articulation of the core values cited by Steele and Redding. The book will also be of help in studying persuasive campaigns. Wills is not very objective about Nixon, but his style is enjoyable, the examples interesting, and much of the criticism is deserved. It also sheds light on motives behind Watergate.

7

The Persuasive
Campaign or Movement

With rare exception, significant changes in attitude, behavior, belief, or action are probably not the result of a "single shot" or single message appeal. If this were the case, persuasion would be hopeless. It would imply that people are so fickle and changeable that they bounce from pro to con minute by minute; and it would be meaningless to try to persuade them to anything, for at any time another persuader could happen along, deliver a single message, and undo all the work done by the first persuader. People are just not that susceptible to single persuasive attempts; they do not sway from pro to con and back again on the slim basis of single messages. They do consider courses of action at length before acting. Of course, all of you can think of cases in which you were "persuaded" by a single message—in an instant, so to speak (e.g., you decided to date or not to date a certain person as the result of a single conversation with him or her, you became convinced of the power of an institution as the result of participating in a demonstration, or a particular teacher was able to open a whole new perspective to you in a single lecture). Most of the time, these instances are not really the result of the single incident you remember. Rather, you were intentionally or unintentionally prepared for the message that changed you—you were exposed to a variety of pieces of information, and the combined effect of them led to your change of mind. In unsophisticated ways and perhaps in unplanned ways you were the recipient of a series of messages that could be called a "campaign." The series led to your decision, not the single message. That is the point—most persuasion occurs as the result of a multitude of message inputs, as the result of a campaign or movement and not as the result of a single well-planned speech. This chapter focuses on this all-important persuasive system—how it works, how it develops, how it relates to the people who work in and respond to it, and on how we, as persuadees, can listen to, analyze, and critique the various campaigns and movements that continually occur around us.

Functional and Formal Aspects of Campaigns and Movements

To investigate the persuasive campaign or movement, we need to look at the key elements that differentiate campaigns and movements from other methods of persuasion. These elements ought to be fairly consistent and similar from movement to movement and from campaign to campaign—and we will look at several of these "universals." Generally, they can be divided into two groups: the first and most important type of universal is the *functional aspect* of campaigns and movements; the second is the *formal aspect*. The functional aspects are those strategic and broad elements that shape the thrust and direction of the movement or campaign; and there are at least two of them. Although there are a variety of formal elements in campaigns or movements, we are concerned here with only one—the *system* of communication used by movements or campaigns.

Functional Aspects

A campaign is different from a series of messages, all of which deal with the same topic or issue. And it is also different from a debate over an issue that may include a variety of information and evidence. What makes the campaign different? One of the differences is that campaigns and movements are *developmental* in nature; that is, they move from stage to stage in fairly orderly fashion—they have a beginning, middle, and end, so to speak. A second characteristic, related to the developmental aspect, is that campaigns and movements must, if they are to succeed, create a sense of the dramatic in the mind's eye of their audiences. (We dealt briefly with this topic in Chapter 5, when we discussed the power of the narrative as evidence.) Movements or campaigns need to depict their cause as one of historic and exciting magnitude, and then they need to invite others to attend to the drama—to join the historic and to share in the great cause in some real or symbolic way.

These two functional characteristics work well together, for the ideal developmental format is one that is also dramatically suitable. It is as if we are seeing a television serial when we watch a movement or campaign; each of its daily "dramas" ultimately leads to the conclusion of the serial. Each "episode" contributes to the overall result of the campaign or movement, and though the episodes can stand alone (each has its own beginning, middle, and end), they draw on one another, rely on one another, and meld into one another until the collage is completed.

Formal Aspects

As already noted, a campaign or movement is not just a collection of messages about the same topic. Not only is this true functionally; it is also true of the formal aspects of campaign persuasion. Here, the thing that differentiates campaign communication from haphazardly collected communication is the *systematic* flow of information and communication through four basic steps. These four steps are analogous to the systematic steps taken by a computer as it processes information: (1) *programming,* (2) information *input and dispersal,* (3) *re-formation* of the information, and (4) the end product of the newly arranged information—the *representation* to the audience of the campaign's central cause.

In what follows, we will first look at the two universals of campaign communication—the formal and the functional—from a theoretical perspective. Then we will look at several campaigns and movements, applying the trends discovered to particular campaigns and movements. For this reason, we shall wait until Chapter 8 to look at political campaigns, protest movements, and other cases of sustained and repeated persuasion. You may want to explore the characteristics of campaigning in much more depth, perhaps by reading accounts of various campaigns, perhaps by participating in one, perhaps even by planning and conducting one. The same for movements—you may wish to read about one or to join and perhaps conduct part of one.

To repeat what must now be a familiar injunction, the student of persuasion must devote time to discovering *how to be persuaded* far more diligently than he needs to discover how to persuade. In finding how we ourselves are affected and swayed by persuasive campaigns, we ought to be able to see trends we can utilize in our own campaigns, whatever they might be—to object to a college or university policy, to get a particular job in the student senate, to change the minds and actions of groups of other persons, or even something as mundane as getting parental support for the purchase of a car or for the right to live in one's own lifestyle.

Campaigns in America

Basically, there are three kinds of movements or campaigns that predominate in America and perhaps elsewhere in the world, too. They are the *politically oriented campaign* for office, the *product-oriented advertising campaign,* and the *issue-* or *cause-oriented social movement or campaign.* At first glance you may think that first and last types are not really different; for the most part, however, political campaigns focus on candidates and not on particular philosophical issues. They are campaigns with the ultimate goal of winning the audience to believe that a particular person is more trustworthy, sincere, wise, resourceful, active, or charismatic than another, while the issue-oriented movement or campaign is concerned with getting audiences to support a certain course of action or to embrace a certain belief.[1] As such, the issue-oriented campaign does not rely on a single leader, and its leadership may shift, with first one individual rising to prominence and then another and with neither the ultimate spokesman for the cause. We might distinguish between the three types of campaigns by saying that the first tries to convince the audience of the value of a man; the second tries to convince the audience of the value of a thing or object; and the third tries to convince the audience of the value or goodness of an idea, a belief, or an ideology. *Person, thing,* and *idea* are the three key words that differentiate these major types of campaigns. We will concentrate on person and idea here, though we shall refer from time to time to advertising campaigns oriented toward products, or things; and it should be noted that many of the characteristics of the person and the idea campaigns relate closely to product-oriented advertising campaigns.

The information discussed here can be used and thought of in connection with campaigns for particular offices in student government organizations or in groups like fraternities or perhaps offices like the campus newspaper. Idea campaigns relate to student attempts to stop tuition hikes, for example, or to religious movements on campuses. In the early 1970s, the Campus Crusade for Christ campaigned on one campus for attendance to listen to a speaker called "Josh," who dis-

---

[1] A good discussion of the differences between the issue and the image of candidates for political office and what that difference implies is available in "Political Myth: Images and Issues in Political Rhetoric" by Dan F. Hahn and Ruth M. Gonchar, *Today's Speech, 20* (Summer 1972), 57–65. Hahn and Gonchar conclude that the image may well be the best indicator of a candidate's future behavior. Issues change and fade, they maintain, but image indicates a pattern of behavior independent of issues.

cussed sex and prophecy—two topics likely to draw a good audience. Though that campaign featured a person, the message was related to an idea associated with the group. In fact, the CCC often angered persons who came to see or hear a particular person (in the past the organization had used illusionists, magicians, former prisoners, etc.) but mostly were subjected to idea-oriented preaching.

Developmental Nature of Campaigns

One of the functional universals that applies to all three types of campaigns is that they are *developmental.* They do not run on the same level or pitch throughout; they do not repeatedly pound away on the same pieces of information; they do not always have the same strategy at various times in their existence. Instead, successful campaigns grow and change and adapt to the change in audience response to them, and as new information and issues become apparent. You might think of it as a fishing expedition in which the strategists of the campaign try in various ways to get the attention of the audience by using different strategies or methods or lures. If one method does not succeed after some use, they try another and perhaps another. As the mood of the audience develops, the mood of the persuasion must also change. The whole thing must be orchestrated so that each shift is reasonable and follows from what preceded it.

For instance, suppose you are hired to establish product X (say, a new kind of building material) in the public eye—to get across the idea that this is the greatest, most impressive development in construction since the steel beam. What would you do first? Think about it. What would you do next? Why? You see, you would not haphazardly go about trying first this method of getting an audience and then that method. Instead, you would carefully contemplate what kinds of points you would want to make about this new product, what kinds of persons would be interested in it, what their values and beliefs about construction probably are, how you could reach them, and several other strategic questions. Now suppose, after your first advertising attempt, you discover that you have miscalculated terribly—people are not, as you originally believed, interested in durability of the product but are much more impressed by its cost. You will have to shift your strategy, but you would never have discovered the variance between what you thought was important to persons building a home and what was actually important if you hadn't first tried to focus on durability. The discovery will affect your next decisions concerning the marketing of the product.

This same kind of adaptation occurs in all campaigns. Campaign planners adapt to their audiences' responses.

Five Stages of Development

Well, how do campaigns develop? There are several possible answers to this question, depending on the theory you begin with. For instance, at one time Theodore H. White seemed to believe that it was the sophisticated and carefully calculated use of the mass media that led to the successful creation of an "image" that could be elected, and that the development of a campaign could be traced through the development of a communication system between the candidate and the press.[2] Four years later, in 1964, he saw the developmental nature of the political campaign as the ongoing revelation of an individual's own potential and worth through the challenge to the daring and imagination of the electorate.[3] Four years later still, White saw the developmental nature of the political campaign as somehow linked to the ability to explain, step-by-step, the chaos and change surrounding the audience.[4]

One particularly interesting developmental theory comes from scholars of national development, or the development of emerging nations, such as Leonard Binder.[5] They suggest that there are five steps in the political development of a national image or character: identity, legitimacy, participation, penetration, and distribution. Logically, each stage must be accomplished before the next can develop and emerge successfully.

Identity For instance, suppose that Transylvania has just declared itself a nation after having seceded from Greater Transylvania. The first step in its development is somehow to characterize itself, metaphorically so to speak, to give itself a mask that will represent what it is to the rest of the world. The new nation must seek an *identity*. There are several ways to do this—Transylvania may design a flag, it may

---

[2] See Theodore H. White's *The Making of the President: 1960* (New York: Atheneum Publishers, 1961). This volume was the first to deal comprehensively with the candidates in a presidential election. It won the Pulitzer Prize in 1961.

[3] See Theodore H. White's *The Making of the President: 1964* (New York: Atheneum Publishers, 1965).

[4] See Theodore H. White's *The Making of the President: 1968* (New York: Atheneum Publishers, 1969).

[5] Leonard Binder, et al., *Crisis and Sequence in Political Development*, (Princeton, N. J.: Princeton University Press, 1971), especially Ch. 1. I wish to thank William Semlak for calling this source to my attention; Mr. Semlak utilized the suggestions offered by the volume to analyze the campaign of George McGovern for the Democratic nomination in 1972 in a paper for a seminar in Movements and Campaigns offered at the University of Minnesota in the summer of 1972. Professor Bernard L. Brock, who taught the seminar, was kind enough to let me join it while I was a visiting professor there in 1972.

develop hero myths, or it may engage in certain actions like wars or building projects.

A movement must do the same thing. Initially a campaign or movement must establish its identity—it must give to the uninformed audience it wishes to persuade some kind of handle or label by which it can be identified. The Black Power movement developed such things as a name, a flag, a salute, a handshake, a hairstyle, and a style of dress.[6] It also developed a certain style of persuasion and certain characteristic issues and methods of presenting them (e.g., speakers in favor of Black Power often used a stereotyped "Nigra" accent to remind audiences of white attitudes toward blacks and to signal to the audience that they, too, were able to "put on" white society). Speakers utilized threats or the implication of violence to excite their black audiences and to speak emphatically to their white auditors. And there are numerous other examples of the development of style in the Black Power movement.

An individual campaign to get parental support for an off-campus apartment must gain attention or identity. A student might appeal to his parents, saying that now that he is legally allowed to drink and get married, he thinks that he could also live off campus. The attention-getting devices identify the cause or object of the campaign. A movement to get a pass-fail grading system introduced might be pushed by several disparate and uncoordinated groups, but still the first step is to gain attention or to get an identity through a name or a slogan.

Product campaigns must do the same thing—they must develop an identity with an audience. The new cigarette designed for women must choose a name (e.g., Virginia Slim or Eve) and an appropriate package and size. These characteristics are emphasized throughout the identity stage of the campaign through mass-media advertisement. Things like the name, the size, and the appropriateness of this cigarette for women are repeatedly called to the consumer's attention; and finally, the product has an identity. The politician also repeatedly seeks to establish an identity for himself. For instance, in the presidential campaign of 1972, George McGovern spent a year establishing an identity for himself as a "man of principles," the carrier of the mantle of Robert Kennedy, as the ideal of youth, and as the prophet of the "New Politics." A recreational land developer must capture attention and get an identity with potential customers. One such developer used the name of Pat Boone to get attention, preceding the name of each development with the singer's name—Pat Boone's Desert Carmel, for instance.

Legitimacy   The second of the five related stages, according to Binder, is to establish a base of *legitimacy* for the now clearly

---

[6] For example, hair and clothing style reflected this new pride and independence —the Afro and daishiki are examples, and later the uniform of the Black Panthers.

defined identity. Transylvania, having established itself as a nation with an identity, may seek alliances, entrance to the United Nations, industrial and commercial agreements, and so forth. All of these give the country a *legitimacy* or a kind of credibility, which is meant to signal that Transylvania is not a fly-by-night operation, that it is a force to be reckoned with. In a sense, the establishment of legitimacy is another way of saying that the movement or campaign demonstrates that it has *power* to support its identity. For the commercial product, a certain threshold of sales may be the legitimacy criterion (e.g., Volkswagen was not able to convince Detroit that it was a "legitimate" threat until it sold close to a half-million vehicles a year—then the industry began to design its own compacts and subcompacts). The Black Power movement of the late 1960s demonstrated that it had power by repeated references to past destruction (e.g., Watts, Detroit, the riots following the assassination of Martin Luther King, Jr.). The credibility or the legitimacy of the Black Power movement prompted such things as governmental programs, laws against incitement to riot, and original charges brought against several Black Power advocates.

A parallel pattern occurred following the Student Power movement of the early 1970s. Legitimacy was demonstrated by the "occupation" or "liberation" of pieces of university property—classrooms, offices, files, flags, and in some cases even deans. That the demonstration of legitimacy was credible is shown by the responses made to it (e.g., student involvement on boards of regents, introduction of nongraded or pass-fail classes, coed dorms, and so forth). The political campaign demonstrates that it has legitimate identity by allying itself with power figures or centers (e.g., the candidate usually is photographed after nomination with all the leadership of his party, no matter how distasteful it may be for him to be seen with his former enemies). The candidate may also choose to demonstrate how his power works, thus convincing the doubtful that he is "legitimate." The student, mentioned earlier, who wishes to campaign for an off-campus apartment establishes a kind of legitimacy or power when he gets a summer job that will allow him to earn his college costs or when he joins ranks with several fellow students who can share apartment costs and help in the persuasive process. The student running for fraternity president establishes legitimacy when fellow group members begin to support him, just as the challenger in a political campaign demonstrates legitimacy when he gets support from the electorate.

In a sense, the incumbent in any election has already demonstrated that he has power; he is in the catbird seat and doesn't need to show his legitimacy. The challenger, particularly in our system of political decision making, is in much more difficult straits. He must first defeat all other challengers to be nominated (he establishes a sort of "apprentice" legitimacy here), and he must also demonstrate his primary legitimacy during the campaign per se. John Kennedy did not do this until the famed "Great Debates" were televised; Goldwater never did establish it; George

Wallace demonstrated his legitimacy by running well in primaries and opinion polls in Northern states and through rallies with huge crowds; McGovern demonstrated his clout on the floor of the convention over the delegate challenges—but after the nomination he was never again able to demonstrate such legitimacy, for he really had only the titular trappings of legitimacy, and he was rebuffed by potentially powerful backers—the president of the AFL-CIO and the party leaders of several large cities and states. This disadvantage, which operates against challengers, perhaps best explains why incumbents are so hard to defeat and why the status quo, regardless of what it is, is so difficult to change.

Participation   The third stage of the five logically related states of development is very similar to the second stage and flows directly out of it. This stage—*participation*—involves more and more people in the campaign or movement in real or symbolic ways. The persons likely to support the campaign or movement are "invited" to join in the activity. They may be asked to fly the flag of Transylvania or join its army or diplomatic corps or to open their houses to foreign tourists, all so that the new country can become better known. They may be asked to share in some project or some challenge—a five-year plan, a redistribution of wealth, or some other change.

Commercially, the distributors and users of products may be asked to participate in the use and profit of the product. Coupon offers may be made to consumers—they buy and use the product and receive money or gifts over and above the actual cost of the product. In some cases distributors are paid for allowing some of their space to be used for special displays of certain soaps, wines, and so forth; or the dealer may get a cut rate for pushing a certain product. Similarly, a movement may ask its followers to participate in real or symbolic ways; women may be asked to stop doing housework in a one-day "strike" for women's rights (the slogan of the women's day strike in 1971 was "Don't iron while the strike is hot!"). In other cases participants may be asked to wear arm bands or badges, to yell slogans at rallies, or to put signs around their homes or on their automobile bumpers. Supposedly, during World War II, it was difficult to get bread sliced at bakeries, and the reason given for the difficulty was to conserve electricity for the war effort. In actuality, the electricity thus saved was never devoted to the war effort, but participation in this symbolic way on the part of the average man was supposed to increase his commitment to the war. The same sorts of stories are told about the scrap collections, the saving of tinfoil, lard, and tin cans. A person running for student body president may ask persons to participate in his campaign by canvassing dormitory floors or student groups. In the Campus Crusade for Christ rally, mentioned earlier, many students were asked to distribute literature and urge others to attend. This kind of participation gets one committed to the campaign or movement and guarantees the active and involved association of the participants. Movements ask supporters to *do* something, even if it is only symbolic, to demonstrate support. The psychological effects of such participation are to increase commitment to the cause and to activate the kind of self-persuasion discussed in Chapter 4.

The political campaign is particularly demonstrative of this participative phase of a campaign. Workers are asked to wear campaign buttons, use the candidate's pencils, nail files, or match packs, apply his bumper stickers to their cars, canvass for him, give money to him, come to dinners for him, and do other acts—all designed to give support to the candidate and more importantly to get the persons actively involved. The author once offered to purchase all ten barbeque tickets given to him to sell if only he didn't have to go to the rally. The offer was refused, and the explanation was that that would do no good—no one was making money on the rally, that it was a breakeven affair—but its purpose was to get persons involved. The purpose of the participation stage is probably twofold: first, it gets participants actively involved and committed to the cause; and second, it underscores the legitimacy of the campaign or movement. Thus, stage three is an extension and an undergirding of the legitimacy stage of a movement or campaign.

Penetration   Stage four—the *penetration* stage—is the most difficult to explain. Think of it this way: Suppose that you are totally unaware of some movement—say, consumerism—and you begin to be exposed to it. You probably first hear about the movement after stages one, two, or three have already been accomplished. At any rate, you are part of the mass of people who will never actively engage in the movement. You will never be the person who brings consumer charges against a product; you will never organize a boycott of inferior products. Instead, you are the recipient of the messages and effects of the movement. Nonetheless, the movement needs your silent support, for without it the persons involved will remain a minority to those who resist the movement. This minority status, shared by all movements and campaigns if we refer only to active participation, must be balanced with a substantial feeling of support among "the people" who are "out there." Various terms have been coined to suggest this supportive sentiment in politics—"the grass roots," "a ground swell of support," "political awareness," and "the silent majority." The penetration stage of a movement or campaign, or that time span when the uncommitted and inactive majority becomes aware of the movement, is the stage that generates an attitude toward the movement—hopefully favorable, but sometimes negative—and reflects this attitude in some way. The reflection may be response on a poll, recognition of the name of a product, awareness of the issues surrounding a certain product, or perhaps the realization of the presence and goals of a candidate. In a sense, the penetration stage is that stage—after the movement or campaign has already established its identity and legitimacy and has engaged the active support of a number of participants—when it moves to impose itself upon the general consciousness of the public.

Though these steps seem distinct and clear, they often merge and flow, usually sequentially, from one to another. The steps flow in a *logical* sequence from one to another, but there are occasions when stages may so merge as to become indistinguishable—and this may occur concurrently or in very rapid sequence. Ultimately, every campaign aims at the penetration stage. The real point at which penetration occurs is when the movement or campaign has succeeded and has power. Transylvania may try again and again to be recognized by the United Nations as a free and separate state—it may invent flags, slogans, and myths; it may get active volunteers for its government—but until it convinces enough persons that it ought to be recognized as a full-fledged nation, it has not succeeded in its penetration. A product may be identified, legitimized, and may even get participation in its campaign; but until it reaches the kind of threshold that Volkswagen reached in the 1950s, it has not penetrated. A candidate for public office may become identified as a certain kind of character (a man of principles, a man with credibility, and so forth), and he may even demonstrate his legitimacy by having large rallies, winning primaries, and identifying himself with power personages or power organizations. He may also get wide participation, with hundreds of volunteers actively working for him; but until he establishes his program and his personage on significant numbers of the large uncommitted and perhaps uninformed mass of the electorate, he has not penetrated.

A movement may go through the same initial stages of getting an identification and a kind of legitimacy or power, coupled with highly active participation on the part of some of its followers; but until a large proportion of the masses supports it or until the movement achieves the change in the status quo which it desires, it too has failed to complete the penetration stage of development. For example, until the Bolsheviks threw out the democratic Duma, or parliament, which followed the abdication of the Czar, they had not achieved penetration. They probably never had a majority of popular opinion on their side, as witnessed by the numerous counterrevolutions and the "Reds" versus the "Whites." At the same time, they did manage to change the status quo—they reached the penetration stage.

In a different case, a majority of persons in the United States probably supported the economic changes initiated by President Roosevelt in the 1930s. Though he did not really "overthrow" the status quo, he did achieve a ground swell of public support that was equivalent to a repudiation of another system of economic policy—he achieved *penetration*. This stage may also be reached in the campaign for an off-campus apartment when one's parents begin to offer less and less resistance to

THE EXISTING STATE OF AFFAIRS

the idea and when they begin to identify reasons of their own for allowing their child to live outside the dorm (it's cheaper, handier, and so
forth). Some products establish a penetration stage rapidly. For example,
Tide, the washing product, was the first detergent to come on the market
in the 1950s. The difference between Tide and soap products was so
obvious that it quickly became the top-selling wash product, thus establishing penetration in a short time. The rotary engine first marketed
by Mazda is another example. Its success created pressure for introduction of similar engine types into American-made autos.

Distribution   In the fifth and final stage of development—
distribution—the campaign or movement becomes institutionalized. That
is, having achieved the control they sought, the leaders of the campaign
or movement must now live up to their promises in some way. They
must make moves that signal to the populace that, with the goal achieved
and with the heights conquered, change is beginning to occur. The likely
moves are the designation of subgroups of the campaign staff or of the
movement's leadership to positions of power with various tasks to complete. These tasks must be consistent with the promises made in the
campaign or with the goals of the movement. This stage probably does
not occur in the object-oriented campaign involving products that are
being sold; but, in the emerging nation, the new government begins land
reform for the peasants, court reform, changes in the social and economic structure, and other changes to indicate that power previously
held by the status quo and its representatives is now being divided and
delivered to the people, the faithful, the party, or the movement leadership.

Unfortunately, this stage is rarely instituted except in symbolic ways.
The overthrow of slavery in 1865 didn't result in a change in the status
of most Negroes in the South; the Black Codes were instituted, and
reconstruction officials neglected to institute much meaningful change
in the daily lives of most former slaves. Following the overthrow of
Fulgencio Batista by Fidel Castro in Cuba, little land redistribution
actually took place. The distribution stage, so it seems, usually contains
within itself the seeds of its own ultimate destruction; by setting itself
up into bureaus, by institutionalizing itself, it is open to the same kinds
of criticism leveled at the old order or the defeated incumbent. Perhaps
that is why most Americans view party platforms with such a jaundiced
eye and why you often hear people say something like "It doesn't make
any difference who gets in; politicians are all crooks anyway."

The first of the *functional* aspects of campaigns and movements,
then, is that they are *developmental* in nature. They go through various
stages, each of which is logically related to each other. Usually these
stages flow sequentially, but at times they may meld into one another.

Nonetheless, the stages must all occur for a campaign or movement to be complete.

As you observe campaigns underway for public office or as you witness movements being conducted to institute some kind of change in social thought or behavior, you ought to be able to identify their developmental stages. The only developmental difference between campaigns and movements is that while the political campaign focuses on the developing image of a *person*, the movement develops acceptance of an *ideology* or lifestyle, and the advertiser develops acceptance and use of an *object*. All three follow the developmental stages of *identification, legitimacy, participation, penetration*, and *distribution*. Many campaigns and movements never reach full bloom and may be stymied at the participation or penetration stage, and most advertising campaigns never do reach the final stage. Social and political movements, upon reaching this stage, usually distribute the power and privilege wrested from the opposition only superficially. Thus, as a movement or campaign develops, it sets for itself not only its next stage of development but ultimately the raw material for a countermovement or countercampaign. This developmental aspect of campaigns is particularly suited for the second *functional* characteristic of campaigns—their reliance upon the dramatic metaphor.

Invitation to the Drama

We have already talked in several places about the importance of the symbolic and dramatic impulse in human beings. We see the world and identify its motivating forces in ordered ways, and our position has been that the most effective and common form of ordering has been the *dramatic episode*. It is interesting to observe in our own lives how often we tend to structure the world in episodal ways: We see meals as having a "plot line," with beginnings sometimes introduced by prayers; certainly as typified by certain foods like salads followed by other courses in a neat, orderly progression to the "peroration" of dessert and perhaps an after-dinner liqueur with coffee. We see our work days as divided into episodes: first-hour class, opening-the-mail time, morning meeting, and others. We see our weeks ordered the same way: Wednesday is sometimes called "humpday," since we get over the halfway point. And we see those around us as actors in the drama. Our parents may be villains and our friends heroes and heroines. Others around us are engaging in apple polishing to get on the good side of the teacher or boss. Our latest job is populated with classic stereotypes—the gossip, the bitter old-timer, the good-natured fellow, the footloose and fancy-free jokester, and so on. This impulse for the dramatic and the momentous is deep and powerful; this characteristic desire to see the world as a drama is one of the universals that link movements and campaigns. In fact, unless a movement or campaign can create a dramatic event or pseudo event, in a dramatic situation or on a dramatic stage, it has little chance of capturing the attention and support of the number of persons it needs. The success of a movement or campaign is dependent upon its ability to create in the minds of its audience the sense of a momentous and incredibly important event or series of events, which must be lived out successfully or else the whole world and all people involved will suffer disastrously. Given the creation of such a drama, the movement or campaign succeeds to the degree that it can also invite the audience to participate in the drama in real or symbolic ways.

Let us look at the dramatic impulse. What is it that creates a sense of the dramatic? How are dramatic elements utilized by persuaders? How do the elements occur? What effects do they have, and what effects have they had in past campaigns or movements?

The first thing we need is a setting or *scene*, to use Burke's terms (see Chapter 3), with at least some dramatic potential. For instance, someone's backyard may have dramatic possibilities, but they are limited. A posh New York nightclub or an impressive apartment or perhaps a deserted junkyard all obviously have dramatic possibilities much broader than the backyard scene.

Given a dramatic scene, we now need the second element—*characters*. To keep it simple, let's limit our characters initially to the good guys and their helpers and the bad guys and their helpers. We need to see our dramatic scene filled with opposing forces that are going to do battle. The forces may be two countries (as was the case in the space race and the arms race utilized by John Kennedy in 1960); the forces may be two systems of economics (as was the case in the 1971 discussions over wage and price controls); it may be between two lifestyles (as is the case in the differences between children of the counterculture and their parents). In any case, a drama necessitates opposing forces—of good and evil, of wisdom and folly, of youth and age, and so forth. Going back to the stylistic attributes of persuasion in Chapter 3, we find that Weaver's notion of "God Terms" and "Devil Terms" relates here. The persuader creates the dramatic mood he desires by choosing hierarchies or families of terms that delineate the good guys and the bad guys in his drama.

The third element of the dramatic characteristic that is common to movements and campaigns is a *plot*. Most movement or campaign plots are also simple. The weak are exploited, and a hero arises in their midst to lead them to liberty (e.g., the Civil Rights movement of the 1960s and its heroes—Martin Luther King, Jr., James Meredith, etc.). Another variation may be the one in which a group is exploited, and through some event becomes aware or conscious of the exploitation, and then as a group tries to overthrow the exploitation (e.g., the Antiwar movement,

the Black Panther party, and so forth). A plot for many dramas is the
search for some goal of high value and the troubles accompanying the
search (e.g., the Horatio Alger myth is such a plot; or the search for
peace in Vietnam carried on by opposing groups or individuals such as
Nixon, McCarthy, and McGovern; or the search for a new style of life,
as exemplified by the movement to communes, natural food, ecology, and
others).[7] We could go on citing numerous examples of dramatic plots,
but generally they are subplots of three or four major lines of action:

1. The overcoming of odds by a group or under the leadership of a
   hero (Franklin D. Roosevelt, the nomination of George McGovern,
   or the legal conviction of an industrial polluter)
2. The quest for a goal or to avoid a pitfall (the Horatio Alger myth)
3. The establishment of long-needed change by a group or through a
   leader (civil rights, women's liberation, the change in grading procedure)
4. The purgation of symbolic *sin* in our midst, or of the removal of
   an evil man, situation, and so on (movements for the consumer or
   for ecological issues)[8]

If one has the raw materials of the drama at hand in the setting or
situation, in the characters, and in the plot, the task of the persuader is
then to utilize the raw material in such a way as to invite the potential
supporter of the movement or campaign to enter into the dramatic setting, to do battle with or to lend support to the characters of the drama,
and to act out a part of the plot line. In this way, the *participation* stage
mentioned earlier is fulfilled, and each supporter of the movement or
campaign feels that he has given of himself and has shared in the victory.
His actions are ego-rewarding, as he sees his efforts to register voters
pay off or as he sees some authority figure lose his temper because of
comments or chanting by the movement supporter. In other words, his
actions become part of the whole artistic collage of the movement or
campaign's themes. He engages in the drama as in a work of art.

Unfortunately, many movements are severely hampered by their
disparate elements, and the drama has difficulty in unifying. At other
times, leaders of the movement or campaign seem unwilling to invite

---

[7] An excellent analysis of this plot line was made by Herman Stelzner, "The
Quest Story of Nixon's November 3, 1969 Address," *Quarterly Journal of Speech*, 57
(April 1971), 163–172. See also contemporary discussions of change such as Charles
Reich's *The Greening of America* (New York: Random House, 1970), Philip Slater's
The Pursuit of Loneliness (Boston: Beacon Press, 1970), and Eldridge Cleaver's
Soul on Ice (New York: Delta Books, 1968).
[8] See Kenneth Burke's *The Rhetoric of Religion* (Boston: Beacon Press, 1961).
"The Epilogue in Heaven" is especially instructive on this point. For three political
plot lines, see Murray Edelman, *Politics as Symbolic Action* (Chicago: Markham
Publishing Co., 1971), pp. 77–79; see also Edelman, *The Symbolic Uses of Politics*
(Urbana: University of Illinois Press, 1967).

participation—they prefer to dwell on ideology or on personal praise for themselves or invective for others. The mudslinging campaign, though interesting for its "fight" aspects (everyone likes to see a scrap), is a risky kind of campaign to run. There is a high risk that it will backfire, bringing the audience to oppose the persuader who is calling names or trying to set up a dramatic "fight" for persuasive purposes. At the same time the mudslinger is besmirching his adversary, he seems to be praising himself. Both arguments are what Aristotle called the *ad hominem*—to the personality or about the man—and audiences are highly suspicious, it seems, of people who compliment themselves while attacking others.[9] The whole strategy seems to reek of self-interest and egotism.

Dramas may also fail to materialize in the audience's eye because leaders focus on ideology and not on the dramatic. Often, the philosophical assumptions of a particular movement or of a particular candidate are not very interesting, except in an abstract "ivory-tower" way. Instead, people want to see assumptions *lived out* and acted out in front of their eyes. Take, for example, the bizarre incident during the presidential campaign of 1972 when Martha Mitchell, the wife of the then Attorney General and chairman of the Committee to Re-Elect the President claimed that she had been beaten and drugged by members of the President's campaign staff and that they had forcibly entered her apartment, scuffled with her, and given her a sedative. When she tried to use the telephone to call for help, the same persons ripped the phone from the wall. She went on to say that she had information they would not want made public and hinted that it related to the wiretapping of the Democratic Party Headquarters. The incident has within it all the elements of a first-rate soap opera. There is the dramatic setting—the apartment of a high government official who is charged with investigating and prosecuting the perpetrators of federal crimes. There are opposing forces—a spunky, outspoken, and almost delightful heroine, and thuglike "enforcers," who may represent the man her husband works for. And we have the potential for a spy-story plot of undercover and double agents trying to trick and outwit one another while trying to cover the tracks of their own federal crime. In other words, all the raw materials are there for a first-rate drama to which the audience could attend. Furthermore, the drama contained within it the kinds of links to philosophical issues that

— EMPIRICAL

---

[9] A good example of the kind of reaction that can be generated when one uses the *ad hominem* is this excerpt from an editorial from the *Chicago Daily News*, October 10, 1972, p. 18 (the *Daily News* is a liberal paper that endorsed John Kennedy, Lyndon Johnson, and Hubert Humphrey): "When McGovern called the Nixon administration the 'most corrupt' in two centuries, he simply went beyond what the public was willing to swallow. More than that, he harmed his own image, with a lot of people feeling that a truly nice fellow wouldn't go around saying such things. . . . So the Democratic candidate appears, once more, to be the victim of the kind of injudicious advice and/or poor judgment that have plagued his campaign since July."

would be ideally fit for a presidential campaign: dishonesty in government, exploitation of individual rights by the government, and government by secrecy. Yet, the McGovern campaign staff never chose to focus on this issue, though later investigation upheld much of what was only hinted at in the Martha Mitchell playlet. Instead, the McGovern strategists chose to focus more on ideological and less dramatic issues and events (the cost of the candidate's welfare reform, the amount of defense spending to be cut, and so forth).[10] Though we can't argue that this choice resulted in the defeat of McGovern, we can say that the incident was clearly a dramatic one, which could have been used to emphasize the philosophical issues associated with McGovern, and we can point out that the issues actually being discussed were more mundane and "boring" for the average voter.[11]

A second characteristic of movements and campaigns, then, is their tendency to succeed when they focus on the dramatic—when they act out their ideology instead of pedantically espousing it. When action invites the audience to the drama in real or symbolic ways, the movement becomes vitalized and attractive. It succeeds to the degree that it is able to avoid the overstatement and abstract espousal of its ideology and to the degree that it can present potential followers of the movement with a sense of historic and dramatic events, which are theirs if they will only follow the movement and its leaders. Hitler's invitation to the German people to join him as he sought Germany's "place in the sun" was such a use of dramatic metaphor; Martin Luther King, Jr.'s invitation to join in his "dream" was another.

When a movement gathers momentum and begins to have effect, the receiver can probably detect other similar dramatic invitations. Though the more ordinary sustained persuasive campaigns do not focus on high drama so obviously, they do nonetheless rely on dramatic raw material. The student trying to get a trip to Europe subsidized may outline the dramatic dangers of staying home during a boring summer, or he may highlight the dramatic potential of exposing oneself to other cultures and languages and of possible advantages that might accrue from exposure (e.g., he may be able to write columns for his hometown newspaper, or he may get a better job later because of the experience). Many product campaigns rely on dramatic input also—many commercials are, in fact, mini-dramas. For example, a girl rushes out of a restaurant crying be-

---

[10] When reporters first asked what her husband thought of the Watergate affair (the electronic bugging of Democratic National Headquarters), Mrs. Patricia Nixon responded: "I don't discuss it, because all I know is what I read in the newspapers"; and she noted that she didn't ". . . know anything about what happened in her [Mrs. Martha Mitchell's] room." *Time*, October 9, 1972, p. 17.

[11] Four weeks before the election, columnists noted voter apathy—people weren't bothering to get registered, weren't contributing money or attending rallies for candidates. William S. White attributed the disinterest not to apathy but ". . . it is likely a far more exact term would be sheer weariness," *Chicago Daily News*, October 8, 1972, Editorial Section, p. 8.

cause her boyfriend has told her that she has horrid-smelling breath. Her friend produces a magic potion in the form of a bottle of Breathsweet and saves the day. The final scene is at the next party where the two lovers gently nuzzle one another at "intimate distance." The story is a minor adaptation of the overcoming of great odds, a plot line already noted.

There are, then, *functional* aspects of campaigns and movements that shape and direct the thrust and course of the movement or campaign. They are the strategic moves campaigners or movement leaders make in attempting to attract supporters and believers. Though there may be many of these functional aspects, two of them—already discussed—are of interest to the persuadee, in that they provide him with a perspective for examining movements or campaigns: the *developmental* nature of the campaign or movement and the need for a *dramatic invitation* to be extended to the audience. These functional characteristics work well together, for the developmental flow of movements and campaigns seems particularly well-suited for dramatic episodes. At the same time, there are several *formal* aspects of campaigns and movements. Here, however, we will consider only one: *the use of communication in systematic ways.*

Power of a Communication System

The basic premise underlying the study of communication as an essential formal characteristic is that movements and campaigns seem to succeed to the degree that they *communicate systematically.*[12] We are not saying that movements succeed by communicating per se, but that they succeed when their communication is *systematic.* Let's look into this characteristic more deeply.

What is a communication system? Begin with what happens in a digital computer, and think about the flow of information from initial input to ultimate output. The computer is a communication system with great power—it communicates with itself and its users or audience in sequential ways. The planner or programmer establishes a path for the flow of communication in the machine, and he programs the "brain" of the machine to "think" in a certain way—to accept and process information in certain sequences. The next step is the introduction of informa-

---

[12] I wish to thank Professor Ernest G. Bormann of the University of Minnesota and the students in his 1972 summer seminar, "The 1972 Presidential Campaign as a Communication System," at the University of Minnesota, for many ideas discussed in this section.

tion or input, which begins to flow through the program. Next comes the processing of the information—the computing and coupling of the many small bits into a complete picture. At this stage, information may be stored in a memory, forgotten if necessary, or it may be sent to another part of the machine—for example, to the printer; that is, the information is dispersed in a variety of ways. Once the information has been sent to various parts of the system (the memory, central processing, etc.), it is considered and combined with other information in new ways and in new configurations—the information is "discussed" by the machine and the program. In a final step, the information (which has now been dispersed, regathered, and discussed) is abstracted and sent out of the system in the form of a printout. The printout does not contain each of the information bits; it does not contain the program of the machine; nor does it contain the combinations of information. It simply contains a new product or message or conclusion, based on all of the forms of information but separate from them.

The communication system in a campaign or movement is similar to that in a computer—we might even use the computer as one of a number of possible models when considering movement or campaign communication. At the initial stage, we find programmers or planners of the campaign or movement. He or they establish the routines by which information will be dispersed, combined, and considered. For instance, in a political campaign the candidate's staff and advance men establish the ways in which messages will be sent to the public (radio, television, newspapers, etc.); they set up speaking engagements and arrange for proper publicity; they prepare pamphlets for distribution; they arrange for rallies, press conferences, and news releases; and they coordinate the candidate's activities as much as possible. In other words, the staff, in conjunction with the candidate, act as programmers for the campaign.[13] The same thing occurs in an advertising campaign when an agency staff is charged with selling a certain product—they, too, determine media, style, occasion, and frequency of messages.

Even in less noticeable persuasive campaigns, we can see a systematic processing of information. For example, one of the ways to conduct a persuasive campaign to get a date with a certain person is to let a friend of the potential date know of one's intentions and hopes. The information input is thus programmed. Taken with the dropped hint, the "accidental" meeting of the potential date, and perhaps the offer of assistance to him or her on a class project, all act in dispersing the information throughout the system. Of course, the degree to which one is successful will be measured, ultimately, by what goes on in the possible

---

[13] For a good discussion of the details of this situation in political campaigns, see Dan Nimmo's *The Political Persuaders* (Englewood Cliffs, N. J.: Prentice-Hall, 1970).

date's mind. This same process can occur when one wants to convince an instructor to change the date of an examination. Several persons can come to the instructor at different times, with varied reasons for changing the date of the exam—there is to be an assembly that day, the debate squad will be out of town, or there are a lot of examinations scheduled for that day. There is a program, in effect, for introducing information or persuasive argument.

In a loosely organized and less disciplined movement, the programmer is of less import; nonetheless, in most movements a staff engages in planning the details and in trying to notify potential followers and the news media of events. A good example is the "Festival of Life" event in the movement against the war and against the Democratic party, planned and sponsored by a number of radical groups in 1968 during the Democratic convention. In fact, the assumption by officials of the city of Chicago was that the planning was coordinated and systematic enough to warrant charging eight persons with conspiracy to incite riot. So also with the campaign for a candidate, with the campaign for a particular product, and with the social movement for or against some change in the status quo, we see that the "programmer" plays a key role.

Given a program, information now can be handled by the dispersal machinery—the local offices of "Citizens for Senator Phogbound" can begin distributing literature, canvassing voters, running television and radio spots. Most of the local campaign headquarters for a presidential candidate do not know what the candidate's particular stands on particular issues are, and they are limited without this information. But in the *dispersal* stage, this information is made available. The same thing occurs in product-oriented campaigns—the local grocer does not know the details about a particular detergent being introduced on the market, so the manufacturer provides him with displays, posters, coupon advertisements, and television spot advertisements to disperse this information to various receivers. In the movement, the coordination is not as strict and systematic, but still pieces of information flow into the system and are dispersed to sectors of it. For example, during the Antiwar movement of the 1960s and 1970s, several "dispersal" organizations were established to spread information to various persons and areas of the country (e.g., Vietnam Veterans Against the War dispersed information to ex-servicemen and to popular audiences; the Coalition to End the War organized several demonstrations against the war and rallies in the nation's capital); and in doing so, they also dispersed information to various sectors of the movement. A group in one of my classes decided to try to get student support for passage of a local school-bond issue. Dispersal was an important element in the campaign planning of the group—they utilized a variety of means to get information spread throughout the student body (door-to-door solicitation, sing-along meetings that ended with explanation of the issue, access to the local cable-television station, and ultimately videotaping and broadcasting a television "documentary" focusing on the condition of schools, and use of the student newspaper and radio station). As noted earlier, the informal persuasive campaign for a date or for delay of an exam also uses various dispersal sources for persuasive information.

One of the most important elements in the dispersion process is the utilization of media, and this applies to movements, campaigns for political office, and product-oriented campaigns. The mass media are channels for the flow of information from programmers, through dispersal centers and to the public. As far back at 1896, and probably much earlier, the power to control these channels became important in presidential politics. In the election of 1896, large numbers of business interests poured in financial support for the faltering campaign of William McKinley. The interests feared William Jennings Bryan's proposal to go off the gold standard. The money was used to purchase newspaper space for the dispersal of information.[14] In the 1930s, with the advent of radio and the widespread use of automobiles, politicians like Huey Long were able to disperse information by utilizing handbills, posters, newspapers, and the radio. In fact, because of his media expertise, in 1936 Long was considered a serious threat as a potential third-party candidate for the presidency on the "Share the Wealth" ticket. Had he not been assassinated, the power of two media masters—Roosevelt and Long—might have been pitted against one another in a way that probably has not been possible since then.[15] Of course, we are all aware of the importance and power of television to disperse the information concerning a particular product, candidate, or movement, but perhaps we ought to look at how important it really is.

In 1950, only about 10 percent of American households had television sets—there were 4.2 million sets. By 1967, 95 percent of American households had television sets (there were 54.9 million sets and 58.2 million households). Furthermore, these sets were being used from three to six hours a day.[16] Clearly, when from one-sixth to one-third of a person's waking hours are spent receiving television messages, this machine has to be the most important channel for message dispersal available to persuaders. Although we will deal more with the power of various media and especially of television in another place, suffice it to say here that, in the dispersal stage, television is an essential and potent channel. The propensity of various movements, persons, and groups to try to attract

---

[14] "Quest for the Presidency," WBBM Radio, Chicago, October 14, 1972.

[15] T. Harry Williams, *Huey Long* (New York: Bantam Books, 1970), pp. 214, 660–661, 850–851. See also "A Rhetorical Analysis of the National Radio Broadcasts of Senator Huey P. Long," Doctoral dissertation by Ernest G. Bormann, University of Iowa, 1953. Long was a contender for the 1936 presidential election and was serious competition for F.D.R. in his ability to use media.

[16] As quoted in *The Image Candidates* by Eugene Wyckoff (New York: The Macmillan Co., 1968), pp. 12–13.

the attention of the television camera testifies to its power and may explain the tactics and strategy behind the use of violence, bizarre events, outlandish costumes, and other attention-getting devices (the staging of fights, the burning of flags, the use of nudity).

In campaigns or movements, programmers have least control over the third stage—or when information is "discussed" and recombined. In a digital computer, recombining and recalling information—putting it together in new configurations—is highly controlled. But in a campaign, the dispersed information is combined with competing information, past history, and other factors in the audience, whereas computers don't have this kind of interference. In campaigns, information is ultimately considered and combined, but not before it has been compared with many elements in a persuadee's image of the world.[17] Clearly, the campaign or movement planners and programmers cannot control the audience's image of the world. All they can do is hope that by exposing and re-exposing the audience to the same or similar pieces of information a number of times, they (the audience members) will incorporate all or part of the message into their image of the world. Of course, the information becomes more or less salient in each audience member's mind depending on the pieces he is exposed to, what his own self-interest happens to be, and such uncontrollable factors as whether he had just had an argument with his wife when he was exposed to the information or what his response might be to a particular kind of clothing worn by a candidate or spokesman. In movements, the philosophical view of life held by audience members plays a part (e.g., some women who oppose women's liberation do so because they view women's natural role as subservient; others oppose it because they may feel that the movement threatens their femininity). In political campaigns, elements other than the candidate himself may influence particular audience members (e.g., supposedly, some persons voted against Thomas Dewey in 1948 because he had a mustache; in 1968 Eugene McCarthy got good audience reactions by appearing on the same stage as Paul Newman; and in 1972 George McGovern's wife probably garnered as much support for him as did his own campaign).[18]

One of the most interesting examples of how this image-building process occurs followed the campaign for the Senate in 1964 in Oklahoma. The G.O.P. candidate was Bud Wilkenson, the former Oklahoma football coach and a person thought to be unbeatable, if for his coaching

---

[17] For an excellent discussion of how one's image of the world is built, see Kenneth Boulding's *The Image* (Ann Arbor: University of Michigan Press, 1961).

[18] For the most part, candidates' wives have been relegated to the status of objects in presidential campaigns—they accept bouquets of flowers, thank mayors for keys to cities, and look pretty. This trend may be changing, however. See, for example, Martha Thompson Barclay's "Distaff Campaigning in the 1964 and 1968 Presidential Elections," *Central States Speech Journal, 21* (Summer 1970), 117–122. In 1972, the McGovern staff decided to produce the *first* five-minute television spot almost entirely about the candidate's wife.

record alone. The Democratic candidate, Fred Harris, faced by a seemingly insurmountable lead, sought to discover what Oklahomans had as "the image" of a senator. Harris won, but needed to know who the probable gubernatorial candidate would be in 1966. His staff asked a sample of Oklahoma voters whom they would rather have as their governor: Ben Cartwright of "Bonanza" fame, Perry Mason, Gomer Pyle, or James Bond—each of whom roughly matched one of the contenders. The overwhelming response was Ben Cartwright—the robust, self-assured, and sincere "Pa" of the Ponderosa. A candidate resembling Lorne Green began to project a "Ben Cartwright" image in as many ways as possible and won the nomination. Though he later lost the general election, the image information was used by Harris's staff in planning the campaign.[19] The same kind of image making occurred in the presi-

---

[19] Private correspondence with Ross Cummings, Oklahoma City, the advertising agent for Senator Harris. The letter is reproduced below:

Thank you for your letter of March 12. For the most part, Bill Carmack's recollection is accurate.

Having served as the advertising agency for Fred Harris' successful campaign in 1964 to fill the unexpired term left by Bob Kerr's death, we were very interested in trying to determine who the Democratic nominee for governor was likely to be in 1966, when Fred would have to run again for a full six-year term.

Most polls conducted by politicians are done on a name basis. They select a number of likely names, attempt to rate them in various degrees of public awareness and acceptance, and match them against each other. As though advertising did not exist.

We had just helped our candidate prevail over two former governors (one an incumbent Senator) and the greatest popular hero in Oklahoma since Will Rogers. Polls taken 60 and 90 days before election day had shown Fred as an unknown and an ignominious third in a field of three seeking the Democratic nomination.

We knew that images can be affected during a campaign, but only during a campaign does the public become sufficiently interested to let an emerging public figure gain massive acceptance. So how can you measure something like this before a campaign starts?

We were not attempting a serious study of issues, since candidates most often join each other in embracing identical issue positions. We only wanted to know what sort of *identity* the people of Oklahoma might prefer for governor.

We had seen "young men's years," when the public swept out the old guard politicians, and other years when established businessmen with mild messages had the greatest appeal.

We first considered a questionnaire describing candidates by personal traits, but discarded that as too wordy and awkward. We then decided to use identities everyone would know—and this led us to the use of TV and movie characters.

We used James Bond, Perry Mason, Ben Cartwright, Andy Griffith, and Gomer Pyle. . . . Our known political contenders fit these characters loosely. . . .

Well, Ben Cartwright won handily, garnering some 60% of the votes, and pointing toward a tendency on the part of the voters to favor an older candidate. Andy Griffith did poorly even in "Little Dixie," indicating a pull-back from an unrelieved rural image. James Bond ran last, indicating dissatisfaction with handsome young playboy types. Perry Mason was second, but far enough behind Ben Cartwright to indicate that rugged, patriarchal directness was a more desirable characteristic than urbane, articulate competence.

We decided the likely winner in the Democratic primary was probably

dential campaign of 1960, when John Kennedy built an image that whittled a 16 percent lead by Richard Nixon to one-half of one percent victory for Kennedy.

At any rate, in the recombination process the re-formation of information takes place in the audience's mind. There it is re-formed with other information into new combinations, each of which is related to what the campaign programmers planned but each is also different from what they planned.

While the re-forming is occurring, parts of it are reflected in two kinds of "images" of the campaign candidate or of the movement's cause. The first is that held by the audience members; the second is that held by the planners or programmers. This image, or these images, is a representation of what was originally fed into the communication system, but it is only that—a representation, a silhouette that resembles but is not identical to the original. At this step, the "computer printout" is not neatly squirted out by a print-gun, but it emerges in uncertain, unclear, and abstract terms. At the end of a campaign we know more about the candidate or product, but we do not know all and we are certainly in error about some of the things we believe. For instance, Richard Nixon was often thought to be "tricky" or "red-baiting," due to his image at the end of various campaigns early in his career. This image was probably partially true, but the "new Nixon" image of 1968 and 1972 was of a masterful political technician. The end product, then, consists of an image about a candidate, product, or cause. Part of the image is true, part of it is part-true, and part of it is false. All three parts yield the final image and also, through feedback, change the initial image the campaign programmers were trying to communicate. After a campaign, even the candidate's staff sees the candidate differently—they see him in their original image of him, in the experiences they have had with him, and in the image the public holds. The same thing happens to causes or issues

---

Preston Moore. Although he still had touches of Perry Mason about him, he fit fairly well with the Ben Cartwright character. We speculated that Raymond Gary's rural image would hold him back under circumstances indicated by the survey. David Hall, the urbane young Tulsa county prosecutor, did not seem to be favored by the results, but a strong possibility for public acceptance if he would avoid being too "country" would be Clem McSpadden, a glib senate leader and linear relative of Will Rogers.

We picked Moore to win the primary and he did. However, in his campaign he failed to show the frontier wisdom of the head of the Cartwrights, and in the fall he was defeated by a Tulsa oilman who never developed a real image of his own, Dewey Bartlett. This candidate, defeated for re-election as governor but beating Ed Edmondson in 1972 by characterizing him as a liberal, is a protest candidate whose victories grow from public dissatisfaction with his opponents. I don't believe our polling method could have picked him up on the radar screen.

. . . I would not seek to palm myself off as a political witch doctor but as a professional communicator.

On second thought, there are some unbelievable fees in being a witch doctor.

in social movements. At the end of the movement for women's suffrage, for example, which culminated in the Eighteenth Amendment to the Constitution, woman's role was seen by the "programmers" of the movement as different from their initial view of that role. Initially, they fought for the right to vote; at the end of their campaign, they saw the need to carry recognition into other areas—job opportunity, birth control, and so forth. In this sense a movement is never really over because the fourth step—representation—does precisely that; it *presents* the cause or issue in a new light. At the end of a personal campaign, such as to have a date with a certain person, one may be disappointed with the outcome, not because he never got the date but because the prize changed in his perception as a result of the campaign. We are all aware of working to attain a goal and then discovering that it was not what we thought it to be. A good example might be what happens to someone who has his heart set on a certain job—he interviews for the job, writes letters to the place of employment, telephones them repeatedly while they are in the decision-making process to remind them that he is still interested; he may seek ways to get further input into the decision-making process (recommendations from prestigious persons, hints from persons who work for the company, etc.). After struggling to land the job, he may discover that the company has changed its image in his perception. It is either much better than he thought it was because he had to fight so hard to get the job, or it is less than he imagined because his campaign may have been frustrating or for other reasons.

A Review and Conclusion

The formal aspect of campaigns or movements we have been concerned with in this chapter is that of systematic communication, or communication that can be thought of as similar to the workings of a computer. *Programmers* plan and design methods by which information is to be dispersed to various persons. *Dispersal* centers or persons utilize media and other means to spread the information provided to them to the public or to potential supporters of the campaign or movement. After a period of time, these supporters or auditors combine the new information with old information in a process of *re-formation*, which ultimately leads to a new "image" of the candidate, product, or cause. This new "image" can be thought of as a meaningful but abstract *representation* of the person, thing, or idea being campaigned for, and that affects not only the audience's attitude toward the object of the campaign but also the actions of planners or programmers of the campaign or movement. The system of communication then loops back on itself, and all elements ultimately affect all other elements in the system. The planners affect the dispersal elements. They, in turn, affect the receiver, who recombines information into a representation, which then affects the planners or programmers as they take other steps to continue persuading audiences.

Earlier, you were asked to think about what you might do to try to promote a new type of building material in a product- or thing-oriented campaign. You tried stressing the durability of the product and then hypothetically dispersed information about the long life of the product through mass-media presentations and so on, only to discover, in a throwaway, disposable society, that durability was not important—cost was the important thing. As a result you had to reorient your frame of reference about your audience, and you changed your campaign. In that imagined example, all the steps in the system of communication outlined in this chapter are evident: *programming* of the durability argument, *dispersal* of it, recombination or *re-formation* of this information with a cultural propensity for nondurable items, and a *representation* in the audience's mind of the new product as too expensive because of its high quality. The final end product, in turn, affects you as planner to adjust the promotional campaign. This circular flow of information typifies all campaign and movement communication and causes successful campaigns to continually adjust, readjust, and readjust again. In the same way that each of the stages in the developmental nature of the campaign prepares the way for following stages, each step or element in the communicative system of a campaign affects each other element or step.

The developmental nature of campaigns or movements consists of five phases or stages that may emerge or develop: the *identification* stage, in which the movement or campaign assembles its ideological identifying characteristics; the *legitimacy* stage, in which power is demonstrated; the *participation* stage, in which large numbers of persons are invited to participate in the movement or campaign in real or symbolic ways, the penetration stage, in which the campaign or movement establishes its image or presence upon the mass of audience members; and the fifth stage, in which *power is distributed.*

Another characteristic of campaigns or movements is the use of the *dramatic* portrayal of *situations*, *persons*, and *events* in which the campaign planner tries to invite the audience to attend to the drama—to become part of it.

Again, the universals pointed out in this chapter work well together; they emphasize the process nature of the campaign or movement (i.e., ongoing, in flux, with each element affecting all other elements) and encourage the dramatic nature of the persuasion in them (i.e., they all lend themselves to a "dramatic" impulse or interpretation). In Chapter 8 we will see how these characteristics operate in specific campaigns or movements.

Questions for Further Study

1. Define each of the developmental terms and identify examples of the first three stages in some magazine or newspaper.

2. What stage of the campaign or movement is represented when we vote for or against a particular candidate or proposition? Why?

3. Recently we have been persuaded more and more frequently that a renewal of trade and cultural ties between our country and others (e.g., Russia, China, and Cuba) is a valuable thing to do. Since there is a feeling against this trend, it must be changed through a persuasive campaign. If you were trying to change the attitudes of the average American, what would you do for identification? What would you do for establishing legitimacy of the movement to reestablish ties? How would you engender audience participation? How has our government done these three things? Rate their success or failure and try to determine why they succeeded or failed and at what stage.

4. As we are exposed to more and more television series like "All in the Family," we are probably being exposed to an informal and vague campaign. Nonetheless, these programs do change ideas and beliefs. At what stage is Archie Bunker as a persuasive symbol at the present time? Is he clearly identifiable? How would you justify your answer? Does the program have legitimacy? Justify? Has it achieved any sort of audience participation? How? Has the point of the program penetrated? What is the point (persuasively speaking) of "All in the Family" and shows like it?

5. Identify a movement of recent times (e.g., the consumer movement or the antiwar movement). Trace its development. Where was it most dramatic? How was this achieved? How effective was or is the movement in communicating its message? Explain.

6. What are the elements in a drama that has or is capturing the attention of the audiences? (*Note:* Look in your local newspaper or at the evening television news program or at a newsweekly. At the time this is being written, the drama that is capturing the attention of the media is the investigation of presidential involvement in the Watergate affair in 1972. Earlier, we had the 1972 political campaign, the killing of the Israeli athletes at the Olympics, and other events that captured the attention of the media and the public.) Who are the heroes? What values do they display? Who are the villains? What values do they display? Does the drama fit into one of the common plot lines? Which ones? Who is playing up the drama? Can you guess at the motive behind continuation of the drama? Is it a part of a movement or campaign? If so, what part or stage is being dramatized? How?

7. Watch the television news for several nights in a row and categorize the various stories into one of several types: *dramatic,* such as the story of a

disaster; *informative,* such as the notification of a defect in the new car models; or *editorial*—those advocating a particular belief or position. Which type predominates? What kinds of issues are involved in each category? Why?

Experiences in Persuasion

1. Trace the history of some recent movement (e.g., the rise of the Black Panther party or the antiwar movement). Use your library resources, and if the movement is still going on, establish a clipping file to gather coverage of the movement in newspapers. You may wish to collect radio and television coverage of the movement or campaign by contacting television or radio stations and by recording commentary off the air. Once you feel that you have collected enough material to give you a good idea of what the movement or campaign is like, begin to search for a pattern in the material. Ask yourself if there is evidence of a dramatic invitation to the audience. Is there a plot? Are there characters, villains, heroes, dramatic settings? Are there favorite metaphors (see Chapter 3 for help in identifying metaphors)? Ask if the campaign or movement is following the developmental stages outlined in Chapter 6. If so, at what stage is the campaign or movement? What has it done to communicate at various stages in its development? In short, do a complete analysis of the campaign or movement.

2. Research a movement of past history (e.g., the labor movement of the 1930s, the suffrage movement, the "Back to Africa" movement, the Populist movement). Use all materials available to you from libraries, interviews, and other sources. Then do the same kind of detailed analysis outlined in project 1. Look at historical novels focusing on the same movement. (*Power* by Howard Fast is a good example; it focuses on the rise of the United Mine Workers and John L. Lewis.) How does the dramatized version compare with the historical facts you gather?

3. Join a campaign or movement on campus or in your community. (This should be easy in alternate years on the political level.) You may have to look around for a movement on campus, but usually one develops—opposition to tuition hikes, religious movements, etc. Keep a communication diary of the experiences you have while you are a member of the movement or campaign staff. Look for dramatic and developmental aspects of the persuasive campaign. Try to identify characteristic metaphors, plots in the dramatic invitations, characters participating in them, and so forth. Report on your findings.

4. Read the reports of various campaigns (e.g., any of the *Making of the President* books on presidential campaigns or reports of any of the other persuasive campaigns that occur frequently, like David Halberstam's *The Best and the Brightest,* which traces the history of the persuasive campaigns to convince several Presidents of the necessity of our involvement in South Vietnam). Do the kind of analysis already outlined. Ask what stages the campaign or movement is in or has passed through. Where did the movement or campaign appear strongest and most persuasive? Why? What was done to exploit this advantage? When was it weakest? Why? How was this used?

5. Research one of the questions raised about persuasion in this chapter. For example, you might want to look at other sources on the use of television and its powerful impact or about the usefulness of metaphor—how to identify it and how to interpret metaphors, or the importance of the dramatic format in modern society. Reanalyze the campaigns or movements sketched out in Chapter 6.

6. Research the journals in speech communication and other disciplines to see what has been done concerning political, advertising, and ideological campaigns or movements. Look for the common assumptions used by the researchers. Are there trends in the ways the researchers describe campaign strategy? Report on your findings.

7. As a class or as a group in class, try to develop a mini-campaign on your own campus. Set your strategy initially to develop in stages. Build in a feedback methodology to determine whether you are being successful. Try various methods suggested here. (*Note:* In the author's class, several groups have run members of their group for political office—alderman, delegate to student senate, and even a delegate to the Democratic nominating convention in 1972. They have also tried to persuade administration and student associations of the need for bicycle paths, no-profit bookstores, and other projects.)

8. Obtain a copy of *Critiques of Contemporary Rhetoric* by Karlyn Kohrs Campbell (Belmont, Calif.: Wadsworth Publishing Co., 1972). Read some of the criticisms of particular kinds of discourse. Follow the directions suggested for analyzing communication used by any of the movements you have chosen to study. Since Campbell focuses on a variety of types and persons (Richard Nixon on the war, the rhetoric of Black nationalism, etc.), the book should provide you with numerous models, one of which is bound to spark your imagination.

Readings for New Dimensions

Andrews, James R., "Confrontation at Columbia: A Case Study in Coercive Rhetoric," *Quarterly Journal of Speech,* 55 (February 1969), 9–16. Professor Andrews was a faculty member at Columbia University when one of the first "campus disturbances" of the 1960s and 1970s occurred there in May of 1968. His case study is excellent for the perspective it offers, and he uses the example to discuss the differences between coercion and persuasion. The question may seem irrelevant to present-day readers, but that it was important only a few short years ago is commentary on how accustomed we have become to movements and campaigns.

Barclay, Martha Thompson, "Distaff Campaigning in the 1964 and 1968 Presidential Elections," *Central States Speech Journal,* 21 (Summer 1970), 117–122. This article traces the campaign activities of Mrs. Barry Goldwater, Mrs. Lyndon Johnson, Mrs. Hubert Humphrey, and Mrs. Richard Nixon. It is of interest in reference to the women's movement discussed here. The perspective that the 1964 and 1968 examples offer is valuable—wives simply did not campaign much.

Binder, Leonard, James Coleman, Joseph La Palombara, Lucian W. Pye, Sidney Verba, and Myron Weiner, *Crises and Sequences in Political Development* (Princeton, N. J.: Princeton University Press, 1972). This book is the original source for the developmental scheme used to describe campaigns and movements in Chapter 7. Though much of this book is devoted to establishing the whole problem of crisis in contemporary Western culture, there are many important implications for the study of movements and campaigns. The book is difficult.

Brock, Bernard L., "1968 Democratic Campaign: A Political Upheaval," *Quarterly Journal of Speech*, 55 (February 1969), 26–35. Brock describes in detail the major persuasive strategies and events in the campaign of 1968 from the Democratic point of view. This article should be of help in doing an extended case study of that campaign. Brock also points out that the problems for the Democrats in 1968 were in leadership, not in ideological differences. That clearly changed with the McGovern movement in 1972. Nonetheless, Brock's observations that politicians of the future will have to be more dynamic, close to the people, and willing to accept "grass roots" inputs are probably still true.

Cathcart, Robert S., "New Approaches to the Study of Movements: Defining Movements Rhetorically," *Western Speech*, 36 (Spring 1972), 82–88. Cathcart observes that one of the problems in the study of movements is adopting a sociological or political science perspective and thus ruling out a communication analysis. He notes that we need a dramatic definition for movements, as opposed to a sociopolitical definition we have been using. Instead of discussing how sectors of the electorate or audience will vote according to income, ethnic origin, and so on, we need to explore how they will react to the dramatic setting and situation presented to them.

Chesebro, James W., "Rhetorical Strategies of the Radical-Revolutionary," *Today's Speech*, 20 (Winter 1972), 37–48. Chesebro explores the various communication attempts by the New Left in America since 1968. The analysis is particularly interesting for our purposes because of its Burkean flavor. Chesebro carefully discusses the use of linguistic symbols (pig, facism, and others) as they reflect dramatic situations. He offers five strategies for revolutionary persuaders, all of which suggest the utilization of the dramatic metaphor. For example, the Political Revolutionary engages in "acting out" his dissatisfaction; the Cultural Revolutionary "lives out" his distaste for the status quo and thus attempts to kill it; the Urban Guerilla actively destroys (bombs, hijacks, etc.) what he cannot abide; the Political Anarchist confronts power symbols and tries to radicalize other persons to oppose this power; while the Superstars ". . . cast themselves as individual personalized forerunners of the new lifestyle." Chesebro notes that the essential metaphor of this last group is the theater. The article is exciting because of its dramatic perspective and for its interesting examples. It might be interesting to use Chesebro's methodology in conjunction with that offered by Karlyn Kohrs Campbell or with the sequential and dramatic trends noted here.

8

Case Studies of
Campaigns and Movements

The task of this chapter is to explore briefly how the three universals—developmental stages, dramatizing the case, and systematic communication—discussed in Chapter 7 have operated in campaigns in the past and in movements that have occurred or are occurring. In each case study of a campaign or movement, we continue to refer to the universals discussed earlier. If any part of the discussion of those universals seems unclear to you, perhaps these case studies will help to dramatize the elements for you. In all of the case studies, the analysis is extremely limited, and you should consider them further or construct other case studies for further study.

We will look at several distinct kinds of campaigns or movements: those that focus on a particular person or candidate and that are well organized and well financed, and with great control over the communication that surrounds them; those that are similarly structured but that focus on an idea; and those movements that are more amorphous and less organized, that may not be financed at all, and that may have limited control over the communication associated with them.

The major distinction between the first two structured types and the third less organized type is that the first two usually have a campaign organizational hierarchy—there is a head planner and subordinates, who are supported by various levels of workers. In the more amorphous movement, there are several different and autonomous organizations all working for the same general goal—some of these groups may be highly organized and efficiently run while others have floating leadership and no real headquarters or staff. Frequently, these separate groups may take action that is detrimental to the goals of the other groups, and there is the likelihood of intergroup conflict and disagreement. A classic example of this kind of disagreement is the splitting of the Students for a Democratic Society (S.D.S.) into at least three separate groups; another is the familiar disagreement between various groups in the "Jesus movement," with some groups suggesting public witnessing, others advocating transcendental meditation, and others operating within traditional student religious organizations like the Newman Center.

The Impact of Television

In 1960 there were nearly 49-million television sets in American households (nearly a 90 percent coverage). Just four years before, during the campaign of 1956 one-third of the homes in America did not have a television set. Most of those that did have one were on their first set, and politicians were not yet aware of the power of this instrument, and their campaign staffs were naive about the use of television to disperse information. Even in 1960, few persons realized that using or not using makeup, having a blue as opposed to a white shirt, and being abstract as opposed to being concrete would all have such powerful effects on a viewing and voting public. Few realized the impact of dramatically staged "events" as opposed to traditional oratory, especially when the two—the dramatic as opposed to the traditional and formal—were viewed on the evening news program—preceded by dramatic programs and followed by others (and contained in the newscast format was a strong need for dramatization). In short, in 1960 Americans *began* to see the power of television in their lives—it developed images and dramatized people and ideas.

In the twelve years between the surprising election of John F. Kennedy in 1960 and the predictable reelection of Richard M. Nixon in 1972, a great deal happened in this country. There were race riots in major American cities; there was an assassination of a President and several other political or controversial figures (Malcolm X, Martin Luther King, Jr., George L. Rockwell, and Robert F. Kennedy); a major war was fought, college campuses exploded; thousands of new products were introduced; many causes were advocated (consumerism, antipollution, legalized abortion, ending of capital punishment, and redefinition of obscenity laws); a drug culture sprang up; a major political scandal reached to the highest levels of government, including the presidency; and people generally experienced a breakdown in old values and patterns and in their ability to feel that they had control over their lives. It is difficult to determine what caused all of this change, but it is certain that each of the trends had an effect on the way people reacted to information and on the way in which they were persuaded. It is also certain that the increased rate of change and the powerful inputs of television influenced campaigns in many ways.[1]

The Political Campaign: 1960–1972

In the period 1960–1972, political campaigning was tremendously influenced by television and its ability to dramatize events and ideas. During that period there were four presidential elections. In each succeeding election campaign, television costs rose higher and higher, and events became more staged on the one hand and more focused on by the media news services on the other hand.

From the beginning of the campaign of 1960 it looked like a lost cause for John F. Kennedy. He was too young to be President; he had limited experience; he was a Roman Catholic; he was unaware of foreign policy and foreign relations; and he was running against the reverence that many held for Dwight D. Eisenhower and his administration. Before he was nominated, Kennedy had *no* real identification in comparison with his opponent. Richard M. Nixon not only had identification, he had legitimacy and power by the time he delivered his acceptance address.[2] Yet Nixon lost a 16 percent lead during the weeks from Labor Day to Election Day. Why?

If we look at the developmental stages of the campaign and at the ability of the candidates to dramatize them, we find part of the answer. Though Nixon had identification and legitimacy, he was never able to get participation by his audience. He gave well-researched speeches that were filled with facts and emotion and that focused on significant issues, but he never was able to invite his audience to join with him in facing the 1960s. Instead, he told of the poverty of his youth, he discussed the economic differences between Keynes and other economists, and he portrayed details of his personality. He came off, according to Theodore H. White, as a "Dagwood Bumstead" sort of character. Kennedy, on the other hand, presented a profile—a silhouette of himself—and let the audience fill in the blank spots. The first of the Great Debates provides a good

---

[1] Bernard L. Brock, "1968 Democratic Campaign: A Political Upheaval," *Quarterly Journal of Speech*, 56 (February 1970), 35.

[2] Eugene Wyckoff, *The Image Candidates* (New York: The Macmillan Co., 1968), pp. 42–43.

example of the difference. While Nixon cited numerous statistics on the issues of the debate, Kennedy stressed the dramatic nature of the events: Consider these two quotations:

> *Kennedy:* In 1933 Franklin Roosevelt said in his inaugural that this generation of Americans has a "rendezvous with destiny." I think our generation of Americans has the same "rendezvous." The question now is: Can freedom ever be maintained? . . . I think it can be, and I think in the final analysis it depends upon what we do here. I think it's time America started moving again.

> *Nixon:* Is the United States standing still? . . . Let's take schools. We have built more schools in the last 7½ years than were built in the previous 20 years. . . . With the previous administration . . . there was a total growth of 11 percent over 7 years; in this administration there has been a total growth of 19 percent over 7 years . . . I costed out the Democratic platform. It runs from a minimum of 13.2 billion a year more than we are presently spending to a maximum of 18 billion a year more than we are presently spending. . . . I know Senator Kennedy feels as deeply about these problems as I do, but our disagreement is not about the goals for America but only about the means to reach these goals.[3]

Clearly, Nixon invited no one to a "drama." Instead he played the pedant and "lectured" his audience. Kennedy's focus was on the dramatic—the historic event in which the audience could participate.

The best description of the differences between the Kennedy and Nixon campaigns—as communication systems—is offered by Theodore H. White in *The Making of the President: 1960.* Both staffs had planners or programmers, but at the dispersal stage the Nixon campaign blundered, or he was difficult to talk with and secretive about what he was going to say or do. Kennedy, on the other hand, made it a point to invite reporters to fly from city to city with him on the campaign plane; he extended invitations to them for in-depth interviews; his staff distributed the details of each day's activities. Reporters following Nixon had to shift for themselves at the airports, and as a result they often missed rally speeches and couldn't file stories on time. Naturally it was easier and more pleasant to disperse the Kennedy news than to disperse the Nixon news. Not only was it more dramatic and entertaining, but it was easier to get and could more readily have the individualistic stamp of each reporter as he, too, "participated" with the candidate in his drama.[4]

---

[3] *Final Report of the Committee on Commerce, Part III* (Washington, D. C.: U. S. Government Printing Office, 1961), pp. 75–78.

[4] Theodore H. White, *The Making of the President: 1960* (New York: Atheneum Publishers, 1961).

By 1964, things had changed dramatically. Now the fight was not over who could get closest to the press, but over who could use the press to suggest and outline and dramatize best. There were several problems for the Republicans—the country was in a period of high prosperity, Lyndon Johnson was popular, and the party was in disarray. Barry Goldwater was never seen as the legitimate nominee of his party but rather as the representative of an extremely dedicated but small minority of right-wing extremists who had captured the G.O.P. Thus he had no identification, and he could not persuade without achieving this necessary stage. Lyndon Johnson, on the other hand, was already legitimate in 1964, since he had run the country for over a year in times of economic plenty and peace. He offered the country the chance to continue the "historic" work begun by John Kennedy. He offered stability and a progression of the drama from "The New Frontier" to "A Great Society."

Both candidates were able to dramatize events for the public but, unfortunately for Goldwater, not in the same ways. To most of the viewing and voting public, Barry Goldwater wanted to involve them in a dangerous drama—he suggested letting NATO commanders and field officers in Vietnam have nuclear weapons; he wanted to defoliate jungles with chemicals; and he once suggested that we saw off the Eastern seaboard states and let them drift away. Nelson Rockefeller, a respected and leading spokesman for the G.O.P., was booed at the 1964 convention and the gallery audience threw food, paper, and firecrackers at him while he spoke. The drama associated with Goldwater was exciting, but not one that encouraged participation—it was seen as too extreme and dangerous for the participants. Johnson, on the other hand, offered a counterdrama by pledging never to send American boys to fight a land war in Asia; he offered an increased participation of federal agencies in fighting a "war on poverty" instead of in Vietnam; and he moved and passed comprehensive civil rights legislation in 1964. The two dramas were vastly different. On the one hand was the risky invitation to tragedy; on the other the warm welcome to setting the wrongs right.

Communicatively, the point of dispersal for the message of Barry Goldwater was never wisely planned. As Theodore White reports in *The Making of the President: 1964*, Goldwater's prime planner, Clifton White, quit after the convention, leaving the candidate without an organized central planning staff. Thereafter, messages against Social Security were foolishly delivered in St. Petersburg to audiences made up of pensioners; and the candidate spoke against the Tennessee Valley Authority in Tennessee, where its positive effects were best known. The press, seeing the dramatic value in these contradictions, emphasized them and coupled them with Goldwater's "extremist" image, which remained from the primary campaigns and from the drama of the "stolen" nomination. In a sense, where Goldwater failed in programming his communication, Johnson was the master of his. He was systematic almost to a fault, while Goldwater simply had little programming. The result was the largest popular majority ever recorded in an election.[5]

By 1968, things had changed again. Now Lyndon Johnson was one of the most unpopular leaders in the history of the country. There were 500,000 men in Vietnam, and the national treasury was being bankrupted by a seemingly endless war. Civil disobedience seemed the word of the day. Legitimacy was the key issue in the campaign of 1968; in fact, the central question was which candidate could demonstrate that he was legitimate, that he had power and credibility. In the primary contests, Eugene McCarthy demonstrated enough power to get a significant minority of the vote in New Hampshire. Later Robert Kennedy demonstrated that he could win in such varied states as Oregon and Nebraska. Hubert Humphrey demonstrated that he could buttonhole delegates without entering primaries. On the Republican side, Richard Nixon did not lose any primaries, and thus he established the legitimacy of the "winner." George Wallace demonstrated a kind of power and legitimacy by organizing a third party. In a sense, the election finally went by default to Nixon, who was the only one to demonstrate a prima facie legitimacy. Humphrey, particularly after the Chicago convention riots, was seen as the "illegitimate" nominee of a legitimate party, while Wallace was seen as the legitimate nominee of an "illegitimate" party. Only Richard Nixon was the legitimate nominee of an established and "legitimate" party. Even after nomination, legitimacy was still the issue. Ultimately, Humphrey had to break with his former commander-in-chief; in a speech in Salt Lake City, he renounced some of the Johnson Vietnam policies.

Beyond the election, legitimacy was the issue in two other ways: Was the Vietnam War legitimate in any sense, and was the American system legitimate in any way? These two issues were the core concepts to be debated. On the one side were masses of the young, the disaffected, the black, and the poor, who argued that the war was not only illegal but that it was morally illegitimate and that it was warping the moral fiber of the country and draining resources from other areas like poverty, pollution, and education—areas desperately needing attention. On the other side were two positions: one that not only was the war legitimate but that it was the only way to make the world safe for democracy and that it ought to be pursued more vigorously (e.g., General Curtis "Bombs Away" LeMay, who advocated using "any weapon" he could dream up, including nuclear weapons, to end the war); the other position was that we must live up to our commitments—hence the war was legitimate. The American system was also questioned, with many persons wondering what had happened to the normal flow of life and to the traditional

---

[5] Theodore H. White, *The Making of the President: 1964* (New York: Atheneum Publishers, 1965).

political campaign—in 1968 legitimacy and power seemed to come from assassination and from threats to line the streets of Washington, D. C., with soldiers with rifles and bayonets every ten feet and from crowds chanting obscenities to stop candidates from speaking.

The most efficient communication *system* was that run by the Republicans. Nixon had learned from 1960 and went about programming messages systematically. (For an excellent description of how carefully this was done, see *The Selling of the President* by Joe McGinniss.) Money was no problem, so millions were spent developing and dispersing a television image of the candidate. The ultimate result was the desired abstract silhouette—the "low profile," as the Nixon staff called it. Wallace was financially hamstrung—people had to purchase the supplies for campaign headquarters before they could open them. Humphrey struggled to get through the programming stage: Was he to be the spokesman for the Johnson years or the populist from Minnesota? Was he to try to be the peacemaker or the social legislator? Should he emphasize the "politics of joy" or the seriousness of the future? All of these and other questions were debated and discussed by him and by his staff. Not until the Salt Lake City speech was Humphrey able to get direction in his campaign—he failed in the first step of the communication system and in being able to achieve legitimacy until it was too late.

In short, 1968 was a campaign year that emphasized legitimacy as the key issue—legitimacy of the primary candidates, legitimacy of the parties, legitimacy of the nominees, legitimacy of the system itself, and legitimacy of the war. It was a dramatic campaign year, with its assassinations and riots, but it was also a year in which candidates had difficulty in creating a sense of the dramatic and historic. Events seemed to overwhelm any drama a candidate might try to enact. The electorate went with the most efficient, legitimate, and calm candidate—Richard Nixon.[6]

Though all of the information is not yet public or even collected, the key issue in 1972 again focused around the idea of legitimacy. This time, though, the question was important on a higher plane, for the nominees from both parties had demonstrated power or legitimacy. George McGovern captured the nomination with thousands of volunteers working precincts door-to-door in primary states and by attending precinct and ward meetings. His legitimacy was clear in his ability to control the nominating convention and its adoption of rules and slates of delegates and in rejecting such traditional powers as Richard J. Daley from the convention. The G.O.P. nominee, Richard Nixon, was also clearly a legitimate figure. Being a successful President, who had man-

---

[6] For a more elaborate discussion of the campaign of 1968, see Theodore H. White, *The Making of the President: 1968* (New York: Atheneum Publishers, 1969); and Lewis Chester, Godfrey Hodgson, and Bruce Page, *An American Melodrama: The Presidential Campaign of 1968* (New York: The Viking Press, 1960).

aged to reduce the American physical and human involvement in the Vietnam war and to renew ties with Russia and China, and who had other accomplishments on his ledger, he was clearly a legitimate and powerful candidate. McGovern, like Goldwater, was seen as having power but as having "stolen" it from the party—his power was "illegitimate" in the eyes of many party faithful.

Following the nominations, the question of legitimacy became even more a focus of debate. On the one side, McGovern denounced the Nixon Administration as "the most corrupt in history" and as an administration lacking in moral posture. McGovern charged that it engaged in lies, spying, intimidation, deceit, and murder. It was not only illegitimate; it was immoral. Nixon avoided the debate, staying away from the mass-media campaign himself until the last few weeks before the election, using instead the voices of his Vice-President, his family, his cabinet, his White House staff, the members of the Committee to Re-elect the President, and Democrats for Nixon. By continuing in his role as President and by moving seemingly closer to a truce in the Vietnam war, Nixon continually emphasized and reemphasized his legitimacy. His image "penetrated" and imprinted itself on the voter. McGovern fell more and more into the image of Goldwater, as the illegitimate thief of the party nomination and as the extremist candidate who repeatedly demonstrated his ineptness and indecisiveness in poor decisions, name-calling tactics, and charges of corruption in high places. His popularity crumpled under the Nixon image as President, peacemaker, and healer.

The chief elements in McGovern's drama were the bad guys and the good guys—the bad guys bugged the Democratic headquarters and drew plans to censor all mail, newspapers, and television programs. They took money from business interests in return for favors, and they used American soldiers, POWs, and Missing-in-Actions as pawns in a giant chess game. The good guys were the simple farm and factory workers, the poor and the young who were being hoodwinked by Machiavellian political technicians. In the Nixon drama the public was never really invited to join in Nixon's program; instead it was invited to repudiate "McGovern the extremist" in a dramatic fashion—to participate in a purgation drama.

The McGovern campaign faltered in both its initial programming and its dispersal stage. In initial programming, the lack of communication between various persons at the programming stage was, in large measure, responsible for the Eagleton affair. At one point McGovern was scheduled to deliver a half-hour television speech, but his staff scheduled him in competition with the award-winning film Love Story, which ultimately drew an unprecedented 80 percent of the viewing audience. This kind of planning typified the programming and dispersal stages of the campaign and hamstrung the candidate's ability to communicate to the electorate. The errors seemed to be a favorite target of the press, which repeatedly noted that "McGovern can't govern" and similar sentiments. Once having re-formed information about staff blunders, reporters picked up on any hint of dissension or disorganization in the McGovern staff. Thus, the feedback process compounded the image of problems with programming and dispersal.

The campaign of 1972, then, was a good example of how one candidate was able to utilize his inherent legitimacy as an incumbent and his opponent's "questionable" legitimacy—and at the same time to convince a large proportion of the voting public that he was the candidate most able to govern the country. Nixon and his staff were able to invite the electorate to join an "anti-McGovern" drama, and they were able to program and disperse the elements in this drama effectively. They never had to engage in a drama that tried to "sell" the President. McGovern, on the other hand, demonstrated a kind of legitimacy in capturing the nomination but was never able to appear the legitimate candidate of the party as a whole. Further, communication deficiencies in two steps of the communicating process—programming and dispersal—caused continuing problems. The result was the overwhelming defeat of the challenger. In 1976, legitimacy may well be the key issue again, especially after the Watergate investigations raised doubts about the power of the presidency.

Social Movements and Persuasive Universals

Political campaigns, such as we have just discussed, are probably the most frequent and common of the campaigns we see in the everyday world. More recently, however, the mass media, and perhaps the rates of change we are witnessing, have given rise to social movements. Social movements are like political campaigns except that they are more loosely structured, and they try to convince the audience of the worth of some *idea* or ideology, whereas political campaigns are focused on the promotion or acceptance of some particular *person*. At times the two seem to blend, and a person-oriented campaign seems also to be idea-oriented (e.g., the "Free Angela Davis" or the "Free Huey Newton" campaigns). In these cases the person probably acts as a symbol for the idea being promoted, with the social impact of the campaign being first and foremost.

These social movements share the universals we have already discussed: (1) they are developmental; (2) they rely upon the creation of a sense of the dramatic and historic; and (3) to a lesser degree than political campaigns, they are communication systems with programs, input dispersal, re-formation, and representation as end products. Of course they differ greatly from political campaigns in their organizational structure and on the degree to which they rely on ideology as opposed to name recognition and other characteristics. The universal characteristics of campaigns and movements provide the beginning point for you as a receiver of campaign and movement persuasion; but it is necessary to go beyond this level of analysis and explore not only the universals in more detail but also the other characteristics of movements—characteristics such as favored metaphors, nonverbal symbolization, the development of camaraderie, and so forth. We will now look briefly at two such movements as they relate to campaign persuasion: the movement for Civil Rights and the movement for Women's Liberation—appropriate movements to investigate, since they have been most active and in flux during the same twelve-year period just examined. Again, the synopses provided here are only beginnings designed to give you an idea of how the universals discussed earlier relate to social movements.[7]

The Movement for Civil Rights

There has been pressure to grant equal rights and privileges to persons of minority races, beliefs, and religions since the beginning of the American republic. In the eighteenth century there was sentiment for ceasing the slave trade from Africa; in the nineteenth century numerous debates were held and pieces of legislation were passed and a war was fought over the issue; and in the twentieth century we have seen the development of the cause of civil rights in a variety of ways ranging from the "Back to Africa" movement of Marcus Garvey to the Black Panthers. What interests us here is the dramatic and powerful development of this pressure for obtaining and guaranteeing civil rights since 1960. The movement of the 1960s began when Martin Luther King, Jr., then an unknown Baptist preacher, was arrested in Birmingham, Alabama, and jailed for activities designed to pressure Southern governments to grant equal rights to blacks. He wrote his now famous "Letter from a Birmingham Jail," and with it really set off the Civil Rights movement of the 1960s. This movement in turn spawned subsequent movements, which will probably continue through the 1970s. Note that we use the word *movements*, for one of the characteristics of a movement which does not apply to a political campaign is that it has many separate and sometimes independent subgroups or submovements,

---

[7] For other examples of critical explorations of movements and campaigns, see *Critiques of Contemporary Rhetoric*, ed. Karlyn Kohrs Campbell (Belmont, Calif.: Wadsworth Publishing Co., 1971).

all of which are working for similar ends. These groups are rarely co-ordinated and often differ bitterly over tactics and even ideology.

The Civil Rights movement of the 1960s had a development that followed the usual stages. It had to establish an *identity;* it had to become recognizable, as different from the traditional civil rights groups like the Congress of Racial Equality, the NAACP, and the National Urban League. Once this difference was articulated and realized, the movement had to demonstrate that it had *legitimacy,* or power. Having established some kind of legitimate image, *participation* had to be encouraged and fostered so that *penetration* would occur, thus allowing *distribution* to take place.

To begin this process, King chose to *dramatize* the plight of black America, using the mass media. He chose to do so in Montgomery, Alabama, against a law common to most Southern cities that forbade blacks from riding in the front of buses or trolleys. King's plan was to boycott buses in Montgomery until the ordinance was rescinded. The tactic was a simple and legal one, which had been used by the Labor movement of the 1930s with great effect and which had been used by Gandhi to realize independence for India in the 1940s. Blacks simply refused to use the rapid transit system, and they publicized their attempts using dramatic examples—a Negro woman, tired and weary, sat down in the front of a bus and refused to move to the back. She was forcibly ejected from the bus and the event became a classic "good guys" versus "bad guys" drama, which captured the attention of the mass media and hence the nation. When the Montgomery Bus Company finally buckled to the pressure, the Southern Christian Leadership Conference (SCLC) had achieved an important identity and had initially demonstrated that it had power—that it was legitimate and could have influence.

Once having established an identity, King and his followers had to keep that identity in the minds of the television audience, and they had to demonstrate it repeatedly in different places and over different issues. In this way the issue was not only repeatedly dramatized for the public, thus preparing it for the penetration stage, but also legitimacy and power were demonstrated to the mass public, to governmental and social agencies, and to participants and potential participants in the movement. There were highly dramatic situations and settings, like the steps of the Lincoln Monument, a courthouse in a Southern town, the admissions offices of large universities, and so forth. The media focused on these elements, which were highlighted by the movement's leadership, resulting in repeated exposure to information with the same theme—"Truth and Justice versus Bigotry and Hatred."

In the middle of these highly dramatic incidents, which were repeated again and again on the mass media, came the highly dramatic and potentially explosive assassination of John F. Kennedy. Not only did this event result in pressure for passage of the Civil Rights Act of 1964, which Kennedy had supported for several years; it also had another kind of effect, which may have led to the splintering of the King non-violent demonstration movement. A few months after the killing of Kennedy (in fact, on the day that Barry Goldwater was nominated in San Francisco) a young Black was killed in Bedford Stuyvesant, New York, and America had its first violent and destructive race riot since World War II. What followed is familiar to anyone who watched tele-vision throughout the 1960s. There were repeated riots in Watts, Detroit, and other large American cities. Stokely Carmichael, the young leader of the Student Non-violent Coordinating Committee, coined the term "Black Power," and the term became a catch phrase for numerous sub-groups within the Civil Rights movement. Soon various groups were competing with one another to gain identity and legitimacy, and King's powerful SCLC began to be viewed as a moderate and only partially successful group. Thus, though the Civil Rights movement continued, the King phase of it began to give way to more active and more violent groups after 1965. King was then forced to take more chances with issues less likely to yield success. His Memphis march in support of city workers in April 1968 resulted in King's own assassination.[8]

Throughout all of its development, the movement demonstrated the power of the dramatic to capture attention and to encourage participa-tion in real or symbolic ways on the part of the mass audience or even parts of it. The prime steps in the development of the movement and its various subparts seemed to be the development of an identity and the demonstration of power or legitimacy in order to get substantial participation. Inevitably, once this was attained, a splinter group began to develop its own identity and legitimacy, only to find itself being supplanted by yet another submovement. Perhaps this is one of the characteristics of movements that set them off from political campaigns —they rarely consummate in a mass acceptance and opportunity for distribution of power and property. Instead, the movement extends goals or increases its demands in order to maintain its own existence. A campaign for political office has an *end*—someone does get elected and does take over the position of power. A campaign for a product also has an end—people do purchase the product, and it becomes estab-lished in the consumer's buying habits. The movement does not seem to consummate this way. Instead, it keeps moving its frontiers forward as it approaches realization of those boundaries.

---

[8] For a further discussion of this dramatic shift of focus in the Civil Rights movement, see "Martin Luther King, Jr., Writes About the Birth of Black Power Slogan" and "Black Power Bends Martin Luther King," by Robert L. Scott, both of which are included in *The Rhetoric of Black Power*, ed. Robert L. Scott and Wayne Brockriede (New York: Harper & Row, 1969); or *Language, Communication, and Rhetoric in Black America*, ed. Arthur L. Smith (New York: Harper & Row, 1971); and see related sections of Campbell's *Critiques* (see fn. 8).

Communicatively, movements do not rely on a *systematic* flow of communication. Its messages are never as coordinated as those in a campaign for political office or for a product; its input is always varied in type and quantity, with many inputs for a period of time and then few; it relies to a greater extent than the campaign on free media exposure, as opposed to carefully planned and purchased media space or time; and it continually depends on new dramatic means to expose and re-expose the audience to its goals and personages to get a re-formation image, which will be favorable and persuasive. We shall see these same characteristics in the other movement to be discussed here —the Women's Liberation movement.

The Women's Liberation Movement

As mentioned earlier, the Women's Liberation movement is not new. Its beginnings relate to abolition and the Civil Rights movement. In 1876 the first woman was nominated for national political office by the Abolitionist Party. In 1918 the first woman was elected to the House of Representatives, and later women served in the Senate and in the cabinet of Franklin Roosevelt and later Presidents. However, as late as 1962, nearly half of the states did not allow women to serve on juries and in 1966—only seven years before the publication of this book—Alabama rescinded its law disallowing women the right to serve on juries. In the 91st session of the Senate (1970), the Senate refused to pass the amendment that guaranteed equal rights for women, though the House of Representatives did.[9] By 1973 the Equal Rights Amendment has not yet been passed.

As with the Civil Rights movement of the 1960s, the Women's Liberation movement had the establishment of an identity as a first priority. This was necessary before the movement could develop further, for the 1960 image of the movement for women's rights was similar to that of the Anti-Saloon league or the Women's Christian Temperance Union (WCTU). As a legitimate and recognizable movement, it simply did not exist in 1960. Unfortunately the identity of this movement was associated, perhaps more than other movements, with personalities. Though the Civil Rights movement was tied to persons like King and Carmichael, its ideology was clear and explicit. With Women's Liberation, the personalities associated with it are clearer than its ideology. For example, following her publication of *Sexual Politics*, Kate Millet was

---

[9] Hamida and Haig Bosmajian, eds., *This Great Argument: The Rights of Women* (Reading, Mass.: Addison-Wesley Publishing Co., 1972), especially pp. 181–200.

the target of unsophisticated and blunt charges of lesbianism from such sources as *Harper's*.

The problem of gaining identity for Women's Liberation revolves around two poles—focus on personalities like Millet, Friedan, and Steinem; and use of bizarre or dramatic events like the bra burnings in Chicago, demands for legalized abortion, and the women's strike against housework. For the most part, this movement remains in the identity stage; it has not demonstrated legitimacy in very many ways.[10]

The mass media, when they do focus on the sex issue, tend to treat it somewhat lightly; they focus on the women who demand jobs as coal miners or telephone linemen; the media emphasizes the physical aspects of job qualifications; they tend to seek out the flamboyant and humorous activities of women's groups (bra burnings, making husbands cook meals, etc.).

In the 1972 presidential campaign, one could see the beginnings of movement toward legitimacy—two women were nominated for the office of President at the Democratic convention, women gave nominating and seconding speeches for both George McGovern and Richard Nixon, and for the first time the wives of the nominees of both major political parties engaged in active campaigning. In fact, Eleanor McGovern was the first candidate's wife to have a television spot that focused on her, not her husband. *Time* magazine devoted one of its issues to the two wives and their campaign activities. These instances are certainly attempts toward demonstrating a kind of legitimacy and power. They are first attempts.

Once this movement attains a legitimate status, the other steps should occur rapidly. Like the Civil Rights movement, Women's Liberation will probably serve to initiate several submovements. Countermovements will also probably emerge; in fact, some have emerged already (e.g., the Pussycat League) and generally can be seen as "backlash" movements favoring femininity over feminism, man-loving instead of man-hating, and sexuality versus sexlessness.

The strength of the women's movement in terms of its communicative abilities has been in the dispersal areas. Articles dealing with feminist issues have appeared in all popular periodicals, ranging from *McCall's* and *Ladies' Home Journal* to *The New Yorker, Saturday Review,* and *Harper's*. Of course, every daily newspaper has had at least two or three series on the movement and many feature articles by leaders of the movement. Television has tended to neglect the movement, except for the bizarre incidents and on talk shows where leaders such as Gloria Steinem appear.

---

[10] For further discussion of Women's Liberation, see Karlyn Kohrs Campbell's "The Rhetoric of Women's Liberation: An Oxymoron," *Quarterly Journal of Speech,* 59 (February 1973), 74–86.

As for the communicative aspects of the women's movement, a sense of legitimacy must be attained before the strength of its dispersal of information will have much effect on public awareness. Instead, except for instances where rights are protected by the law, most persons of both sexes will not re-form a representation of the Women's Rights movement as one of any real impact or power. The need for dramatization—to emphasize the legitimacy and power of this movement—is clear. The potential for social change of tremendous impact is available to the Women's Liberation movement, but it needs to establish itself as a power to be reckoned with and as a movement with the ability to dramatize its ideology. Until then it will continue to seek further means of gaining identity and of dispersing its message—two tasks already carried out to a great degree.

Nonpolitical Campaigns and Movements

We have been discussing campaigns and movements that are national in character and that focus on issues one could roughly label "political" in nature—campaign for office, movements for social justice, and movements for equal treatment. There are other campaigns and movements, which are less flamboyant and noticeable, that nonetheless aim to persuade us. They are even more familiar, because they occur so often and are so widespread. We tend not to take special notice of them because of their very familiarity—the campaign to get financial pledges for a new addition to one's church, the campaign for adoption of a school bond issue, the campaign for a new product or idea, the revivalist movement or the Jesus movement, and others typify this kind of persuasive attempt. The universals, so often mentioned already, also apply to this type of campaign.

When one wants to raise money, say for the United Fund, he must gain *identification.* This is usually done by choosing and publicizing a campaign staff. In one town, the co-chairmen of the United Fund drive were a prominent white businessman and one of the few black businesswomen in town. The values gained from choosing these persons are obvious—various sectors of the community could feel a sense of identification with one or both of the leaders—students who often visited the black woman's soul food restaurant would identify with her if not with the businessman; and local merchants would identify with the businessman. Members of both the black and white communities in town would identify with the drive for funds. *Legitimacy* for the campaign was achieved by having employers send letters to their employees soliciting funds and underwriting the fund drive. Political officials, like the mayor, voiced positive sentiments for the United Fund and the work it does, and the town erected a huge thermometer replica showing how far the campaign had succeeded in reaching its goal. *Participation* occurred in several ways—students canvassed from door-to-door; speeches were delivered in local churches; in some cases pledging ceremonies were held; and every donor was asked to wear a button showing that he had contributed or to put an emblem up on his door showing that he was a contributor. Ultimately, as the campaign neared its goal, one could say that *penetration* had occurred. Of course, at the end of the campaign the funds were *distributed* to the agencies.

In another example, several students in a persuasion class decided to conduct a campaign for the institution of bicycle paths on campus. They sought *identification* by placing ads in the personals column of the student newspaper and by placing posters around campus. They achieved a sense of *legitimacy* when they were able to convince several student senators to introduce a measure in the student association proposing bicycle paths. Unfortunately, funds ran out and the program was never adopted.

Several groups tried to stop the construction of a new psychology building on campus because contractors would have to destroy most of the trees in a memorial arboretum on campus. To get *identification*, several persons made speeches and wrote letters to the student and town newspapers. Some even chained themselves to trees to prevent the workmen from cutting the trees. This action was so dramatic that the story was highlighted on several of the news reports on major radio and television stations in Chicago and in newspapers there as well. The group never seemed to move beyond this identification stage, however. It is easy to imagine what they might have done to demonstrate *legitimacy* (attend a board of regents meeting in large numbers or present a petition to save the trees to the board or to other university officials).

One of the common kinds of campaigns on campuses is the religious campaign, usually sponsored by groups like the Campus Crusade. These campaigns often capture attention by advertising some spectacular individual as a main speaker or feature in a rally (e.g., "Josh," mentioned earlier, who was ballyhooed using signs like the one in Figure 8–1). Notice that the sign focuses on the words "Sex" and "Prophecy" and then on the name "Josh" and the meeting place and time. Only as an addendum is the sponsorship of the rally included. At such a rally (the feature speakers are often reformed sinners like prisoners, dope addicts, or professional gamblers) the speaker usually tells his story or performs his acts (in some cases professional illusionists, mimics, or magicians might be used) and then relates it to the overall theme of the campaign. If the group has planned wisely, this *participation* stage has been preceded by a *legitimacy* stage, in which the rally is suggested by persons

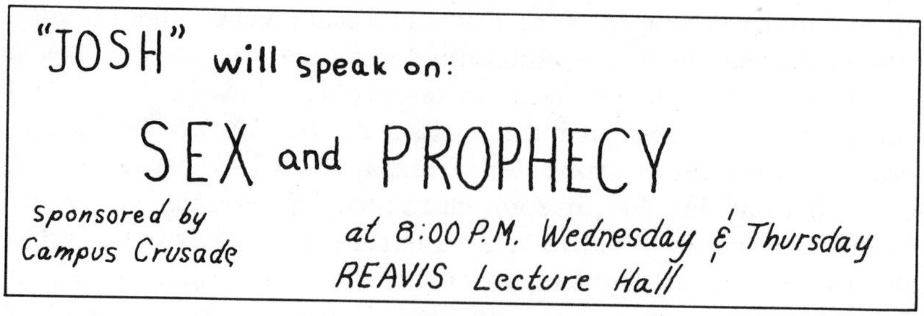

Figure 8–1

handing out leaflets or by student leaders in newspaper endorsements. The event is dramatic, and *dramatization* is furthered in the *penetration* stage, when converts are asked to "act out" their conversion by overtly and publicly making a decision and confessing. Thus the model, presented earlier, is also applicable in the activities of religious rallies and campaigns.

A Review and Conclusion

As one thinks of the total number of movements and campaigns that have taken place since 1960—political, product, and ideological, it is incredible that any receiver of persuasion would even conceive of messages coming to him in "single-shot" formats. When we think of persuasion, we ought to couple it immediately with the idea of a campaign.

If you reexamine the definition of persuasion offered in Chapter 1, you will see that it suggests that *decision options are altered* in persuasion, due to the input of information that changes the receiver's frame of reference. If we were to define "frame of reference" as a person's image or perception of the world, we would clearly see the necessity for an extended and repeated series of messages. To change someone's image of the world, we need to appeal to various aspects of that image; and since the image is probably composed of many aspects, some of which have existed for a long time in one's image of the world, we clearly need to offer many and varied appeals (i.e., a campaign) to the persuadee. Further, the appeals will best succeed when they capture the imagination of the audience and invite the audience member to participate in the campaign in real or symbolic ways. This ability to dramatize, coupled with a developmental strategy, typifies the successful campaign or movement. Finally, even if the ability to dramatize is given and the campaign or movement manages to engage in identification, legitimacy, participation, and penetration tactics, it is doomed to failure unless it communicates these dramas and strategies effectively. It must plan and disperse its messages so that re-formation of an end product or representation can occur. Inevitably, this end product is a combination of the receiver's inputs and the planner's or campaigner's inputs. Both combine to result in the final "image" of the world or frame of reference from which decision options are altered.

Readings for New Dimensions

Gonchar, Ruth M., and Dan F. Hahn, "Predicting Nixon's Rhetoric," *Today's Speech*, 19 (Fall 1971), 3–13. This article is a good example of what can be done with stylistic analysis. In that sense it relates to Chapters 2 and 3, as well as this chapter. Though Gonchar and Hahn may let their biases enter into this analysis, they offer good proof for what they claim—that Nixon's rhetoric *is* likely to reflect his personalization of the presidency, his Horatio Alger conceptualization of leadership, and his predilection for control, especially for self-control. These will be reflected in justificatory persuasion, rhetoric that casts the audience into polar positions, among other characteristics.

Hahn, Dan F., and Ruth M. Gonchar, "Studying Social Movements: A Rhetorical Methodology," *Speech Teacher*, 20 (January 1971), 44–52. Hahn and Gonchar offer a methodology for studying social movements that does not rely on simple description but looks at the language and communication activities used in movements. They focus this methodology around the traditional Aristotelian ethos, pathos, and logos. Also included is a section dealing with style; of particular interest in this section is a brief but exciting probe into the power of various metaphors. The dramatic setting, mentioned in Chapter 6, is affected by such metaphorical settings (e.g., Goldwater's "sea" or "water" metaphor). The article is well worth reading, especially by readers investigating movements as persuasion for the first time.

Ling, David A., "A Pentadic Analysis of Senator Edward Kennedy's Address to the People of Massachusetts, July 25, 1969," *Central States Speech Journal*, 21 (Summer 1970), 81–86. Ling uses the dramatic methodology mentioned in detail in Chapter 3 and suggested here in Chapter 8 to analyze the speech delivered by Senator Edward Kennedy following the highly publicized death of Mary Jo Kopechne. This analysis is interesting in several ways: First, it demonstrates the value of the dramatic metaphor; second, it reveals trends in the Kennedy style that are now interesting for comparative purposes; and finally, Ling suggests that Kennedy depicts himself as trapped by circumstance. This last possibility may be one of the universal plots that persuaders use as dramatic skeletons for the dramas to which they hope to invite persuadees.

McBath, James H., and Walter R. Fisher, "Persuasion in Presidential Campaign Communication," *Quarterly Journal of Speech*, 55 (February 1969), 17–25. This is one of the early attempts to suggest direction for a theory of campaign persuasion. Although it focuses on the 1968 presidential campaign and is therefore somewhat limited in scope, several aspects are very useful for the analysis of other campaigns. Interestingly, McBath and Fisher observe that campaigners do not seek ideological conversion and that the job of the campaigner is to attract attention of the middle majority while not alienating his most zealous supporters. This observation is insightful, particularly in light of the campaign of 1972. McBath and Fisher also note the importance of image and the necessity for the electorate to see itself in the campaign— to be invited to the drama, in the words of Chapter 6.

Rosenfield, Lawrence, "George Wallace Plays Rosemary's Baby," *Quarterly Journal of Speech*, 55 (February 1969), 36–44. The particular value of this selection is the dramatic format used by Rosenfield in analyzing the Wallace campaign. He also applies some of the tools of Chapter 3 (e.g., God terms, Devil terms, and the paranoid style) to the campaign. Thoroughly enjoyable and particularly apropos to this book.

Scott, Anne Firor, ed., *The American Woman: Who Was She?* (Englewood Cliffs, N. J.: Prentice-Hall, 1971). This would be a good book to begin with in a study of the Women's Liberation movement. It provides a good collection of public documents, speech excerpts, and other material that traces the development of the women's issue since the nineteenth century. Although there is no "speech criticism" of the movement included in the volume, the perspective and introductory essay material deal directly with problems in persuading audiences, with particular reference to the feminism issue.

Scott, Robert L., and Bernard L. Brock, eds. *Methods of Rhetorical Criticism: A Twentieth Century Perspective* (New York: Harper & Row, 1972). Though this book looks at criticism in general, much of it deals with persuasion and with persuasive campaigns in particular. The selections by Lawrence Rosenfield ("The Anatomy of Critical Discourse" and "A Case Study in Speech Criticism: The Nixon-Truman Analog") are helpful in setting a critical perspective for students. Examples of the uses of dramatic interpretation of persuasion are David A. Ling's analysis of Edward Kennedy's Chappaquiddick speech, Kenneth Burke's own analysis of *Mein Kampf* (which might prove an interesting starting point for a student wishing to study the Nazi movement), and Bernard Brock's discussion of Burkean criticism. Several articles dealing directly with movements are included.

Scott, Robert L., and Wayne Brockriede, eds. *The Rhetoric of Black Power* (New York: Harper & Row, 1969). This is one of the first collections of speeches and articles related to the Black Power movement. It traces a variety of issues and speakers in relation to this movement. The book would be a good place to start researching the movement and would also be of help in setting the stage for study of other related movements like the Black Panther party.

Scott, Robert L., and Donald K. Smith, "The Rhetoric of Confrontation," *Quarterly Journal of Speech*, 55 (February 1969), 1–8. Scott and Smith discuss radical movements and their strategies. Their analysis of the rhetoric of confrontation typical of the 1960s is dramatic in many ways. They discuss the rite of the kill, a Burkean notion wherein one declares himself symbolically "dead" in order to be resurrected by "killing" the enemy in real or symbolic ways. The article provides excellent insights into some of the underlying aspects of confrontation as a strategy in movements, although it may be difficult for some readers.

Simons, Herbert W., "Requirements, Problems, and Strategies: A Theory of Persuasion for Social Movements," *Quarterly Journal of Speech, 56* (February 1970), 1–11. Simons approaches the social movement by looking at the kinds of problems it faces—usually they are essentially rhetorical problems. Since movements are required to attract, keep, and shape workers, to appeal to a constituency larger than their own supporters, and to react to resistance from forces outside the movement, certain rhetorical problems arise for a movement and its leaders. They need to distort information at times, to suppress it at others, to appear to be inconsistent sometimes, and to adapt to audiences. Simons notes several rhetorical strategies that leaders of movements can utilize.

Smith, Arthur L., ed. *Language, Communication, and Rhetoric in Black America* (New York: Harper & Row, 1972). Smith has collected a large number of varied sources in this book—grouped under various headings, some of which apply directly to the notion of campaigns and movements. For example, see the sections entitled "Rhetorical Case Studies," "Criticism and Social Change," and "Social and Historical Dimensions," containing articles of help to students studying various phases of the Civil Rights and/or Black Power movements.

Swanson, David L., "The New Politics Meets the Old Rhetoric: New Directions in Campaign Communication Research," *Quarterly Journal of Speech, 57* (February 1972), 31–40. Swanson discusses the necessity for altering methods of research when we look at campaigns. His emphasis on the importance of the receiver is interesting; he suggests that the criteria for evaluation of political persuasion be drawn from the audience—the voters. Swanson handily discounts some of the traditional criteria used by researchers (argument strength, logicalness, and others).

Trent, Judith S., "Richard Nixon's Methods of Identification in the Presidential Campaigns of 1960 and 1968: A Content Analysis," *Today's Speech, 19* (Fall 1971), 23–30. This article is interesting for its method of analysis and the categories suggested by Trent. Furthermore, it demonstrates the changes between the persuasive attempts of 1960, which tended to be highly ideological, and those of 1968, which employed less direct appeal and more dramatic invitation.

White, Theodore H., *The Making of the President: 1960; The Making of the President: 1964; The Making of the President: 1968;* and *The Making of the President: 1972* (New York: Atheneum Publishers, 1961, 1965, 1969, and 1973). All of these volumes provide excellent detailed descriptions of all the candidates in both the primary and general election campaigns. They are filled with detail that should be of value in researching a campaign or in discovering about campaigning in general. The formerly unknown details are fascinating (e.g., that John Wayne contributed large sums to the George Wallace campaign in 1968). Any group project involving the study of a campaign and subsequent reports on it would be the kind of assignment in which these books would be of help. They are also enjoyable reading for one's own general knowledge.

Perspectives on Ethics in Persuasion

Richard L. Johannesen
Northern Illinois University

> To point out persuasion is not to condemn it;
> the practical problem is not to avoid all
> persuasion, but to decide which to avoid and
> which to accept.—Charles L. Stevenson, *Ethics
> and Language*

As receivers and senders of persuasion, we have the responsibility to uphold appropriate ethical standards in discourse, to encourage freedom of inquiry and expression, and to promote the health of public debate as crucial to democratic decision making.[1] To achieve these goals, we must understand their complexity and recognize the difficulty of their implementation.

The process of persuasion involves a message source's presenting good reasons to receivers for a specific choice among probable alternatives. Whether the persuader is a candidate seeking votes, an elected official urging citizens to adopt a governmental policy, a protestor demanding institutional reform by the Establishment, an advertiser appealing to consumers to purchase a product, a citizen urging others to accept his belief as correct, or a mass movement advocating major social change, alternatives are present and the persuader marshals logical and psychological supports for the choice of a specific alternative.

---

[1] This chapter is adapted and revised from some of the author's previous writings on the topic. See Johannesen, ed., *Ethics and Persuasion: Selected Readings* (New York: Random House, 1967); "Ethics of Persuasion: Some Perspectives," in Robert L. King, ed., *Marketing and the New Science of Planning*, 1968 Fall Conference Proceedings of the American Marketing Association (Chicago: American Marketing Association, 1968), pp. 541–546; "On Teaching the Social Responsibilities of a Speaker," in J. Jeffery Auer and Edward B. Jenkinson, eds., *Essays on Teaching Speech in the High School* (Bloomington: Indiana University Press, 1971), pp. 219–243. This particular version is printed here for the first time. All rights reserved. This chapter, in whole or part, may not be reproduced without permission in writing from the publisher and from the author.

Receivers of persuasive messages evaluate them according to standards they perceive as relevant. For example: Is the message interesting and directly relevant to my concerns? Am I clearly understanding the message as intended by the persuader? What is the persuader's purpose? Do I perceive the persuader as a credible source on this subject (expert, competent, trustworthy, experienced, sincere, honest, concerned)? Has the persuader presented sufficient evidence and reasoning for me to accept his message as reasonable (workable, practical, efficient, etc.)?

As a receiver do I see a legitimate connection between the persuader's message and my related needs, motives, and goals? Is the persuader's message consistent with my related beliefs and attitudes? Is the message sanctioned by my relevant value standards, by my conceptions of the good or the desirable? As a receiver do I feel that the nonverbal elements of the persuader's message reinforce or conflict with the verbal aspects? How do I perceive the persuader's view of my personal worth or abilities? What role does the persuader's message play in some larger, continuous campaign of persuasion? To what degree are the persuader's techniques, appeals, arguments, and purpose ethical?

Ethical issues focus on value judgments concerning right and wrong, goodness and badness, in human conduct. Criteria of potential impact on other human beings, and conscious choice of means and ends, mark the existence of potential ethical issues in human behavior. A persuasive transaction, as an instance of human behavior, inherently contains potential ethical issues because persuasion (1) involves a persuader attempting to influence other persons by altering their beliefs, attitudes, values, and overt actions, (2) involves conscious choices by the persuader among ends sought and rhetorical means used to achieve the end, and (3) necessarily involves a potential judge (any or all of the receivers, the persuader, or an independent observer).

How receivers and senders of persuasion evaluate the ethics of a persuasive instance will differ, depending upon the ethical standards they are using. Some may even choose to ignore ethical judgment entirely. Nevertheless, *potential* ethical questions are there, regardless how they are answered. And whether a persuader wishes it or not, consumers of persuasion generally will judge, formally or informally, the persuader's effort in part by *their* relevant ethical standards. If for none other than the pragmatic reason of enhancing his chances of success, the persuader would do well to consider the ethical standards held by his specific audience.

As receivers of persuasion, we must realize that accurate *understanding* of a persuader's message may be hindered by our attempt to *impose* our ethical standards on him. Our immediate, "gut-level" ethical judgments may cause us to distort the intended meaning. Only *after* reaching an accurate understanding of the persuader's ideas can we reasonably *evaluate* the ethics of his communicative strategies and purposes.

The ethical analysis of any persuasive situation may be aided by focusing on some basic elements. A *persuader* attempts to achieve a specific *end* with a specific *audience* by choosing to employ persuasive *means* or techniques to influence that audience. The persuader's message and techniques may also have *effects* on the audience in addition to, or in spite of, the end he seeks. The entire persuasive transaction occurs within a *rhetorical situation* of factors that stimulate the persuader's effort and constrain his choices. And the persuasive attempt also occurs within an *ethical context* of value standards held by the persuader, his audience, and society at large.

Some Ethical Perspectives

We can identify and employ at least seven major ethical perspectives as vantage points for analyzing specific ethical issues in persuasion.[2] As categories, these perspectives are not exhaustive, mutually exclusive of one another, or given in any order of precedence.

As receivers of persuasion we can employ one or a combination of such perspectives to evaluate the ethical level of a persuader's use of language (such as metaphors, ambiguity, and what Richard M. Weaver labels God terms and Devil terms—see Chapter 3 of this book) or of evidence and reasoning (such as what Stephen Toulmin calls data, warrant, backing, rebuttal, qualifier, and claim—see Chapter 6). We also can utilize them to assess the ethics of psychological techniques, such as appeals to needs and values, the stimulation and resolution of dissonance and imbalance, or the capitalization on pervasive cultural images and myths—all discussed in earlier chapters. And the persuasive tactics of campaigns and social movements can (indeed must) be subjected to ethical scrutiny.

---

[2] For other approaches to categorization of ethical viewpoints, see Kenneth E. Andersen, *Persuasion: Theory and Practice* (Boston: Allyn and Bacon, 1971), Ch. 16; James Chesebro, "A Construct for Assessing Ethics in Communication," *Central States Speech Journal*, 22 (Summer 1969), 104–114. General overviews of ethical standards and issues in communication may be found in Wayne C. Minnick, *The Art of Persuasion*, 2nd ed. (Boston: Houghton Mifflin Co., 1968), Ch. 11; Lee Thayer, ed., *Communication: Ethical and Moral Issues*, 2 vols. (New York: Gordon and Breach, 1973); J. Vernon Jensen, *Perspectives on Oral Communication* (Boston: Holbrook Press, 1970), Ch. 4; Robert T. Oliver, *The Psychology of Persuasive Speech* (New York: David McKay Co., 1968), Ch. 2; John R. Wenberg and William W. Wilmot, *The Personal Communication Process* (New York: John Wiley & Sons, 1973), Ch. 4. A case study based on several perspectives is Patricia L. Freeman, "An Ethical Evaluation of the Persuasive Strategies of Glenn W. Turner of Turner Enterprises," *Southern Speech Communication Journal*, 38 (Summer 1973), 347–361.

Religious Perspective

First is the *religious* perspective. One can turn to the sacred literature, such as the Bible or the Koran, of various religions to extract moral and spiritual injunctions to be employed as standards for evaluating the ethics of persuasion. The Bible, for example, warns against lying, slandering, or giving false witness. The New Testament records Jesus' proclamation: "I tell you, on the day of judgment men will render account for every careless word they utter; for by your words you will be justified and by your words you will be condemned." Of course such ethical guidelines for human communication behavior may vary from one religion to another.

Philosophical Perspective

Philosophical, or ontological, premises concerning the essential nature of man afford a second ethical perspective.[3] Some writers isolate unique characteristics of man's nature that should be nurtured. These characteristics can then be used to judge the ethics of specific persuasive techniques. A determination can be made of the extent to which a technique fosters or undermines the development of a uniquely human attribute. Enhancement of these attributes, so this perspective argues, promotes fulfillment of maximum individual potential. Among the characteristics suggested as marks defining man as man are these: the capacity to reason; the capacity and compulsion to utilize symbols; the need for mutual understanding; the capacity to *generate* knowledge *by* and *in* communication; and the capacity for conscious, free, informed, responsible choice making. Any one of these essentially human attributes could be used in a largely absolute way to judge the ethics of persuasion regardless of situation, form of government, culture, or religion—man would be man wherever he is found.

---

[3] For illustrative philosophical perspectives, see Lawrence J. Flynn, "The Aristotelian Basis for the Ethics of Speaking," *Speech Teacher,* 6 (September 1957), 179–187; Karlyn Kohrs Campbell, "The Ontological Foundations of Rhetorical Theory," *Philosophy and Rhetoric,* 3 (Spring 1970), 97–108; Henry N. Wieman and Otis Walter, "Toward an Analysis of Ethics for Rhetoric," *Quarterly Journal of Speech,* 43 (October 1957), 266–270; Thomas R. Nilsen, *Ethics of Speech Communication* (Indianapolis: Bobbs-Merrill Co., 1966), pp. ix, 8–9, 37; Paul N. Campbell, *Rhetoric-Ritual* (Encino, Calif.: Dickenson Publishing Co., 1972), pp. 226–228; Robert L. Scott, "On Viewing Rhetoric as Epistemic," *Central States Speech Journal,* 18 (February 1967), 9–17; Thomas M. Garrett, S.J., *An Introduction to Some Ethical Problems of Modern Advertising* (Rome: Gregorian University Press, 1961), pp. 39–47; Clarence C. Walton, "Ethical Theory, Societal Expectations, and Marketing Practices," in John S. Wright and Daniel S. Warner, eds., *Speaking of Advertising* (New York: McGraw-Hill Book Co., 1963), pp. 359–373.

Political Perspective

Political systems provide a third perspective. Implicit or explicit within a specific political system are values and procedures basic to the health and growth of that system. Once these essential political values are identified, they can function as criteria for assessing the ethics of persuasive means and ends within that particular political system. Within the context of American representative democracy, for instance, analysts pinpoint values and processes fundamental to the optimum functioning of our political system.[4] Among the political values and procedures suggested as standards for evaluating persuasion in our society are these: enhancement of man's capacity for rational thought; freedom of inquiry, expression, and criticism; wide diffusion of and access to information; adequate existence of and access to channels of communication. Thus, for example, if a persuasive technique aimed at circumventing or bypassing the citizen's capacity for rational choice, it might be condemned as unethical because it undermines achievement of a value crucial to the functioning of our representative democracy. Naturally other political systems, such as Soviet Communism or German Nazi National Socialism, could embody different values leading to different ethical judgments.[5]

---

[4] For sources propounding variations on what I label "the democratic premise," see Franklyn S. Haiman, "Democratic Ethics and the Hidden Persuaders," *Quarterly Journal of Speech, 44* (December 1958), 385–392; Haiman, "A Re-examination of the Ethics of Persuasion," *Central States Speech Journal, 3* (March 1952), 4–9; Arthur N. Kruger, "The Ethics of Persuasion: A Re-Examination," *Speech Teacher, 16* (November 1967), 294–305; Karl R. Wallace, "An Ethical Basis of Communication," *Speech Teacher, 4* (January 1955), 1–9; Thomas R. Nilsen, "Free Speech, Persuasion, and the Democratic Process," *Quarterly Journal of Speech, 44* (October 1958), 235–243; Nilsen, *Ethics of Speech Communication,* pp. 13, 88–89 (see fn. 3); Nilsen, "Ethics and Argument," in Gerald R. Miller and Thomas R. Nilsen, eds., *Perspectives on Argumentation* (Chicago: Scott, Foresman and Co., 1966), pp. 176–197; Nilsen, "The Ethics of Persuasion and the Marketplace of Ideas Concept," in Donn V. Parson and Wil A. Linkugel, eds., *The Ethics of Controversy: Politics and Protest* (Lawrence, Kan.: The House of Usher, 1968), pp. 7–49; Dennis G. Day, "The Ethics of Democratic Debate," *Central States Speech Journal, 17* (February 1966), 5–14; Sidney Hook, "The Ethics of Controversy," *The New Leader,* February 1, 1954, pp. 12–14; Hook, "The Ethics of Political Controversy," in Parson and Linkugel, eds., *The Ethics of Controversy,* pp. 50–71; Wayne Flynt, "The Ethics of Democratic Persuasion and the Birmingham Crisis," *Southern Speech Journal, 35* (Fall 1969), 40–53.

[5] See, for example, Jack H. Butler, "Russian Rhetoric: A Discipline Manipulated by Communism," *Quarterly Journal of Speech, 50* (October 1964), 229–239; Alex Inkeles, *Public Opinion in Soviet Russia: A Study in Mass Persuasion* (Cambridge, Mass.: Harvard University Press, 1962), pp. 6, 22–25, 123, 317–320, 325–327, 337–338; Stefan Possony, *Wordsmanship: Semantics as a Communist Weapon* (Washington, D.C.: U.S. Government Printing Office, 1961), pp. 2, 14–15; Adolf Hitler, *Mein Kampf,* trans. Ralph Manheim (Boston: Houghton Mifflin Co., 1943), pp. 80–81, 106–107, 177–179, 231–232, 236, 342; Z. A. B. Zeman, *Nazi Propaganda* (London: Oxford University Press, 1964), pp. 25–26, 37, 86; Ernest K. Bramstead, *Goebbels and National Socialist Propaganda* (East Lansing: Michigan State University Press, 1965), pp. 56, 174, 193–195, 455–457.

Utilitarian Perspective

A fourth perspective is a *utilitarian* emphasis.[6] Criteria of usefulness and expediency are used to analyze the ethics of persuasion. The utilitarian standard for assessing persuasive means and ends could be phrased as a question: Does the technique or goal promote the greatest good for the greatest number in the long run? A determination could be made of the usefulness to people affected and the survival potential for groups involved. One should be careful, however, to consider the interests of minorities when judging the greatest good for the greatest number. Furthermore, this utilitarian perspective usually is applied in combination with other perspectives. The definition of "good" often is derived from religious, philosophical, political, or other vantage points.

Situational Perspective

A fifth perspective can be labeled *situational*.[7] Here only elements of the specific persuasive situation at hand are used to make the ethical judgment. Absolute, universal standards are avoided and criteria from broad religious, philosophical, or political viewpoints are minimized. Among the situational or contextual factors relevant to making an ethical judgment may be the following: the role or function of the persuader for his audience; expectations held by the audience; ethical standards of the specific audience; degree of urgency for implementation of the persuader's proposal; degree of audience awareness of the persuader's means; goals and values held by the audience.

Using this situational perspective, it could be argued that unlabeled hyperbole is ethical in a political speech but unethical in a classroom lecture, that imperiled national survival might sanction otherwise unethical techniques, or that an acknowledged leader has the responsibility

---

[6] For some utilitarian emphases, see Winston L. Brembeck and William S. Howell, *Persuasion: A Means of Social Control* (Englewood Cliffs, N.J.: Prentice-Hall, 1952), pp. 444–464; A. K. Rogers, "Prolegomena to a Political Ethics," in *Essays in Honor of John Dewey* (New York: Holt, Rinehart and Winston 1929), pp. 324–335.

[7] Illustrative discussions of situational perspectives are found in Edward Rogge, "Evaluating the Ethics of a Speaker in a Democracy," *Quarterly Journal of Speech*, 45 (December 1959), 419–425; Saul Alinsky, *Rules for Radicals* (New York: Random House, 1971), pp. 24–47, 125–164; B. J. Diggs, "Persuasion and Ethics," *Quarterly Journal of Speech*, 50 (December 1964), 359–373; Joseph Fletcher, *Situation Ethics: The New Morality* (Philadelphia: Westminster Press, 1966); Fletcher, *Moral Responsibility: Situation Ethics at Work* (Philadelphia: Westminster Press, 1967); Charles Stevenson, *Ethics and Language* (New Haven, Conn.: Yale University Press, 1944), pp. 163–164.

in some situations to rally support and thus could employ emotional appeals that circumvent man's rational processes of choice. This perspective might justify a persuader's use of techniques such as guilt-by-association, innuendo, and unfounded name calling if the audience recognized his use of these devices and approved of that use.

We can suggest a number of questions that highlight issues arising from a contextual viewpoint: Should ethical standards be more stringent for persuasion aimed at children than for adults? Should ethical standards for persuasion be higher in peacetime or in time of declared war? Should ethical standards vary for persuasion in different fields such as politics, religion, education, and advertising? Is the use of so-called obscene words ethical in some public persuasive situations?[8] As a final observation we note that some analysts ethically justify on pragmatic or situational grounds (such as political powerlessness and inadequate functioning of traditional communication channels) the acceptability of some techniques of "confrontation" rhetoric.[9]

Legal Perspective

A *legal* perspective represents a sixth vantage point from which to evaluate the ethics of persuasion. This view would take the general position that things that are illegal are unethical. Such a perspective certainly has the advantage of allowing simple ethical decisions; one need only measure persuasive techniques against current laws and regulations, such as Federal Trade Commission regulations for advertisers, to determine whether the technique is ethical. But we must also consider whether this perspective leads to oversimplified, superficial judgments of complex persuasive situations.

---

[8] Haig Bosmajian, "Obscenity and Protest," in Bosmajian, ed., *Dissent: Symbolic Behavior and Rhetorical Strategies* (Boston: Allyn and Bacon, 1972), pp. 294–306; J. Dan Rothwell, "Verbal Obscenity: Time for Second Thoughts," *Western Speech*, 35 (Fall 1971), 231–242.

[9] In light of such situational constraints, Franklyn S. Haiman has somewhat modified his political perspective involving a "degree of rationality" standard by pragmatically justifying some confrontation rhetoric techniques. See Haiman, "The Rhetoric of the Streets: Some Legal and Ethical Implications," *Quarterly Journal of Speech*, 53 (April 1967), 99–114; Haiman, "The Rhetoric of 1968: A Farewell to Rational Discourse," in Wil Linkugel, R. R. Allen, and Richard L. Johannesen, eds., *Contemporary American Speeches*, 3rd ed. (Belmont, Cal.: Wadsworth Publishing Co., 1972), pp. 133–147. For defenses of the view that, depending on contextual factors, persuasion may be used ethically to *promote* social conflict, see Herbert W. Simons, "Persuasion in Social Conflicts: A Critique of Prevailing Conceptions and a Framework for Future Research," *Speech Monographs*, 29 (November 1972), 227–247, esp. 238–240; Parke G. Burgess, "Crisis Rhetoric: Coercion vs. Force," *Quarterly Journal of Speech*, 59 (February 1973), 61–73, esp. 69–73.

Dialogic Perspective

The *dialogic* perspective, a seventh viewpoint, emerges from current scholarship on the nature of ethical human communication as dialogue rather than as monologue.[10] This perspective contends that the attitudes participants in a communication transaction have toward one another are an index of the ethical level of that communication. Some attitudes are held to be more fully human, humane, and facilitative of personal self-fulfillment than are other attitudes.

Communication as dialogue is characterized by such attitudes as honesty, concern for the welfare and improvement of others, trust, genuineness, open-mindedness, equality, mutual respect, empathy, humility, directness, lack of pretense, nonmanipulative intent, sincerity, encouragement of free expression, and acceptance of others as unique individuals with intrinsic worth regardless of differences over belief or behavior. Communication as monologue, in contrast, is marked by such qualities as deception, superiority, exploitation, dogmatism, domination, insincerity, pretense, personal self-display, self-aggrandizement, distrust, coercion, possessiveness, condescension, self-defensiveness, judgmentalism that stifles free expression, and viewing others as objects to be manipulated.

In the case of persuasion, then, the techniques and presentation of the persuader would be scrutinized to determine the degree to which they reveal an ethical dialogic attitude or an unethical monologic attitude toward the audience. Even though using this perspective, however, a devotee of the alternative situational viewpoint could argue that the ethics of at least some dialogic qualities, such as honesty or truthfulness, depends on the circumstances of the specific persuasive situation. In some situations certain dialogic characteristics, such as concern for the psychological welfare of others, could take precedence over other dialogic elements, such as total frankness.

---

[10] For a general analysis of communication as dialogue and monologue, see Richard L. Johannesen, "The Emerging Concept of Communication as Dialogue," *Quarterly Journal of Speech*, 57 (December 1971), 373–382. See also Paul Keller and Charles T. Brown, "An Interpersonal Ethic for Communication," *Journal of Communication, 18* (March 1968), 73–81; Thomas R. Nilsen, *Ethics of Speech Communication*, Ch. 5; John R. Stewart, ed., *Bridges Not Walls: A Book About Interpersonal Communication* (Reading, Mass.: Addison-Wesley Publishing Co., 1973); Richard M. Weaver, *The Ethics of Rhetoric* (Chicago: Henry Regnery Co., 1953), Ch. 1; Douglas Ehninger, "Argument as Method: Its Nature, Its Limitations, and Its Uses," *Speech Monographs, 37* (June 1970), 101–110; Wayne Brockriede, "Arguers as Lovers," *Philosophy and Rhetoric*, 5 (Winter 1972), 1–11; Everett L. Shostrom, *Man, the Manipulator* (New York: Bantam Books, 1968); David W. Johnson, *Reaching Out: Interpersonal Effectiveness and Self-Actualization* (Englewood Cliffs, N. J.: Prentice-Hall, 1972).

Some Fundamental Ethical Issues

With the above seven ethical perspectives (religious, philosophical, political, utilitarian, situational, legal, dialogic), we can confront a variety of questions that underscore difficult issues relevant to ethical problems in persuasion. As receivers constantly bombarded with a variety of verbal and nonverbal persuasive messages, we continually face resolution of one or another of these fundamental issues.

To what degree should ethical criteria for assessing persuasion be either absolute, universal, and inflexible or relative, context-bound, and flexible? Surely the more absolute our criteria are, the easier it is to render simple, clearcut judgments. But in matters of human behavior and public decision making, the ethics of persuasive ends and means are seldom simple. In making ethical evaluations of persuasion, we probably should avoid snap judgments, carefully examine the relevant circumstances, determine the perspectives most appropriate to the instance, and consider the welfare of all involved.

Do the ends justify the means? Does the necessity of achieving a goal widely acknowledged as worthwhile justify the use of ethically questionable techniques? To say that the end does not *always* justify the means is different from saying that ends *never* justify means. The persuasive goal is probably best considered as one of a number of potentially applicable criteria, from among which the most appropriate standards (perspectives) are selected. Under some circumstances, such as threat to physical survival, the goal of personal security—temporarily —may take precedence over other criteria. In general, however, we can best make mature ethical assessments by evaluating the ethics of persuasive techniques apart from the worth of the persuasive goal. We can strive to judge the ethics of techniques and ends separately. In some cases we may find ethical persuasive devices employed to achieve an unethical goal. In other cases unethical techniques may be aimed at an entirely ethical goal.

Are the traditional "propaganda devices" always to be viewed as inherently unethical?[11] Textbooks in fields such as social psychology, journalism, and speech communication often discuss the devices of name calling, glittering generality, transfer, testimonial, plain-folks, card stacking, and bandwagon. Such a list does not constitute a sure guide to exposure of unethical persuasion. The ethics of at least some of these

---

[11] For a discussion of propaganda devices largely viewed as unethical, see W. H. Werkmeister, *An Introduction to Critical Thinking*, rev. ed. (Lincoln, Neb.: Johnson Publishing Co., 1957), Ch. 4.

techniques depends on how they are employed in a given context. For example, the plain-folks technique of stressing humble origins and modest backgrounds shared by the persuader and his audience may not be uniformly unethical. In his "whistle-stop" speeches to predominantly rural, Republican audiences during the 1948 presidential campaign, Democrat Harry Truman typically used the plain-folks appeal to establish common ground in introductions of his speeches. He used the device to accomplish one of the purposes of the introductory segment of most speeches—namely, establishment of rapport, and he did not rely on it for proof in the body of his speeches. But if a politician relied primarily on the plain-folks appeal as pseudoproof in *justifying* the policy he advocated, such usage could be condemned as unethical. Furthermore, Truman really was the kind of person who could legitimately capitalize on his actual plain-folks background. But a more patrician politician, such as Edward Kennedy, could be condemned for using an unethical technique if he were to appeal to farmers and factory workers by saying "you and I are just plain-folks."

Are all so-called "emotional appeals" inherently unethical? Although a countertrend seems to be emerging, as reflected by encounter groups and sensitivity training, our culture traditionally has viewed with suspicion the expression of or capitalization on emotion. And the Aristotelian heritage in rhetorical theory has perpetuated the primacy of logic over emotion in selecting ethical persuasive strategies.[12] But one point that has emerged from behavioral science research on persuasion is that receivers of persuasive messages find it difficult to categorize appeals or supporting materials as either emotional or logical in exactly the same manner as the persuader intends them. Differing audiences may view the same appeal differently. A given technique, such as a set of statistics indicating the high probability of falling victim to cancer during one's lifetime, may be perceived as possessing both logical and emotional components.

Since neither logical nor emotional appeals are inherently unethical, but depend largely on manner and circumstance of usage, the need to dichotomize persuasive appeals into logical and emotional categories is not very great. But if one does wish to evaluate the ethics of a persuasive technique he perceives as emotional appeal, the following guideline is suggested. Assuming that the appeal is ethical in light of other relevant perspectives, the "emotional" device is ethical if it is undergirded by a substructure of sound evidence and reasoning to support it. Presentation of this substructure could accompany the appeal in the persuasive message or the substructure could exist apart from the

---

[12] See Edwin Black, *Rhetorical Criticism* (New York: The Macmillan Co., 1965), Chs. 4 and 5.

message and be produced upon the request of a critic. And the emotional appeal is ethical if the audience is asked to view it not as proof for justification but as the expression of the persuader's internal emotional state. Generally, the emotional appeal is unethical when it functions as pseudoproof giving the appearance of evidence or if it functions to short-circuit the receiver's capacity for free, informed, responsible choice.

Does sincerity of intent release a persuader from ethical responsibility relative to means and effects? Could we say that if Adolf Hitler's fellow Germans judged him to be sincere, his fellow citizens could not assess the ethics of his persuasion? In such cases, evaluations probably are best carried out if we appraise sincerity and ethics separately. Thus, for example, a persuader sincere in his intent may be found to utilize an unethical strategy.

To what degree is it ethical for a persuader to alter his proposal to adapt to the needs, capacities, desires, and expectations of his audience? What are the ethics of audience adaptation? Some persuaders adapt to an audience to the extent of so changing their ideas—to secure acceptance—that the idea no longer really is theirs. These persuaders merely say what the audience wants them to say. On the other hand, some degree of adaptation in language choice, supporting materials, organization, and message transmission to reflect the specific nature of an audience is a crucial part of successful persuasion. No ironclad rule can be propounded here. Each persuader and receiver must decide the ethical balance point between the persuader's idea in its pure form and that idea modified to achieve maximum impact with the audience.

The foregoing questions highlight only some of the complex issues involved in determining the ethics of persuasion. Several additional issues—such as ghostwriting and the crisis in public confidence in public communication—can be analyzed at greater length.

The Ethics of Ghostwriting

Is a persuader unethical when he employs a ghostwriter?[13] Should a speaker use a person, or staff, to write his speech, to write parts of his speech, to contribute ideas, or to do research? Nationally prominent figures, such as Franklin D. Roosevelt, Adlai Stevenson, John F. Kennedy, and Richard M. Nixon, relied on ghostwriters. But rhetorical critics stress that these speakers frequently played an intimate role in the creation of his own speeches. Were they, nevertheless, socially irresponsible in using speech writers? We can explore a number of interrelated issues when analyzing the ethics of ghostwriting.

---

[13] For one interpretation, see Ernest Bormann, "The Ethics of Ghostwritten Speeches," *Quarterly Journal of Speech*, 47 (October 1961), 262-267.

First, what is the speaker's intent and what is the audience's degree of awareness? Clearly condemned by some critics is the speaker who deceives his audience by pretending to write his own speeches when in fact they are ghostwritten. However, if the audience is fully aware that ghostwriting is a normal circumstance, such as for Presidents and congressmen, then no condemnation is warranted. Everyone seems aware that certain classes of speakers use ghostwriters and make no pretense of writing, in toto, each of their speeches.

Second, does the speaker use ghostwriters to make himself appear to possess personal characteristics he really does not have? Eloquent style, wit, coherence, and incisive ideas are qualities all speakers desire, but some speakers can obtain them only with the aid of ghostwriters. We must consider the extent to which ghostwriters are used to improve a speaker's image without unethically distorting his true character.

Third, what is the speaker's role and what are the surrounding circumstances? Pressures of time and duty are invoked to sanction the necessity of ghostwriting for some speakers. In a speech-communication course, most people agree that the student is entirely responsible for creating his own speech. Training in analysis, research, and speech composition is subverted when a student relies on someone else to do all or part of his work. However, the President of the United States, a senator, a college president, or a corporation head may, because of job demands and lack of time, be unable to avoid using ghostwriters. But what about a college professor, state senator, or local businessman? Are they unethical when they use a ghostwriter? Should a clergyman use a ghostwriter? Although a minister has written his own sermon, is he ethical if he repeats the same speech again and again? And some critics would argue that when the President of the United States speaks, not as the head of the executive branch, as in a State of the Union message, but as an individual politician, as in a presidential campaign, he should avoid using ghostwriters.

Fourth, to what degree does the speaker himself participate in the writing of his speeches? Adlai Stevenson and Franklin D. Roosevelt participated extensively in the writing of their major addresses, even though each used a staff of speechwriters. They are not often condemned for employing ghostwriters; their speeches accurately reflected their own style and intellect. But what of the speaker who lets his ghostwriter research and write the entire speech and then simply delivers it?

Finally, does the speaker accept responsibility for the speech he presents? Some argue that even if a speaker did not write his speech, or help write it, he still is ethical as long as he accepts responsibility for the accuracy and ethics of its content. When his address is criticized, he should not disclaim authorship and "pass the buck" to his ghostwriters.

By fully exploring these five issues, then, we should be able to assess perceptively the ethics of a speaker who employs ghostwriters. Depending upon the standards we employ, our judgment may not always be clearcut. Through such analysis, however, we may avoid over-simplification inherent in most either-or evaluations.

Public Confidence in Public Communication

Whether a message goes from government to governed, political candidate to voter, news media to citizen, or advertiser to consumer, mutual confidence and trust are desirable for complete communication. Although we are now witnessing a mounting crisis in public confidence in the truthfulness of public communication,[14] such confidence is a goal or value integral to the optimum functioning of American representative democracy.[15] And enhancement of public confidence can be employed as a standard for judging the ethics of public persuasion in our society. When contents or techniques of public persuasion weaken or undermine that confidence, they should be condemned as unethical.

Democratic decision making through vigorous and free debate of issues assumes access to accurate and trustworthy information. With the veracity of government pronouncements, campaign speeches, news reports, and advertising appeals increasingly questioned, clearly public confidence in the process of democracy is dangerously shaken. Citizens today complain more and more of "managed news" and a "credibility gap" in communications from federal, state, and even local governments. They tend to dismiss as untrue, without analysis, much governmental communication. During political campaigns, citizens also dismiss many persuasive appeals, often characterized by extreme exaggeration, as "mere campaign oratory." They have so little confidence in campaign persuasion that they believe a substantial portion of it is not worthy of thoughtful scrutiny.

Presently, in the arena of political protest, we are witnessing a turning from persuasive approaches based upon conciliation and identification with common interests to an aggressive, abrasive, nonconciliatory rhetoric of confrontation, coercion, and demand. One rationale some use to justify the ethics of confrontation rhetoric is that traditional standards do not apply—normal channels and modes of communication are inadequate. This inadequacy, so the argument goes, stems from methods

---

[14] For a more detailed discussion, see Richard L. Johannesen, "The Crisis in Public Confidence in Public Communication," in Thomas Tedford, ed., *Free Speech Yearbook: 1971* (New York: Speech Communication Association, 1971), pp. 43–49.
[15] For instance, see Bruce Ladd, *Crisis in Credibility* (New York: New American Library, 1968), p. 9; Thomas Nilsen, *Ethics of Speech Communication*, p. 13; Bill D. Moyers, "The Press and the Government: Who's Telling the Truth?" in Warren K. Agee, ed., *Mass Media in a Free Society* (Lawrence: University of Kansas Press, 1969), pp. 20, 36; Hans Morgenthau, "What Ails America?" *The New Republic*, October 28, 1967, pp. 19–20.

that are too slow to meet crucial problems, channels that are inaccessible to aggrieved segments of the public, an Establishment that will not listen, an Establishment that uses the normal channels for delaying tactics, and an Establishment that cannot be trusted to communicate truthfully.

What are some of the effects of weakened public confidence in the truthfulness of public communication?[16] Sincere human communication is thwarted, and democratic decision-making processes are hampered. Alienation from the "system" and polarization of attitudes increase. Distrust and suspicion poison a widening variety of human relationships. Untruthfulness in *some* advertising tends to breed consumer distrust of *all* advertising. The veracity and objectivity of the news media are more and more suspect. Voters give up in dismay and vote blindly or not at all. Receivers of all types of public persuasion develop a habitual re-action pattern of rejecting *all* public persuasion simply because it *is* public persuasion, not because of the content of the persuasion. People come to feel that nothing is to be believed.

We must combat the growing assumption that most public com-munication inherently is untrustworthy. Just because a communication is of a certain type or comes from a certain source (government, candi-date, news media, advertiser), it must not be *automatically* rejected as tainted or untruthful. Clearly, we must always exercise caution in ac-ceptance and care in evaluation, as emphasized throughout this book. Using the best evidence available to us, we may arrive at our best judg-ment. But to condemn a message as untruthful *just* because it stems from a suspect source and *before directly* assessing it is to exhibit decision-making behavior detrimental to our political system. Rejection of the message, if such be the judgment, must come *after*, not before, our evaluation of it. As with a defendant in the courtroom, public com-munication must be presumed innocent until we have proved it guilty. And when techniques of persuasion weaken or undermine confidence in public communication, they can be condemned as unethical.

Two Examples for Analysis

To illustrate the complexity involved in assessing the ethics of persuasion and to encourage sensitivity to the variety of issues related to such judgments, we offer two examples for analysis and dis-cussion.

---

[16] Bruce L. Felknor, *Dirty Politics* (New York: W. W. Norton & Co., 1966), p. 129; Robert K. Merton, *Mass Persuasion* (New York: Harper & Row, 1946), p. 189; William McGaffin and Erwin Knoll, *Anything but the Truth: The Credibility Gap—How News Is Managed in Washington* (New York: G. P. Putnam's Sons, 1968), pp. 35–36.

First, let us consider a hypothetical example of a persuasive transaction. Imagine that you are an audience member listening to a speaker,
call him Mr. Bronson, representing the American Cancer Society. His
aim is to persuade you to contribute money to the research efforts of
the American Cancer Society. Suppose that, with one exception, all of
the evidence, reasoning, and motivational appeals he employs are valid
and above ethical suspicion. But at one point in his speech Mr. Bronson
consciously chooses to use a *false* set of statistics to scare the audience
into believing that, during their lifetime, there is a much greater probability of their getting some form of cancer than there actually is.

To promote exhaustive analysis of the ethics of this persuasive situation, consider these issues: If the audience, or the society at large, views
Mr. Bronson's persuasive end or goal as worthwhile, does the worth of
his end justify his use of false statistics as a means to help achieve that
end? Does the fact that he *consciously* chose to use false statistics make
a difference in your evaluation? If he used the false statistics out of
ignorance, or out of failure to check his sources, how might your ethical
judgment be altered? Should he be condemned as an unethical *person*,
as an unethical *speaker*, or as one who in this instance used a *specific*
unethical technique?

Carefully consider the standards you would employ to make your
ethical judgment of Mr. Bronson. Are they purely pragmatic? In other
words, he should avoid the false statistics because he might get caught.
Are they societal in origin? If he gets caught, his credibility as a *representative* would be weakened with this and future audiences. Or his
getting caught might weaken the credibility of *other* American Cancer
Society representatives. Explore in detail the ways in which the ethical
perspectives or standards discussed in this chapter may be used to
evaluate the persuasive ethics of this example. How might Mr. Bronson's
use of false statistics be assessed according to religious, ontological,
political, utilitarian, situational, legal, or dialogic perspectives?

To provide further opportunity for analysis, we now examine an
actual example of a persuasive technique advocated by Robert Welch,
founder of the conservative John Birch Society. At one point in *The
Blue Book of the John Birch Society*, Mr. Welch outlines various persuasive strategies and techniques designed to expose Communists in
American public life. He explains at length one specific persuasive technique:[17]

> There is the head of one of the great educational institutions in
> the East (not Harvard, incidentally) whom at least some of us believe
> to be a Communist. Even with a hundred thousand dollars to hire

---

[17] *The Blue Book of the John Birch Society* (Belmont, Mass.: 1961), pp. 95–96.

sleuths to keep him and his present contacts under constant sur-
veillance for awhile, and to retrace every detail of his past history, I
doubt if we could prove it on him. But—with just five thousand
dollars to pay for the proper amount of careful research, which could
be an entirely logical expenditure and undertaking of the magazine, I
believe we could get all the material needed for quite a shock. Of
course we would have to satisfy ourselves completely as to whether
our guess had been correct, from the preliminary research, before
going ahead with the project and spending that much money.

But if we are right, and with the research job done and the
material assembled which I think would be available, we would run
in the magazine an article consisting entirely of questions to this man,
which would be devastating in their implications. The question technique, when skillfully used in this way, is mean and dirty. But the
Communists we are after are meaner and dirtier, and too slippery
for you to put your fingers on them in the ordinary way—no matter
how much they look and act like prosperous members of the local
Rotary Club.

What ethical considerations concerning means and ends can be
extracted from Mr. Welch's proposal? How does his explanation illustrate
the rationale of the end justifying the means? What is your assessment
of the ethics of an innuendo technique, a barrage of questions "devastating in their implications"? Does Mr. Welch believe, in this case,
that a standard argumentative approach could be utilized, that charges
could be directly stated and then proved with evidence and reasoning?
Finally, from among the ethical perspectives previously discussed, apply
the most appropriate ones to make an evaluation.

A Review and Conclusion

The process of persuasion necessitates that the persuader
make choices about the methods and content he will use in influencing
his receivers to accept the alternative he advocates. These choices involve
issues of desirability and of personal and societal good. What ethical
standards are to be used in making or judging these choices among
techniques, contents, and purposes? What should be the ethical responsibilities of a persuader in contemporary American society?

Obviously, answers to these questions have not been clearly or universally established. But the questions are ones we must face squarely.[18]

---

[18] Ralph T. Eubanks and Virgil Baker, "Toward an Axiology of Rhetoric,"
Quarterly Journal of Speech, 42 (April 1962), 157–168; Karl R. Wallace, "The Substance of Rhetoric: Good Reasons," *Quarterly Journal of Speech*, 49 (October 1963),
239–249.

In this chapter, we have explored some perspectives and issues useful in evaluating the ethics of persuasion. Our interest in the nature and effectiveness of persuasive techniques must not outstrip our concern for the ethical use of such techniques. We must examine not only *how* to, but also *whether* to, employ persuasive techniques. And the issue of "whether to" is both one of audience adaptation and one of ethics. We should formulate meaningful ethical guidelines, not inflexible rules, for our persuasive behavior and for use in evaluating the persuasion to which we are exposed. Hopefully, we will share the sincere concern for ethical communication expressed by the late Secretary General of the United Nations, Dag Hammarskjöld, in his book *Markings:*

> Respect for the Word—to employ it with scrupulous care and an incorruptible heartfelt love of truth—is essential if there is to be any growth in a society or in the human race.
>
> To misuse the word is to show contempt for man. It undermines the bridges and poisons the wells. It causes Man to regress down the long path of his evolution.[19]

Questions for Further Thought

1. Why are potential ethical issues inherent in every persuasive situation?

2. What are the basic elements of a persuasive situation to be considered in making a comprehensive analysis of the ethics of that persuasion?

3. Can you briefly and clearly explain the nature of the seven perspectives suggested for possible application in judging the ethics of persuasion?

4. Should criteria for assessing ethics of persuasion be absolute or relative?

5. To what degree can a worthy end justify use of unethical persuasive techniques?

6. In what ways may some of the traditional propaganda devices not be inherently unethical?

7. To what degree are all emotional appeals unethical?

8. Does sincerity of intent abrogate a persuader from ethical responsibilities toward his audience? Explain.

9. What are the ethics of audience adaptation by the persuader?

10. What guides could be used to determine whether a specific instance of ghostwriting should be viewed as unethical?

11. Why might enhancement of public confidence in truthfulness of public communication be urged as a standard for appraising persuasive ethics?

---

[19] Dag Hammarskjöld, *Markings* (New York: Alfred A. Knopf, 1964), p. 112.

Experiences in Persuasion

1. Suppose a persuader employs techniques of guilt-by-association, unproven innuendo, and unwarranted name calling to defame the President of the United States; his immediate audience readily recognizes and encourages his use of these techniques. Write a paper in which you apply three of the ethical perspectives discussed in this chapter to judge the ethics of this persuader.

2. Develop a written rationale for including or excluding *tact* as an ethical criteria for judging persuasion. In your rationale consider the meaning not only of tact but also of *candor, frankness,* and *appropriateness.*

3. With the most recent national presidential campaign as your focus, hold a small-group discussion of four to six people, in which you assess the persuasive ethics of the major candidates. Be sure you clearly identify the ethical perspectives you employ.

4. In Saul Alinsky's *Rules for Radicals,* read pages 24–47 and then present your assessment of the soundness of his suggested ethical guidelines. As an alternative, read pages 125–164 and then present your evaluation of the ethics of the tactics he discusses.

5. Read a chapter in Bruce Felknor's *Dirty Politics,* and give your assessment of the ethics of the political campaigning practices discussed in that chapter.

6. Select a chapter on a twentieth-century politician in Reinhard Luthin's *American Demagogues.* Based on your reading of that chapter, present your evaluation of the persuasive ethics of that politician.

7. Read Chapter 4 on propaganda devices in W. H. Werkmeister's *An Introduction to Critical Thinking* (rev. ed., 1957). Select three propaganda devices, and describe how they might each be unethical or ethical in two different situations or from two different ethical perspectives.

8. Read one of the following two journal articles on use of obscenity as a tactic in the rhetoric of protest. Write your analysis of the ethics of obscenity as a confrontation rhetoric technique. See Haig Bosmajian, "Obscenity and Protest," *Today's Speech, 18* (Winter 1970), 9–14; J. Dan Rothwell, "Verbal Obscenity: Time for Second Thoughts," *Western Speech, 35* (Fall 1971), 231–242.

9. Using the premise that "the speaker who appeals to emotions which short-circuit the auditor's normal critical facilities uses unethical and undemocratic methods," Wayne Flynt has assessed the persuasive ethics of the 1963 Birmingham civil rights efforts. Read his essay and present your view of the soundness of his analysis and also your view of how the same situation could be judged by a different ethical perspective. See Wayne Flynt, "The Ethics of Democratic Persuasion and the Birmingham Crisis," *Southern Speech Journal, 35* (Fall 1969), 40–53.

10. Write your reply to the following questions concerning the ethics of advertising (questions adapted from Vance Packard, *The Hidden Persuad-*

ers, Ch. 24): (1) What is the morality of the practice of encouraging house-wives to be nonrational and impulsive in buying the family food? (2) What is the morality of playing upon hidden weaknesses, such as aggressive feelings, dread of ¬nonconformity, infantile hangovers, and sexual yearn-ings, to sell products? (3) What is the morality of manipulating small children to pressure their parents to buy products? (4) What is the morality of encouraging a public attitude of wastefulness toward national resources by promoting the planned "psychological obsolescence" (out-of-style view) of products already in use?

Readings for New Dimensions

Alinsky, Saul, *Rules for Radicals* (New York: Random House, 1971). One of America's most successful community organizers explains his aims and meth-ods. Pages 24–47 and 125–164 in particular, focus on tactics and on a situa-tional ethic of means and ends.

Bowers, John, and Donovan Ochs, *The Rhetoric of Agitation and Control* (Reading, Mass.: Addison-Wesley Publishing Co., 1971). Analyzes the nature of contemporary confrontation rhetoric and rhetorical responses of the Estab-lishment. Three chapters are case studies appropriate for ethical scrutiny: nonviolent protest in Birmingham, 1963; confrontation at the 1968 Democratic Convention in Chicago; and confrontation at San Francisco State College, 1968–1969.

Felknor, Bruce L., *Dirty Politics* (New York: W. W. Norton & Co., 1966). As former director of the nonpartisan Fair Campaign Practices Committee, Felk-nor is uniquely qualified to assess the ethics of political campaigning. A fasci-nating sourcebook of examples.

Johannesen, Richard L., ed., *Ethics and Persuasion: Selected Readings* (New York: Random House, 1967). An anthology of thirteen essays by experts who probe ethical problems in persuasion within contexts of public address, political campaigning, public relations, and advertising. Included in this an-thology are many of the essays noted in this chapter.

Lomas, Charles W., ed., *The Agitator in American Society* (Englewood Cliffs, N. J.: Prentice-Hall, 1968). In the initial three theoretical chapters, the author discusses the nature and analysis of agitative persuasion and distinguishes between an agitator and a demagogue. Among the thirteen speeches re-printed are ones by Joseph R. McCarthy, Stokely Carmichael, and Billy James Hargis.

Luthin, Reinhard H., *American Demagogues* (Boston: Beacon Press, 1954; reprinted Russell and Russell, 1959). Analyzes in depth ten American dema-gogues of the twentieth century, including Huey Long and Joseph R. Mc-Carthy. Chapter 12 discusses the characteristics of a demagogue.

Nilsen, Thomas R., *Ethics of Speech Communication* (Indianapolis: Bobbs-Merrill Co., 1966). An original treatise that provocatively blends the political, philosophical, and dialogic ethical perspectives for judging the ethics of oral communication.

Thayer, Lee, ed., *Communication: Ethical and Moral Issues* (New York: Gordon and Breach, 1973). Includes essays by such scholars as Jurgen Ruesch, Anatol Rapoport, Hugh D. Duncan, J. L. L. Aranguren, Martin E. Marty, Kenneth Boulding, William Stephenson, Frank E. X. Dance, Alfred G. Smith, and Kenneth Burke.

10

The Role of the Persuadee
in a Mass Society

We live in a mass society. Everything is affected by that fact—the way we think, the way we live, the alternatives open to us, the degree to which we are able to discover the information around us —what we believe and what we do. Nearly all social critics agree that this "mass" aspect of society is quite recent, probably developing only since the 1920s.

In the 1970s, the mass society in which we live is characterized by two seemingly contradictory trends, both of which are inextricably tied to persuasion and how it operates. The first trend has been developing for some time but seems to have become more pronounced since the initiation of the atomic age and the widespread use of television—the trend for people to become increasingly skeptical about their futures, their government, their leaders, and perhaps even such traditionally stable institutions as the family. In short, we have become doubters. The second trend that has developed, particularly since the early 1960s, is almost contradictory to the notion of becoming cynical and skeptical—the tendency for people to become more involved in a variety of activities— politics, sports, leisure-time activities, social institutions, and so forth. Perhaps we simply have more leisure time now than ever before and so have the opportunity to become involved more than ever. Or it may be that increased educational levels allow more and more persons to become involved in activities and institutions than ever before.

The existence of these two trends has been in the background throughout this book. In many ways, the book encourages you to be skeptical and doubting as a persuadee and also to involve yourself in the persuasive process, especially as persuadee. In fact, all of the tools for analysis of persuasion have been aimed at these two trends—the tools allow you to become both cynical and involved. Perhaps, in closing this consideration of the process of persuasion, it would be worthwhile to investigate the possible causes of these two trends. There are dangers and promises in both trends. While it is good to be somewhat cynical, we may become so doubtful that we refuse to believe *any* persuasion (and we need to be persuaded in a mass society, if only because of the increase in available alternatives). At the same time that we become skeptics, we may become so apathetic that we totally atrophy our power to reject almost all persuasion—an equally odious alternative. While it is good to become involved in political and social affairs, there is a cost for the involvement—we cannot become involved in everything we would like to or even in all of those issues that necessitate our involvement. So we must choose, and understanding the causes of our discontent may make the choice easier. There have been three premises repeatedly articulated in this book:

1. That man is a symbol-making and symbol-using creature who becomes involved with his own symbols, thus revealing himself

2. That the role of the persuadee in persuasion is becoming more and more important and that he must, therefore, become increasingly critical as he responds to persuasion

3. That the basic unit of human interaction, especially persuasive interaction, is perceived by participants or observers as dramatic —we see ourselves or others as actors in dramatic episodes

There is a fourth premise that we have not articulated so directly or as often—that the increasing sophistication of television has enabled it to shape and direct our thinking and our responses to the society around us. Further, television is at the heart of both the developing cynicism and the need for involvement. It is reasonable that this should be the case. Who wouldn't be a skeptic, as each dramatic adventure he watches is repeatedly interrupted with commercial messages in which little men in rowboats paddle around toilet bowls advising housewives that Tidy Bowl does the job? The nature of our programming encourages skepticism, for we willingly suspend our objectivity to enter the fantasy world, only to have that world continually disrupted or repeated on instant replays or reruns. What about involvement as a trend, though? It, too, has developed as a result of television in our mass society.

Television and Involvement

In several other places, we have briefly discussed the development of the television media from feeble and unsophisticated moorings in 1960 (when Richard Nixon refused even to wear makeup for his television debates with John Kennedy) to the highly orchestrated and clever uses in the 1970s. What are the implications of these changes?

The McLuhan Perspective

Perhaps the best known commentator on the implications of television is Marshall McLuhan. Though he is a popularizer, and though his style smacks of Madison Avenue and the advertising business, he has identified at least one aspect of television that seems to be extremely critical—the degree to which it "involves" its observer. We tend to think of television as a passive medium for viewers; they don't have to do anything to observe it, except to sit fairly still and attend to the picture and sound coming out of the machine. This approach seems much different from what we must do with a book, where it is essential to imagine and build characters in the mind's eye, or with radio, where one must try to visualize the face of the announcer or the actor or the speaker. McLuhan reverses these two conceptions and calls television (the medium that seems to require passivity, dullness, and insensitivity) a "cool" and "involving" medium, while books and radios (which require more intellectual "filling in" and seem to ask for more imaginative involvement) are labeled "hot" media.

The distinction between hot and cool media is fairly simple. A *hot* medium provides a maximum number of potential message bits to its respondent (e.g., a photograph that gives an accurate and complete two-dimensional image) and thus requires *low participation* in completion of the image. As such, McLuhan says, it is a *high definition* medium. A *cool* medium, on the other hand, is one which provides a minimum amount of potential information bits to its respondents (e.g., a cartoon that only suggests an image) and thus requires *high participation* in order to complete the image. It is a *low definition* medium, according to McLuhan. Table 10–1 labels several media in McLuhan's terms.

Table 10–1

Medium	Source of Information	Definition	Participation	Type of Medium
Television	Lighted dots	Low	High	Cool
Books	Completed letters	High	Low	Hot
Cartoons	Dots on paper	Low	High	Cool
Photographs	Image on film	High	Low	Hot
Telephone	Low-fidelity sound wave	Low	High	Cool
Movies	Moving image on film	High	Low	Hot
Telegraph	Dots and dashes in sound	Low	High	Cool
Stereo	High-fidelity sound wave	High	Low	Hot

You will notice that there is a distinction made between the *medium*, which conveys the message bits, and the *content* of the message bits. A novel may be very intellectually involving and may require imagination on the part of the reader, but as a *medium* print does not require participation ("filling in") in the same way that a cartoon does; that is, you must "fill in" the medium as well as the content with a cartoon—you don't "fill in" a book or a photograph. Television, according to McLuhan, is unlike novels. It is a cool medium. The picture is composed of over 500 lines with numerous dots of light possible on each line. The participant, using only a few of these dots, has to put them together for himself. McLuhan compares this process with its seemingly similar cousin—film—this way:

> The T.V. image is not a *still* shot. It is not a photo in any sense but a ceaselessly forming contour of things . . . The T.V. image offers some three million dots per second to the receiver. From these he accepts only a few dozen each instant, from which to make an image.

> The film image offers many more millions of data per second and the viewer does not have to make the same drastic reduction of items to form his impression. He tends instead to accept the full image as a package deal.[1]

If you have a cool, involving medium, which is tuned in seven hours per day on the average, McLuhan argues it would be foolish not to expect an increase in the desire to involve one's self in a variety of other things. Thus, according to McLuhan, the medium trains us to become physiologically involved with itself *sans* content, and by our nature as symbol makers we become involved with the dramatic content of television. We imagine ourselves in the drama. The next logical step is to become equally involved outside the television room. Television thus not only entertains its audience, but it shapes their response patterns by conditioning them to the involvement. From the McLuhan perspective,

---

[1] Marshall McLuhan, *Understanding Media: The Extensions of Man* (New York: Signet Books, 1964), p. 273.

the most effective programs are those that "fit" the medium—programs with low definition (minimal character development, fast plot lines, flashy but incomplete images, etc.), thus requiring high intellectual as well as physical involvement. Candidates, according to McLuhan, need to be low definition and involving characters.[2] Earlier we said that, in the 1960 debates and campaign, Kennedy was incomplete (McLuhan says he was "shaggy")—he allowed his audience to participate or become involved with him, while Nixon was clearcut—he seemed like the man next door, a Dagwood Bumstead of sorts—and his audience could not find a way to become involved with him. There were no "blanks" to "fill in." In 1968 Nixon had a low profile and was ambiguous, while it was Humphrey who was clearly defined. Television thus encourages involvement, not only through its nature as a medium but also in the kind of images it encourages. This penchant for involvement or participation may explain the increased involvement in other things like drugs, politics, the occult, bizzare events like happenings, or nude theater.[3]

Other Perspectives

If one does not accept McLuhan's theory to explain increased involvement, there are alternative explanations. The interesting thing about them is that they, too, begin with the "given" that television is a pervasive influence and the cause of increased involvement.[4] The involvement discussed and considered by these sources deals with the content level of involvement, in contrast to the cultural, technological, and perhaps physiological involvement treated by McLuhan. The recent Surgeon General's report on violence and television maintains that children become psychologically "involved" with the violent acts they witness on television shows ranging from the highly symbolic violence in cartoons, through the slapstick violence of the three stooges, to the sophisticated physical and psychological violence in television dramatic presentations.[5]

---

[2] A good discussion of this notion is presented by McLuhan in a film entitled *This is Marshall McLuhan: The Medium is the Message* (New York: McGraw-Hill Book Co., 1968). See also Raymond Rosenthal, ed., *McLuhan: Pro and Con* (New York: Funk and Wagnalls, 1968).

[3] Ross Snyder, "Architects of Contemporary Man's Consciousness: The Content Television Puts in Our Minds," included in *Broadcasting and the Public Interest*, eds. John H. Pennybacker and Waldo Braden (New York: Random House, 1969), pp. 166–167.

[4] There are several good examples of these varied perspectives. For instance, see Fred Friendly, *Due to Circumstances beyond Our Control* (New York: Random House, 1967); or Nicholas Johnson, *How To Talk Back to Your Television Set* (New York: Bantam Books, 1970); or Robert Cirino, *Don't Blame the People* (Los Angeles: Diversity Press, 1971).

[5] *Television and Growing Up: The Impact of Televised Violence*, a report to the Surgeon General (Washington, D. C.: U. S. Government Printing Office, 1972).

Others argue that an important factor in the involving nature of television is that it is a presentational medium—it acts out a dramatic episode to the viewer, with which he symbolically and mentally interacts (i.e., he "lives" the experience in a passive and symbolic state by inviting himself into the world of Archie Bunker, deep-sea diving with Jacques Cousteau, or the six o'clock news). The fact that the content is a "presentation" served up to the viewer in organized (usually dramatic) form encourages him to involve himself in the content of the presentation.[6] Proponents of this position would probably agree with some politicians who maintain that by broadcasting the details of riots, campus disruptions, sniper incidents, hijackings, and other such dramatic episodes, we encourage repetition of these incidents—someone sees how to hijack an airplane and then, having symbolically experienced the event, is prone to experience it by hijacking a plane himself.

Others argue that one becomes addicted to television as he observes more and more of it, thus "involving" himself with the medium to the detriment of other activities—some even maintain that he "uneducates" himself by becoming a television junkie. Some argue further that the viewer becomes passive through his involvement and is thus more easily manipulated.[7] Finally, some persons observe that since television must choose to present only a part of reality, and even that in secondhand fashion, that involvement with the medium channels one's distrust and imagination.[8]

Regardless of the perspective one chooses, he is bound to find that a recurring area of concern in a mass society is the incredible power of television to reach cross sections of whole nations and perhaps even cultures, and that this power is highly correlated with an increase in emotional and intellectual involvement with events—riots, demonstrations, violent acts, and other political and social activity. At the same time, theorists writing about the power of television express fear that one or the other of the two extremes expressed earlier may be emerging: complete distrust of all persuasion or complete apathy toward and acceptance of all persuasion. A problem for the persuadee in a mass society is to learn how to be persuaded, particularly how to be persuaded by television. Because if we don't teach ourselves or our children to watch television and to respond to it and other mass media, we may be encouraging either a new generation of cynics and skeptics or a generation of automatons too dulled by simplistic television fare to respond critically to anything. We need only to watch a single day's pro-

---

6 Snyder, pp. 167–172 (see fn. 3).

7 Hilde Himmelweit, A. N. Oppenheim, and Pamela Vince, "Television and the Child," *Reader in Public Opinion*, 2nd ed., by Bernard Berelson and Morris Janowitz, eds. (New York: The Free Press, 1966), pp. 418–445.

8 Kurt Lang and Gladys E. Lang, "The Mass Media and Voting," Berelson and Janowitz, pp. 466–469.

gramming on any of the major networks critically to distinguish what the media masters think the average intelligence of its viewers is.

Perhaps the classic piece of evidence that demonstrates the power of television to encourage involvement is the invention of an "electronic game of the future" called "Odyssey," which was being marketed by Magnavox in the early 1970s. Similar toys are available from other sources. The interesting thing about the toy Odyssey is that it attaches to one's television set and the viewer then "plays" a variety of games with his own set, thus participating or becoming totally involved with the medium—psychologically or intellectually involved in the content of the game, physiologically (in McLuhan's view of the world) by watching the medium, and physically by manipulating what happens on the screen. Consider the promotional material about Odyssey: "With *Odyssey* you participate in television . . . you're not just a spectator . . . . Odyssey is thought, action, and reaction."[9]

Clearly, we are experiencing an increasing trend toward involvement on all levels of human interaction—television is doubtless one of the causes of this trend, if only for its informational attributes. Because of the nature of the medium and its fantasy aspects, it may also encourage the apathy so often commented on by observers of American culture.

Television, Mass Society, and Skepticism

As we have already noted, there is something in the nature of American television programming that seems inherently destined to produce skepticism. Whenever you purposely interrupt the viewer's fantasy world to tell him to buy some product or to believe that a character called "Mother Nature" is fooled by Chiffon margarine or that a "Man from Glad" flies down out of the sky to deliver cellophane wrap, you are also bound to create a skeptical reaction. One group of critics puts it this way:

> The constant exposure to this shower of matter—half-true, true, or even true, but always simplified, always loud, always self-serving—induces a peculiar mixture of gullibility and cynicism that is close to neurosis. It is not an attitude that is well adapted for distinguishing between bullshine and brass tacks, rhetoric and reality.[10]

---

[9] Form ASDM-731, entitled "Factory Sponsored Annual Magnavox Sale," an advertising brochure distributed in January 1973 by Magnavox.

[10] Lewis Chester, Godfrey Hodgeson, and Bruce Page, *An American Melodrama: The Presidential Campaign of 1968* (New York: The Viking Press, 1969), p. 47. This observation is particularly interesting since the authors are British and perhaps more objective in viewing American culture.

Thus, not only does the form of our television programming encourage a skeptical reaction, but so does the content—we are asked to believe the ridiculous in the middle of the serious and imagined. At the same time, the serious and imagined fantasy we are attending to is shattered by constant interruption, thereby further convincing the viewer that little is real or sincere.

These feelings of doubt and skepticism are bound to affect us in other ways. Like the trend to become involved in television, which causes us to become involved outside our television world, the doubt engendered by the television world is bound to spill over outside that fantasy world. Not surprisingly, then, we find that people, in the past ten years, seem to have become less sure of themselves. (You can pick up almost any contemporary magazine and find several articles dealing with this problem—how to deal with depression, when to partake in sensitivity group training, what to do when your husband leaves you.) The problem is further underscored when you look at other developments of the technological age. For example, most of us get a lot of third-class mail that tries to induce us to buy some product or to subscribe to some magazine or insurance policy. In almost every one of these pieces of mail, there is a "personal" letter in which our very own names and address have been printed in order to fool us into believing that we are one of a select few chosen to receive the letter. Or we are aware that the world is rapidly becoming polluted beyond redemption—the seas, the land, the air—yet no one seems to be able to do anything about it. Another example of this sense of helplessness and uncertainty is seen in the difficulties associated with finding employment. At least in the mid-1970s, the passport to success—a college degree—was no longer a guarantee that you would find a job and be happy. Paradoxically, the college degree often deterred your job-getting ability. The evening news on any night of the year would underscore the cynical and doubting frame of mind we have been describing. If the politicians are not being exposed for flim-flamming the public, someone has discovered a new source of pollution, or someone is going on strike, or another airliner has been hijacked or a sniper is picking people off in a large city, or another public figure has been shot at or assassinated.

Certainly the American involvement in the Vietnam war has been a major element in inducing feelings of helplessness and doubt about our individual ability to control our destinies. As late as January of 1973, Mike Mansfield, the Senate majority leader, observed that even if the entire Senate were to vote to cut off funds for fighting the war or for supporting the Saigon government, the President would still be able to continue giving aid for a considerable length of time. During the 1960s and early 1970s, the war seemed totally uncontrollable by the average individual. Even when hundreds of thousands of demonstrators gathered in Washington, D. C., to demonstrate against the war, little changed, and

President Nixon talked about football with the demonstrators. The very technological neatness of the war was depressing—killing was depersonalized when you could drop bombs using homing devices. The way the government and the military talked about the war certainly re-emphasized the skepticism described above—villages were "saved" by obliterating them, and air attacks into Cambodia were once called "anticipatory protective reaction strikes."

Finally, the speed with which we are now able to do things induces a kind of doubt in our ability to control our environment—the best example is probably the digital computer. To anyone who has had a billing confused by the computer and has found that he owes more than he knows he spent, this feeling of lack of control is familiar. A friend who repairs computers once related this story, which exemplifies the kind of frustration and skepticism that can occur:

> A man was billed by a large catalog sales house for several hundred dollars more than he spent. Further, every time he would make a payment, it would be recorded as a purchase. He telephoned the credit department several times and was repeatedly assured that the problem would be corrected. Still, he kept getting larger and larger bill notices and letters warning him of dire results if he did not make an effort to pay his delinquent bill. He attached notes to his bill telling of the error and referring the reader to someone in the credit office. Finally one day the entire computer billing machine came to an abrupt halt. The repairmen were called and discovered the difficulty. The card from the overbilled customer was stuck in the card feeder. It had been filled with staples so that no space on the card could be seen. After removing the staples, the repairmen found a note that said, "Now I'll bet you S.O.B.'s will get your damned machine to check with the credit office—I'll keep doing this until you get un-screwed up!!!"

We have all had experiences similar to these. In a mass society such as we live in, things happen so fast that we cannot keep up with them—change overwhelms us and we feel helpless to keep up, let alone to regain control. This feeling of helplessness, coupled with the natural doubt engendered by television, news reporting, the breakdown of traditional values and patterns of behavior, and the inaccessibility of our government, is bound to create feelings of skepticism. We inevitably begin to doubt a little bit of everything—to take everything with a grain of salt.

A Final Note

Kenneth Boulding, author of *The Image,* recently noted in an interview that one of the major problems in our society is not a loss of confidence but the deterioration of legitimacy. He argues that, with the development of nuclear missiles, the "unconditional viability of the national state" (i.e., legitimacy) is destroyed and that the Vietnam War has destroyed the legitimacy of the military:

> If you don't have what we call internal legitimacy—which is the equivalent of morale or self-confidence or nerve—you obviously can't function. . . . And you can't function without external legitimacy, without having people accept the role structure and the authority structure and so on . . . The erosion of legitimacy is a profound problem in society but we mustn't overestimate it.[11]

He goes on to argue that though much of this loss of legitimacy or believability can be attributed to the effects of mass society and to the information explosion, the case is not hopeless. Information, he says, is not knowledge—"Knowledge . . . is attained much more by a loss of information than by the gain of it."[12]

This loss of information—another way of saying deciding or putting information together in order to discard some of it and to act on the basis of what is left—is similar to the definition of persuasion we used in Chapter 1 of this book:

> *Persuasion* is a process whereby options are intentionally limited or extended through the interaction of messages, sources, and receivers, and through which attitudes, beliefs, opinions, or behaviors are changed by a cognitive restructuring of one's image of the world or of his frame of reference.

In other words, though things seem to be uncontrollable and depersonalized we can control them by becoming involved in the world of persuasion around us—the ultimate error would be to allow our cynicism and skepticism to cause us either to accept all persuasion *carte blanche*

---

[11] Interview with Kenneth Boulding, "Aristocrats Have Always Been Sons of Bitches," by Robert W. Glasgow, *Psychology Today,* January 1973, pp. 61 and 63.
[12] *Ibid.,* pp. 63–64.

or to reject all persuasion as manipulation. We need to be persuaded in a mass society, but it needs to happen only after we have critically lost or rejected some of the information surrounding us. In the same interview cited above, Boulding replied to a question about how he could remain optimistic in spite of all of the fears expressed by himself and others concerning the problems of the future. He answered the question this way:

> Your perception is accurate. The only unforgivable sin is despair, because that will justify itself. I believe man is very far from exhausting the potential of his extraordinary nervous system.[13]

We need to avoid despairing because the world seems so uncontrollable and uncertain. One of the ways to avoid that feeling is to become actively involved in the persuasion that is continually aimed at us. We need to become alert and critical persuadees so that we can responsibly practice the reception of persuasive messages.

---

[13] *Ibid.*, p. 87.

Name Index

Subject Index